Also by Graham Seal

Great Australian Stories
Great Anzac Stories
Larrikins, Bush Tales and Other Great Australian Stories
The Savage Shore
Great Australian Journeys
Great Convict Stories
Great Bush Stories

Praise for other books by Graham Seal

Great Australian Stories
'The pleasure of this book is in its ability to give a fair dinkum insight into the richness of Australian story telling.' —*The Weekly Times*

'A treasure trove of material from our nation's historical past.' —*The Courier Mail*

'This book is a little island of Aussie culture—one to enjoy.' —*Sunshine Coast Sunday*

The Savage Shore
'A fascinating, entertainingly written voyage on what have often been rough and murky seas.' —*The Daily Telegraph*

'Colourful stories about the spirit of navigation and exploration, and of courageous and miserable adventures at sea.' —*National Geographic*

'. . . a gripping account of danger at sea, dramatic shipwrecks, courageous castaways, murder, much missing gold, and terrible loss of life.' —*The Queensland Times*

Larrikins, Bush Tales and Other Great Australian Stories
'. . . another collection of yarns, tall tales, bush legends and colourful characters . . . from one of our master storytellers.' —*The Queensland Times*

Australia's FUNNIEST YARNS

A humourous collection of colourful yarns
and true tales from life on the land

GRAHAM SEAL

ALLEN&UNWIN
SYDNEY·MELBOURNE·AUCKLAND·LONDON

Allen & Unwin
83 Alexander Street
Crows Nest NSW 2065
Australia
Phone: (61 2) 8425 0100
Email: info@allenandunwin.com
Web: www.allenandunwin.com

A catalogue record for this book is available from the National Library of Australia

ISBN 978 1 76052 845 4

Set in 11.5/15 pt SABON by Midland Typesetters, Australia
Printed and bound in Australia by Griffin Press, part of Ovato

10 9 8 7 6 5 4 3 2 1

The paper in this book is FSC® certified. FSC® promotes environmentally responsible, socially beneficial and economically viable management of the world's forests.

*Dedicated to the bull artists, jokers and yarn-spinners
of the great Australian tradition*

CONTENTS

INTRODUCTION: An edge like a chainsaw   1

1   BULL   7
   What a hide   7
   The split dog   8
   Drop bears   9
   Hoop snakes   10
   Giant mozzies   11
   Crooked Mick and the Speewah   13
   Dinkum!   17
   The exploding dunny   18
   The well-dressed 'roo   19
   Loaded animals   20
   The blackout babies   29
   The most beautiful lies   30
   The Pommies and the Yanks   35
   Aussie efficiency   38

2   CHARACTERS   41
   The Drongo   41
   Cousin Jacks   42
   Tom Doyle   43
   The Widow Reilly's pig   44
   The Convict's Tour to Hell   45
   Make it hours instead of days   48
   Who was Billy Barlow?   51

	Jacky Bindi-i	54
	Jimmy Ah Foo	58
	Snuffler Oldfield	59
	Corny Kenna	60
	The Hodja	60
	Dad makes a blue	61
	Dad, Dave and Mabel	64
	Anzac characters	67
	How he worked his nut	69
	Tom 'n' Oplas	72
	Three blokes at a pub	74
3	HARD CASES	77
	The cocky	77
	'Hungry' Tyson	79
	Ninety the Glutton	82
	Galloping Jones	83
	Christy Palmerston	84
	Moondyne Joe	85
	The Eulo Queen	87
	Wheelbarrow Jack	88
	Long Jack	92
	Diabolical Dick	94
	Puppy pie and dog's dinner	95
	The World's Greatest Whinger	96
	The Captain of the Push	99
	The Souvenir King	102
	Mrs Delaney	104
	Dopes	105
	Taken for a ride	105
	Bea Miles	106
	Doing business with Reg	109
	An unwelcome miracle	110
4	DIGGEROSITIES	115
	A million cat-calls	115
	Religion	116
	Monocles	117
	Food and drink	118
	Army biscuits	120
	Babbling Brooks	123
	The casual digger	126
	Officers	128

Birdie   133
The piece of paper   135
Parables of Anzac   137
Baldy becomes mobile   139
The Roo de Kanga   141
Blighty   143
Very irritated   146
Thinking ahead   147
Finding the 'Awstralians'   148
Please let us take Tobruk!   149
Count your children   150
Parable of the kit inspection   151
The air force wife   153

5 WORKING FOR A LAUGH   157
The garbos' Christmas   157
A Christmas message   159
Rechtub Klat   160
The wharfie's reply   161
The union dog   161
Working on the railway   162
High-octane travel   163
Railway birds   164
Total eclipse of communication   165
The laws of working life   167
Somebody else's job   168
The basic work survival guide   169
Twelve things you'll never hear an employee tell the boss   169
Excessive absence   170
The end of a perfect day   172
Total Quality Management (TQM)   172
Policy development   173
The boat race   174
Prospective Employee Assessment   175
Specialised High-Intensity Training (S.H.I.T.)   176
Early retirement   178
Differences between you and your boss   179
What do they really mean?   180
The little red hen   180
The airline steward's revenge   182
The boss   183
After work . . .   184
Meetings   185

Prayer for the stressed   185
The job application   186
The boss's reply   188
Ode to public servants   189
Jargoning   190
The Jargon Generator   191
Governmentium   192
The surprise party   193
The sex life of an electron   193
Death of employees   194
Workplace agreements   195
Population of Australia   197

6   A SWAG OF LAUGHS   201
The Great Australian Yarn   201
The Bagman's Gazette   202
A stump speech   203
The phantom bullocky   205
A fine team of bullocks   206
Language!   207
Droving in a bar   208
Slow trains   209
Service!   210
Meekatharra ice blocks   211
The redback spider   212
The Great Australian Adjective   213
Lore of the track   218
Sniffling Jimmy   220
The poetic swaggie   222
Where the angel tarboys fly   224
Bowyang Bill and the cocky farmer   227
A good feed   229
The Swagman's Union   230
A glorious spree   232
The Dimboola cat farm   234
A farmer's lament   236
What's on, Cookie?   237
The maiden cook   238
The farmer's will   240

7   THE LAWS OF LIFE   243
Rules for being human   243
Application for Australian Citizenship   244
Children's proverbs   247

To the citizens of the USA   249
Signs of your times   253
Facebook for the chronologically challenged   255
Making a difference   255
Go Aussie, go!   256
25 lessons in life   258
Why cucumbers are better than men   260
Why beer is better than women   262
Personal growth and development courses   263
Lifetime horoscope   264
A rotten day   266
What they wanted   267
The impossible examination   267
Do not break the chain   272
An invitation   273
The army recruit's letter   274
Application for an Australian passport   275
Take a running jump at yourself!   277

8   MOMENTS LIKE THESE . . .   281
Up, up and away!   281
All's well that ends well   283
The Oozlum bird   286
The black stump   292
Yearning for yowies   294
My boyfriend gave me an apple   297
A seasonal guide to wives   300
Henry spruiks Heenzo   300
Spifler- ——— -cate Him!   301
Tough times   305
Australian tourism   305
The naked caravanner   308
Roaming gnomes   309
Her Majesty responds   310
Tigga's travels   311
Running naked with the bulls   312
You need Minties   314

ACKNOWLEDGEMENTS   317

NOTES   319

PHOTO CREDITS   336

*Campfire in the bush with mates, some tucker and a good yarn,
Victoria, 1920s.*

INTRODUCTION

AN EDGE LIKE A CHAINSAW

Australians traditionally like their humour irreverent, crude and with very sharp teeth. The 'politically correct' is out and the 'isms' of sex, race and a swag of other prejudices abound. Pretty well anything and anyone is fair game.

Through the tall tales of the bush, the yarns of Anzac diggers, the antics of larrikins and workplace laughter, our jokes are often at the expense of others, particularly newcomers. Remember the one about the strange whining sound heard at airports as planes from Britain landed? It was eventually realised that this was the whingeing of 'Pommie' migrants dissatisfied with what they found in Australia.

On the other hand, we are also adept at 'taking the piss' out of ourselves. One of the lampoons in this book is titled 'Application for Australian Citizenship', and it begins with this question:

How many slabs can you fit in the back of a Falcon ute while also allowing room for your cattle dog?

And it goes rapidly downhill from there, pillorying our prejudices and preferences.

1

This tendency could come from the history of modern Australia. The need to deal with an unforgiving environment meant that those from the softer northern hemisphere had to toughen up very quickly to survive, never mind thrive. The fabled Australian lampooning of 'new chums' in the nineteenth century and our notorious jokes against 'new Australians', 'reffos', 'boat people' and so on are reprehensible, but perhaps explainable through these circumstances.

Those who are the targets of such humour, of course, are unlikely to see things the same way. But they can and do get their own back through the same process of sending up, making light and generally turning the joke back upon the jokers.

Apart from making us laugh—and, sometimes, cringe—humour can be a great leveller, a safety valve, a consolation or all of these things. It can also be a way to cope with difficult situations, from the everyday trivialities of 'Minties moments' to the often-grim realities of war, tensions at work or just with life in general. It is also something that works best when it is shared. Research shows that people laugh much more frequently when they are in a social situation. When Australians share a joke or swap a yarn, we are so pleased with sending things up that we include ourselves in the humour.

And that humour comes in many forms—yarns, anecdotes, jokes, satires, parodies, cartoons, send-ups and even the ways in which we like to amuse ourselves. Even our fabled slang is not only colourful but frequently humorous in itself. 'In a pig's arse', or simply 'pigs', is a well-worn expression of disbelief. Just what the rear end of the poor old porker has to do with truth or lies is a mystery, but the expression is inherently humorous. Other terms, such as to 'perform like a pork chop' or be as 'happy as a frog in a sock' or 'flat to the boards like a lizard drinking', like many other Australian idioms, use absurdity to produce the kind of humorous talk we find screamingly funny. At least, it is to us; others often find it incomprehensible, vulgar or just plain weird.

Demanding a 'fair suck of the sav(eloy)'—or the sauce bottle, according to some—reminds us of another important characteristic of Australian humour: it is fiercely democratic, insisting on a 'fair go' and 'cutting down tall poppies' at every opportunity. Our parodies and satires often undercut authority figures, whether they be politicians, bureaucrats, experts or just the boss, always fated to be an 'arsehole'. We relish taking someone or something down a peg or three, particularly the prominent and the pompous.

Most of the humour in this book comes from the rich traditions of Australian laughter. The yarns, jokes and sayings that have been handed down from generation to generation still raise a smile. Others are more recent examples of modern traditions of send-up and satire associated with working life or parodying some aspect of politics, economics or society. Some items are humorous anecdotes and stories that have been turned into literature, such as Henry Lawson's 'The Loaded Dog', or literature turned into folklore, like the Dad and Dave stories based on the writings of Steele Rudd. Some are retellings of humorous incidents and events in history, official and otherwise. They all draw on the same native wit that delights in puncturing pretensions and generally giving anyone and anything a 'bit of a serve' or 'stirring the possum' a bit.

We begin with 'bulldust', or just 'bull'. The American humorist Mark Twain was greatly impressed with the Australian ability to generate 'the most beautiful lies' when he visited in the 1890s. He was a man who told more than a few tall stories of his own and so was well qualified to judge. Whether Australians enjoy a good lie more than other nations is a debatable point, but we have an impressive repertoire of 'bullshit', and it is not all slung in Canberra! The country has been blessed with some prodigious liars and you will find some of their greatest works here.

Australian humour is also populated with an amazing array of quirky 'characters'. They range through the funny, the cranky, the weird and the wonderful. Some are mythical, like Sandy the shearer. When told that some lambs were for sale at five shillings each, Sandy complained bitterly that this was far too expensive. When the seller said that he could have them for three pounds a dozen, Sandy was overjoyed and bought the lot.

The intelligence-challenged Drongo is another, hopefully, imagined character of this kind. But other figures, like Bea Miles, actually existed and brightened things up for years with her crazy antics. Memorable eccentrics of all kinds, they are a staple of our folklore.

Another type of identity is the hard case. These types are often battlers, like the cocky farmer or the swaggie, though skinflint tycoons like the miserly grazier 'Hungry' Tyson are not unknown. They may also be stupendous whingers or ratbags, like the bloke who swapped his wife for a billy and a pup because the dog was an extra good one. Whoever they are, real or fictional, they demonstrate the very angular Australian sense of humour, with its sharp elbows and shouldering, four-square attitude. Tough customers all, their doings have delighted us throughout our history and still raise a laugh today.

One of the distinctive elements of Australian humour revolves around the character of the 'Digger', the idealised soldier of the Anzac tradition. While most Digger jokes and japes take place on active duty, they follow the style of bush humour and reflect the biases as well as the delights of the Aussie at war. Digger humour reflects the famous larrikinism and anti-authoritarianism of the Anzacs, from Gallipoli and onwards.

If most of us have to work for a living, we might as well have a laugh about it as often as possible. And we do. Whatever the trade, occupation or profession, there is no shortage of humour about working life, whether we earn our daily crust in the bush, in an office, in a factory or anywhere else. Some yarns and jokes are peculiar to certain industries, trades or workplaces, others are immediately understandable to outsiders. These may be told, suitably adapted, in other industries, like the yarn about the employee who is supposed to keep the workplace clean and tidy. When the boss makes an inspection, he finds the place in a mess and the surfaces thick with dust. He berates the worker, saying, 'The dust on that table is so thick I could write my name in it.' The worker agrees, replying, 'But then, you're an educated man.'

The bush is an inescapable location for a great deal of humour, past and present. Pioneering, settlement, battling fire, flood and drought are all activities that have produced yarns of tough cocky farmers, shearers, bush workers, swaggies and dreadful cooks. Much of this humour relates to the resilience and fortitude necessary to endure the realities of rural life, as well as the need of bush and outback folk to have a very well-developed sense of humour in order to get by.

The trials and tribulations of everyday life are a fertile ground for humour, in the bush and in the city. Wherever we live and work, the same problems perplex us all and we've come up with an endless succession of send-ups, spoofs and satires to raise a laugh or two. Exercising the facial muscles helps us weather the inevitable challenges and disappointments of existence and the seemingly endless absurdities of the laws of life.

Lastly, amusing events and situations, quirky comments and excruciatingly embarrassing moments are a big part of the Australian idea of what is funny, absurd and just odd.

As well as amusing ourselves with quirky characters, jokes about the boss and all those yarns about three blokes in a pub, we even invent quirkily humorous activities, like running naked with the bulls and other odd sporting events such as cockroach racing, boating regattas held in desert river beds or Port Lincoln's famous Tuna Toss competition.

And then, there are always those moments we'd rather forget or, even better, never experience at all. Excruciating embarrassments and cringeworthy exploits are in the 'moments like these' category of great Australian humour. You'll definitely need a Mintie or two.

In the end, the essential ingredient in making humour funny, rather than simply crude or offensive, is to keep it playful. Wit, cleverness, satire and the puncturing of officialdom and pretence are the hallmarks of our best humour. Whatever the circumstances, Australians have found something to laugh about, laugh at, or laugh off.

Prepare for blasting! Cataganga Dam site, Tasmania, 1958.

1

BULL

He's the man who drove the bull through Wagga and never once cracked the whip.

Traditional saying

WHAT A HIDE

This whopper from Western Australia is attributed to a famous north-western yarn-spinner known as 'Lippy the Liar'. Like most tellers of such tales, Lippy was a shearer's cook. He'd grown up, so he said, living with his mother in poverty on a cockatoo farm:

We was so poor we lived on boiled wheat and goannas. The only thing we owned was an old mare.

One bitter cold night Mum and me was sittin' in front of the fire tryin' to keep from turnin' into ice blocks, when we hear a tappin' on the door. The old mare was standin' there, shiverin' and shakin'. Mum said, 'It's cruel to make her suffer like this; you'd better put her out of her misery.'

7

Well, I didn't want to kill the old mare, but I could see it was no good leavin' her like that. So I took her down to the shed. We was too poor to have a gun, so I hit her over the head with a sledgehammer. Then I skinned her and pegged out the hide to dry.

About an hour later, we're back in front of the fire when there's another knock on the door. I open it and there's the old mare standin' there without her hide. Me mother was superstitious and reckoned that the mare wasn't meant to die and that I'd better do somethin' for her. So I took her back down the shed and wrapped her up in some sheep skins to keep her warm.

And do you know, that old mare lived another six years. We got five fleeces off her and she won first prize in the crossbred ewes section of the local agricultural show five years runnin'.

THE SPLIT DOG

A popular bush tale is one also widely told in Britain and America. Usually called 'The Welded Dog' or 'The Split Dog', the story involves a hunter and his dog, which has a painful but, as it turns out, useful accident.

One day while out hunting kangaroos the hunter wounds a beast and his dog tears off to locate the unfortunate 'roo. The dog either runs through some barbed wire or across an opened tin can left by some careless camper and is cut in half, head to tail. Unperturbed, the hunter then puts the two halves of the dog back together.

Unlikely as this may seem, the story continues with the teller claiming that, in his haste, he put the dog back together the wrong way round, leaving the dog with two legs on the ground and two sticking into the air. This does not slow down the dog. The reconstructed canine continues chasing down the 'roo until he gets too tired, whereupon he simply rolls over and continues running with the other two legs. The story ends with the dog catching the 'roo and biting both ends of the animal at the same time.

DROP BEARS

Drop bears are mythical creatures of Australian tall-tale tradition that fall from the trees onto unsuspecting dupes walking below. They are often described as koalas with large heads and sharp teeth. Like a good portion of Australian folktales, drop bears are more of a floating motif around which brief narratives can be constructed by the teller for the edification or, in these cases, the trepidation, of audiences, rather than fully formed, elaborate tales.

The following account of a drop bear yarn in action is a classic example of the Australian love of 'trying on' a 'new chum', or newcomer. It is not unique to Australia, though we do seem to take a particular relish in giving new arrivals a hard time. The account given here includes parenthetical comments from the teller on exactly how to tell such a tall tale for maximum effect on the unsuspecting:

I was working at . . . the hardware shop in 1987 when some Pommy backpackers came in to get some fly screen to cover the bull bar of their Dodge van to stop the insects clogging the radiator. A bit of a slow day so I helped them attach it. When I was finished I stood up and stated, 'That'll stop anything from a quokka to a drop bear.'

'A what?'

'Well, a quokka is a small wallaby-looking thing from Western Australia.'

'Yeah, but what's a drop bear?' (Made them ask.)

'You guys don't know what a drop bear is?' (Disbelief at their lack of knowledge.) 'Okay, they are a carnivorous possum that lives in gumtrees but then drops out the branches, lands on the kangaroo or whatever's back and rips their throat out with an elongated lower canine tooth. Sort of looks like a feral pig tusk. Then laps the blood up like a vampire bat.' (A couple of references to existing animals with known characteristics.)

'My God, have you ever seen one?'

'Well, not a live one. During the expansion of the 1930s the farmers organised drives because they were killing stock. There is a stuffed one in the museum in town.' (Offering verification if they want to stay another day. But they had already established they were heading for Mount Isa as soon as I was finished.)

'They're not extinct but endangered; just small isolated groups now.' (More believable that there are only limited numbers as opposed to saying they are everywhere.)

'Really, whereabouts?'

'Here in Queensland; well, the Western bits at least.' (Which direction are they heading? Townsville to Mt Isa.)

'But how will we know if it's safe to camp?' (Concern now; they can't afford motels.)

'Oh, well, it's a local thing. As you're going through the last town before you stop for the night, just go into any pub and ask what the drop bear situation is like. Bye . . . have a nice trip.'

The teller of this tale accurately concluded his account with the comment: 'Jeez, there are some bastards in this world.'

In one of a number of drop bear stories collected in Queensland during the 1980s, the creature is said to have size 10 feet, which it uses to kick in the head of its unfortunate victims. More recently, there have been several bands and a sports team using the name and the little beasts also lead a busy life on the internet, the modern-day home to many older traditions.

HOOP SNAKES

Hoop snakes are another species of mythical creature sharing the bush story space with drop bears and giant mozzies. They have been rolling through Australian tradition since at least the mid- to late nineteenth century, and are said to put their tails in their mouths and then roll after their intended victims, as in this typical hoop snake yarn:

> Well, there I was, slogging through this timber country, and just as I gets to the top of the hill I almost steps on this bloody great snake. Of course, I jump backwards pretty smartish-like, but the snake comes straight at me, so off I went back down the hill, fast as I could go. Trouble was, it was a hoop snake. Soon as I took off, the bloody thing put its tail in its mouth and came bowling along after me. And it was gaining on me, too—but just as I reached the bottom of the hill, I jumped up and grabbed an overhanging branch. The hoop snake couldn't stop. It just went bowling along and splashed straight into the creek at the bottom of the hill and drowned. Well, of course it's a true story. I mean—if it weren't true the snake would have got me and I wouldn't be telling you about it, would I?

Hoop snakes can be found on the internet and have also been known in North America since at least the 1780s, in which country they sometimes wriggle into tales of Pecos Bill, the superhuman occupational hero of cowboy legend, similar in some ways to the Australian shearers' hero, Crooked Mick.

GIANT MOZZIES

Old bush favourites are the giant mosquitoes who wear hobnail boots, carry off cows and bullocks, and may be seen later picking their teeth with the unfortunate beast's bones. Sometimes these are located in particular areas and attract a variety of ever-taller tales about their doings, as in the cases of 'The Mozzies of Giru' in Queensland and 'The Hexham Greys' in New South Wales, as described in an anonymous twentieth-century folk ballad:

Now the Territory has huge Crocodiles,
Queensland the Taipan snake
Wild scrub bulls are the biggest risk,
over in the Western state
But if you're ever in NSW, 'round Hunter Valley way
Look out for them giant mozzies, the dreaded
Hexham Grey.

They're the biggest skeetas in the world,
and that's the dinkum truth
Why, I've heard the fence wire snappin',
when they land on them to roost
Be ready to clear out smartly,
when you hear the dreaded drone
They'll suck the blood right out ya' veins,
and the marrow from ya' bones.

Now some shooters on the swamp one night,
waiting for the ducks to come in
Loaded their guns in earnest
at the sound of flappin' wings
As the big mob circled overhead
they aimed and blasted away
But by mistake they'd gone and shot,
at a swarm of Hexham Greys.

And a bullocky in the early days, bogged in swampy
    land
Left his team to try and find, someone to lend a hand
When he returned next morning, he found to his dismay,
His whole darn team had perished, devoured by Hexham
    Greys.
Oh his swearin' they say was louder,
than any thunder storm
When he spotted a pair of Hexham Greys,
pickin' their teeth with his leader's horns.

And ya' know, twenty men once disappeared,
to this day they've never been found
They'd been workin' late on a water tank,
by the river at Hexham town.
The skeetas were so savage,
the men climbed in that tank's insides
Believin' they'd be protected,
by the corrugated iron.

But when the skeetas bit right through that tank,
determined to get a meal
The apprentice grabbed his hammer,
clinched their beaks onto the steel.
Well it wasn't long before they felt,
that big tank slowly rise
You see them skeetas lifted it clear from the ground
Then carried 'em all off into the sky.

Well they're just a few of the facts I've heard,
concernin' the Hexham Grey
Passed on to me by my dear old dad,
who would never lie they say.
So if you're in NSW, 'round Hunter Valley way
Look out for them giant mozzies,
the dreaded Hexham Grey.

There is a three-metre statue of a grey mosquito outside the
Hexham Bowling Club. The locals say that it is a life-sized
model of a Hexham Grey. Other giant mozzies may feature in
tales of the Speewah.

CROOKED MICK AND THE SPEEWAH

Fabled figures of bush lore and legend, shearers created a rich
body of humorous stories about themselves and aspects of
their calling. Many of these stories have a strong tendency to
exaggeration, an important aspect of their appeal.

Crooked Mick is the legendary occupational hero of Australian shearers and other outback workers. Mick can shear more sheep, cut more trees and do anything faster than anyone else. Julian Stuart, one of the leaders of the 1891 shearer's strike in Queensland, provides the earliest known reference to Crooked Mick, writing in *The Australian Worker* during the 1920s:

I first heard of him on the Barcoo in 1889. We were shearing at Northampton Downs, and we musterers brought in a rosy-cheeked young English Johnny who, in riding from Jericho, the nearest railway station to Blackall, where he was going to edit the new paper, had got lost and found himself at the station, where we were busily engaged disrobing about 150,000 jumbucks.

He was treated with the hospitality of the sheds, which is traditional, and after tea we gathered in the hut—dining room and sleeping accommodation all in one in those days—and proceeded to entertain him.

Whistling Dick played 'The British Grenadiers' on his tin whistle; Bungeye Blake sang 'Little Dog Ben'; Piebald Moore and Cabbagetree Capstick told a common lie or two, but when Dusty Bob got the flute I sat up on my bunk and listened, for I knew him to be the most fluent liar that ever crossed the Darling.

His anecdotes about Crooked Mick began and ended nowhere, and made C.M. appear a superman—with feet so big that he had to go outside to turn around.

It took a large-sized bullock's hide to make him a pair of moccasins.

He was a heavy smoker. It took one 'loppy' (rouseabout) all his time cutting tobacco and filling his pipe.

He worked at such a clip that his shears ran hot, and sometimes he had a half a dozen pairs in the water pot to cool.

He had his fads, and would not shear in sheds that faced north. When at his top, it took three pressers to handle the wool from his blades, and they had to work overtime to keep the bins clear.

He ate two merino sheep each meal—that is, if they were small merinos—but only one and a half when the ration sheep were Leicester crossbred wethers.

His main tally was generally cut on the breakfast run. Anyone who tried to follow him usually spent the balance of the day in the hut.

Between sheds he did fencing. When cutting brigalow posts he used an axe in each hand to save time, and when digging post holes a crowbar in one hand and a shovel in the other.

This slightly idealised depiction gives a good idea of the context in which Crooked Mick tales were told and also the ability of the fluent liar, Dusty Bob, to string otherwise unconnected, fantastic events into a crude but engaging narrative, a practice sometimes noticed among bush yarn-spinners.

Another of many such related incidents is the story of how Mick came to be called 'Crooked'. As Mick tells it (and there are other versions, of course), he was ploughing one day and it got so hot that the fence-wire melted. When he took the horses to have a drink after the day's work, he placed one leg in the water bucket. The leg was red hot and when he lifted his other leg and put his weight on the one in the water, it buckled. It's been that way ever since, which is why Mick walks with a slight limp.

In later life, Mick's escapades include attempting to stone the crows by throwing Ayer's Rock (Uluru) at them, harnessing willy-willies to improve the flow of a water windmill, and becoming the ringer of the Speewah shed with an unbeaten tally of 1847 wethers and twelve lambs, all shorn in just one day using hand blades.

The Speewah is closely associated with Crooked Mick. It is an outback never-never land where everything grows in unnaturally large proportions: the pumpkins are so big that they can be used as houses, the trees are so tall that they have to be hinged to let in the sunlight, the sheep are so large that they cannot be shorn without climbing up a ladder. Many strange and wondrous sights can be witnessed on the Speewah, which is variously said to be located out the back of beyond, where the crows fly backwards. The Speewah is so hot in summer that its freezing point is set at 99 degrees. It is so cold in the winter that even the mirages freeze solid and the grasshoppers grow fur coats to keep themselves warm. Droughts are not over until the people of the Speewah are able to have water in their tea.

The creatures of the Speewah form a strange and exotic menagerie that includes the small Ker-Ker bird, so named from its habit of flying across the Speewah in summertime crying 'ker-ker-kripes, it's hot!' Then there is the Oozlum bird that flies tail-first and in smaller and smaller circles until, moaning, it disappears inside itself head-first. Hoop snakes and giant mosquitoes are commonplace on the Speewah, as are giant emus, wombats, crocodiles and boars. The 'roos are so big that they make the emus look like canaries and the rabbits so thick, large and cunning that Mick had to go to war to save himself.

As well as Mick himself, the Speewah is peopled with other larger than life characters. These include Prickly Pear Polly, so plain that a cocky farmer hired her as a scarecrow. She was so good at scaring the birds that they even started returning the corn they'd stolen two seasons before. Another was Old Harry, the building worker with one wooden leg. He came home from work one night and his wife noticed that he only had one leg left. Harry looked down and was amazed to discover that she was correct. No idea how he'd lost it, just hadn't noticed. Irish Paddy was so good at digging post-holes that he would wear his six-foot crowbar down to the size of a darning needle. There was Bungeye Bill the gambler and Greasy George, the third assistant shearer's cook, a man who rarely bathed and was so greasy that your eyes slid right off him as you looked.

The Speewah shearing shed itself was said to be so large that it needed two men and a boy standing on each other's shoulders to see the whole of it and the boss would take a day or more to ride its length on horseback. Traditions of outsize shearing sheds and stations featuring men of the stamp of Crooked Mick are also found under names like Big Burrawong and Big Burramugga (WA), suggesting that the tales of Mick's doings and those of the mythic stations may have been independent.

A number of Australian folklorists and writers recall speaking and corresponding with individuals who told Crooked Mick tales or knew of him and his exploits on the Speewah, suggesting a strong currency in oral as well as literary tradition. On the other hand, collections of shearer anecdotes made in the late twentieth and early twenty-first centuries make no reference to these tales, suggesting that Crooked Mick may be having a tough time surviving change, despite his prowess.

DINKUM!

A perennial favourite of the Australian yarning tradition is the one-upmanship of American 'skiters', as boasters used to be called. There are many tales of this type; this one was told in World War I:

In a London café last month a soldier who hailed from the other side of Oodnadatta fell into a friendly argument with an American, as to the relative greatness of the two countries.

'Wal,' said the Yankee, 'that bit o' sunbaked mud yew call Australia ain't a bad bit o' sile in its way, and it'll be worth expectoratin' on when it wakes up and discovers it's alive, but when yew come to compare it with Amurrica, wal, yer might 'swell put a spot o' dust alongside a diamond. Y'see, sonny, we kinder do things in Amurrica; we don't sit round like an egg in its shell waitin' fer someone tew come along and crack it; no, we git hustling' till all Amurrica's one kernormous dust storm kicked up by our citizens raking in their dollars. Why, there's millions of Amurricans who 'ave tew climb to the top of their stack o' dollars on a ladder every morning, so's they ken see the sun rise. We're some people!'

The Australian took a hitch in his belt, put his cigarette behind his ear, and observed:

'Dollars! Do yer only deal in five bobs over there! We deal in nothin' but quids in Australia. Anything smaller than a quid we throw away. Too much worry to count, and it spoils the shape of yer pockets. The schoolboys 'ave paper-chases with pound notes. Money in Australia! Why, you can see the business blokes comin' outer their offices every day with wads of bank notes like blankets under each arm. I remember before I left Adelaide all the citizens was makin' for the banks with the day's takin's, when a stiff gale sprung up pretty sudden. Them citizens let go their wads ter 'old their 'ats on and immediately the air was full of bank notes— mostly 'undred quiders. Yer couldn't see the sun fer paper. The corporation 'ad to hire a thousand men ter sweep them bank notes in a 'eap and burn 'em. Dinkum!'

THE EXPLODING DUNNY

This is an update of an old bush yarn from the days before septic tanks and sewers. Back then, the traditional dunny was a hole in the ground. Every week or two, as the hole began to fill, the usual practice was to pour kerosene down to disguise the smell and aid decomposition. One day someone mistakenly poured petrol down the hole and the next person to use the dunny dropped his lighted cigarette butt down. The resulting explosion variously blows up the dunny, its contents and the unfortunate smoker.

In the modern version, the woman of the house is trying to exterminate an insect, often a cockroach. It won't die by the normal methods, so she throws it into the toilet bowl and gives it a good spray of insecticide. Immediately afterwards, the husband rushes in with an urgent need to use the convenience. Comfortably seated and enjoying the relief along with a cigarette, he finishes smoking and drops the lighted cigarette butt into the bowl. Still filled with the flammable residue of the insecticide and other gaseous elements, the bowl immediately ignites and burns his backside.

With badly burned rear and genitals, the husband is in need of hospitalisation. When the ambulance arrives, the ambulance men are so amused that they cannot stop laughing. They get the husband onto the stretcher, but on the way out their laughter becomes uncontrollable. They drop the stretcher. The burned husband hits the concrete floor and breaks his pelvis.

The continued popularity of this fable is perhaps due to its moral—even the most mundane domestic places and activities can be dangerous. Old though it is, the exploding dunny continues to amuse us.

THE WELL-DRESSED 'ROO

The well-dressed 'roo is, not surprisingly, an old favourite, and probably derives from bush yarns about a kangaroo mimicking the actions of humans. It was probably not new when it was published in a 1902 book of humour titled *Aboriginalities*. The story was also told in the 1950s about visiting English cricket sides and, in the mid-1980s, about an Italian America's Cup team in Western Australia. It has been frequently aired in the Australian press.

A group of tourists (sometimes Japanese, sometimes American) is being driven through the outback to see the sights. The bus runs down a kangaroo and stops to assess the damage. The tourists are all excited at this bit of authentic Australiana and rush out to have a look. After the cameras have been clicking for a while, someone gets the bright idea of standing the dead 'roo up against a tree and putting his sports jacket on the animal for a bit of a different souvenir photo.

Just as the tourist is about to snap his photo, the 'roo, only stunned by the bus, returns to consciousness and leaps off into the scrub, still wearing the tourist's expensive jacket, which also contains his wallet, money, credit cards, passport . . .

Despite its Australian pedigree, the tale is not unique to these shores. The theme of poetic justice meted out to the human by a supposedly dumb animal has many international variations, including the American bear that walks off into Yellowstone Park carrying a tourist's baby and the deer hunter who loses his expensive rifle by placing it in the antlers of a deer he has just shot. Like the 'roo, the deer is only stunned and races off with the weapon still fixed in its horns. Versions of the tale are also told in Germany and Canada.

LOADED ANIMALS

A relatively recent urban legend concerns a rabbit and a stick of gelignite:

A rabbit-o, new to the task of catching bunnies, was not having too much luck. No matter what he did he couldn't seem to bag a single bunny. The old hands were doing well, so the new bloke decided to ask them for some advice. They told him to get himself a rabbit, tie a stick of gelignite to its tail, light the 'gelly' and send the rabbit down the nearest burrow. This would guarantee a big, if messy, haul.

The new bloke thought that this was a fine idea. The only trouble was, he couldn't catch a rabbit in the first place to start off. So he decided to buy himself a rabbit at the pet store in town. Back in the bush, he gets the rabbit out of its cage, ties the gelly to it, lights the fuse and points it towards the burrows. Off the rabbit goes. But, being a pet-shop rabbit, it had been born in captivity and didn't know what to do in the wild. It circled round and ran back towards the bloke, fuse sputtering, and scurried straight underneath his expensive new jalopy, blowing the whole thing to buggery.

This is another old bush yarn modernised. It also has a lengthy history as an international tale, being known at least as early as the Middle Ages in Europe, and also in India. Like many other such widely distributed tales, it has been traced to the Bible, though its more modern versions tend towards the 'biter bitten' category of stories. In the updated versions, it is usually a couple of blokes, often out hunting, who tie the gelignite to the rabbit out of cruelty. The rabbit, which is a wild one rather than a tame one, is terrified and does the same thing as the traditional bunny, running under the blokes' $50,000 four-wheel-drive where, of course, it explodes.

Other modern versions of this are reported widely in North America and in New Zealand, and it often pops up in the press when journalists are desperate to fill a few empty column centimetres. There is even an exploding fish variation, sometimes said to be a shark. In Queensland they seem to prefer exploding pigs that write off the ute in exactly the same way. But as far as the Australian renditions, old and new, are concerned, Henry Lawson knew the yarn and used it in his well-known short story 'The Loaded Dog'.

Dave Regan, Jim Bently, and Andy Page were sinking a shaft at Stony Creek in search of a rich gold quartz reef which was supposed to exist in the vicinity. There is always a rich reef supposed to exist in the vicinity; the only questions are whether it is ten feet or hundreds beneath the surface, and in which direction. They had struck some pretty solid rock, also water which kept them baling. They used the old-fashioned blasting-powder and time-fuse. They'd make a sausage or cartridge of blasting-powder in a skin of strong calico or canvas, the mouth sewn and bound round the end of the fuse; they'd dip the cartridge in melted tallow to make it water-tight, get the drill-hole as dry as possible, drop in the cartridge with some dry dust, and wad and ram with stiff clay and broken brick. Then they'd light the fuse and get out of the hole and wait. The result was usually an ugly

pot-hole in the bottom of the shaft and half a barrow-load
of broken rock.

There was plenty of fish in the creek, fresh-water bream,
cod, cat-fish, and tailers. The party were fond of fish, and
Andy and Dave of fishing. Andy would fish for three hours
at a stretch if encouraged by a 'nibble' or a 'bite' now and
then say once in twenty minutes. The butcher was always
willing to give meat in exchange for fish when they caught
more than they could eat; but now it was winter, and these
fish wouldn't bite. However, the creek was low, just a chain
of muddy water-holes, from the hole with a few bucketfuls
in it to the sizable pool with an average depth of six or seven
feet, and they could get fish by baling out the smaller holes
or muddying up the water in the larger ones till the fish rose
to the surface. There was the cat-fish, with spikes growing
out of the sides of its head, and if you got pricked you'd
know it, as Dave said. Andy took off his boots, tucked up
his trousers, and went into a hole one day to stir up the mud
with his feet, and he knew it. Dave scooped one out with his
hand and got pricked, and he knew it too; his arm swelled,
and the pain throbbed up into his shoulder, and down into
his stomach too, he said, like a toothache he had once, and
kept him awake for two nights only the toothache pain had
a 'burred edge', Dave said.

Dave got an idea.

'Why not blow the fish up in the big water-hole with a
cartridge?' he said.

'I'll try it.'

He thought the thing out and Andy Page worked it
out. Andy usually put Dave's theories into practice if they
were practicable, or bore the blame for the failure and the
chaffing of his mates if they weren't.

He made a cartridge about three times the size of those
they used in the rock. Jim Bently said it was big enough to
blow the bottom out of the river. The inner skin was of stout
calico; Andy stuck the end of a six-foot piece of fuse well

down in the powder and bound the mouth of the bag firmly
to it with whipcord. The idea was to sink the cartridge in
the water with the open end of the fuse attached to a float
on the surface, ready for lighting. Andy dipped the cartridge
in melted bees'-wax to make it water-tight. 'We'll have to
leave it some time before we light it,' said Dave, 'to give the
fish time to get over their scare when we put it in, and come
nosing round again; so we'll want it well water-tight.'

Round the cartridge Andy, at Dave's suggestion, bound
a strip of sail canvas that they used for making water-bags
to increase the force of the explosion, and round that he
pasted layers of stiff brown paper on the plan of the sort
of fireworks we called 'gun-crackers'. He let the paper dry
in the sun, then he sewed a covering of two thicknesses of
canvas over it, and bound the thing from end to end with
stout fishing-line. Dave's schemes were elaborate, and he
often worked his inventions out to nothing. The cartridge
was rigid and solid enough now—a formidable bomb; but
Andy and Dave wanted to be sure. Andy sewed on another
layer of canvas, dipped the cartridge in melted tallow,
twisted a length of fencing-wire round it as an afterthought,
dipped it in tallow again, and stood it carefully against a
tent-peg, where he'd know where to find it, and wound the
fuse loosely round it. Then he went to the camp-fire to try
some potatoes which were boiling in their jackets in a billy,
and to see about frying some chops for dinner. Dave and
Jim were at work in the claim that morning.

They had a big black young retriever dog or rather an
overgrown pup, a big, foolish, four-footed mate, who was
always slobbering round them and lashing their legs with
his heavy tail that swung round like a stock-whip. Most
of his head was usually a red, idiotic, slobbering grin of
appreciation of his own silliness. He seemed to take life,
the world, his two-legged mates, and his own instinct as a
huge joke. He'd retrieve anything: he carted back most of
the camp rubbish that Andy threw away. They had a cat

that died in hot weather, and Andy threw it a good distance away in the scrub; and early one morning the dog found the cat, after it had been dead a week or so, and carried it back to camp, and laid it just inside the tent-flaps, where it could best make its presence known when the mates should rise and begin to sniff suspiciously in the sickly smothering atmosphere of the summer sunrise. He used to retrieve them when they went in swimming; he'd jump in after them, and take their hands in his mouth, and try to swim out with them, and scratch their naked bodies with his paws. They loved him for his good-heartedness and his foolishness, but when they wished to enjoy a swim they had to tie him up in camp.

He watched Andy with great interest all the morning making the cartridge, and hindered him considerably, trying to help; but about noon he went off to the claim to see how Dave and Jim were getting on, and to come home to dinner with them. Andy saw them coming, and put a panful of mutton-chops on the fire. Andy was cook to-day; Dave and Jim stood with their backs to the fire, as Bushmen do in all weathers, waiting till dinner should be ready. The retriever went nosing round after something he seemed to have missed.

Andy's brain still worked on the cartridge; his eye was caught by the glare of an empty kerosene-tin lying in the bushes, and it struck him that it wouldn't be a bad idea to sink the cartridge packed with clay, sand, or stones in the tin, to increase the force of the explosion. He may have been all out, from a scientific point of view, but the notion looked all right to him. Jim Bently, by the way, wasn't interested in their 'damned silliness'. Andy noticed an empty treacle-tin, the sort with the little tin neck or spout soldered on to the top for the convenience of pouring out the treacle, and it struck him that this would have made the best kind of cartridge-case: he would only have had to pour in the powder, stick the fuse in through the neck, and cork and seal it with bees'-wax. He was turning to suggest this to Dave, when Dave glanced over his shoulder to see how the chops were doing and bolted. He explained afterwards that he thought he heard the pan spluttering extra, and looked to see if the chops were burning.

Jim Bently looked behind and bolted after Dave. Andy stood stock-still, staring after them. 'Run, Andy! run!' they shouted back at him. 'Run!!! Look behind you, you fool!' Andy turned slowly and looked, and there, close behind him, was the retriever with the cartridge in his mouth wedged into his broadest and silliest grin. And that wasn't all. The dog had come round the fire to Andy, and the loose end of the fuse had trailed and waggled over the burning sticks into the blaze; Andy had slit and nicked the firing end of the fuse well, and now it was hissing and spitting properly.

Andy's legs started with a jolt; his legs started before his brain did, and he made after Dave and Jim. And the dog followed Andy.

Dave and Jim were good runners, Jim the best for a short distance; Andy was slow and heavy, but he had the strength and the wind and could last. The dog leapt and capered round him, delighted as a dog could be to find his mates, as he thought, on for a frolic. Dave and Jim kept shouting back, 'Don't foller us! Don't foller us, you coloured fool!' but Andy kept on, no matter how they dodged. They could never explain, any more than the dog, why they followed each other, but so they ran, Dave keeping in Jim's track in all its turnings, Andy after Dave, and the dog circling round Andy—the live fuse swishing in all directions and hissing and spluttering and stinking. Jim yelling to Dave not to follow him, Dave shouting to Andy to go in another direction to 'spread out', and Andy roaring at the dog to go home.

Then Andy's brain began to work, stimulated by the crisis: he tried to get a running kick at the dog, but the dog dodged; he snatched up sticks and stones and threw them at the dog and ran on again. The retriever saw that he'd made a mistake about Andy, and left him and bounded after Dave.

Dave, who had the presence of mind to think that the fuse's time wasn't up yet, made a dive and a grab for the dog, caught him by the tail, and as he swung round snatched the cartridge out of his mouth and flung it as far as he could: the dog immediately bounded after it and retrieved it. Dave roared and cursed at the dog, who seeing that Dave was offended, left him and went after Jim, who was well ahead. Jim swung to a sapling and went up it like a native bear; it was a young sapling, and Jim couldn't safely get more than ten or twelve feet from the ground. The dog laid the cartridge, as carefully as if it was a kitten, at the foot of the sapling, and capered and leaped and whooped joyously round under Jim. The big pup reckoned that this was part of the lark, he was all right now, it was Jim who was out for a spree.

The fuse sounded as if it were going a mile a minute. Jim tried to climb higher and the sapling bent and cracked. Jim fell on his feet and ran. The dog swooped on the cartridge and followed. It all took but a very few moments. Jim ran to a digger's hole, about ten feet deep, and dropped down into it—landing on soft mud—and was safe. The dog grinned sardonically down on him, over the edge, for a moment, as if he thought it would be a good lark to drop the cartridge down on Jim.

'Go away, Tommy,' said Jim feebly, 'go away.'

The dog bounded off after Dave, who was the only one in sight now; Andy had dropped behind a log, where he lay flat on his face, having suddenly remembered a picture of the Russo-Turkish war with a circle of Turks lying flat on their faces (as if they were ashamed) round a newly-arrived shell.

There was a small hotel or shanty on the creek, on the main road, not far from the claim. Dave was desperate, the time flew much faster in his stimulated imagination than it did in reality, so he made for the shanty. There were several casual Bushmen on the verandah and in the bar;

Dave rushed into the bar, banging the door to behind him. 'My dog!' he gasped, in reply to the astonished stare of the publican, 'The blanky retriever—he's got a live cartridge in his mouth—'

The retriever, finding the front door shut against him, had bounded round and in by the back way, and now stood smiling in the doorway leading from the passage, the cartridge still in his mouth and the fuse spluttering. They burst out of that bar. Tommy bounded first after one and then after another, for, being a young dog, he tried to make friends with everybody.

The Bushmen ran round corners, and some shut themselves in the stable. There was a new weather-board and corrugated-iron kitchen and wash-house on piles in the back-yard, with some women washing clothes inside. Dave and the publican bundled in there and shut the door, the publican cursing Dave and calling him a crimson fool, in hurried tones, and wanting to know what the hell he came here for.

The retriever went in under the kitchen, amongst the piles, but, luckily for those inside, there was a vicious yellow mongrel cattle-dog sulking and nursing his nastiness under there, a sneaking, fighting, thieving canine, whom neighbours had tried for years to shoot or poison. Tommy saw his danger, he'd had experience from this dog, and started out and across the yard, still sticking to the cartridge. Half-way across the yard the yellow dog caught him and nipped him. Tommy dropped the cartridge, gave one terrified yell, and took to the Bush. The yellow dog followed him to the fence and then ran back to see what he had dropped.

Nearly a dozen other dogs came from round all the corners and under the buildings, spidery, thievish, cold-blooded kangaroo-dogs, mongrel sheep- and cattle-dogs, vicious black and yellow dogs that slip after you in the dark, nip your heels, and vanish without explaining and yapping, yelping small fry. They kept at a respectable distance round the nasty yellow dog, for it was dangerous to go near him when he thought he had found something which might be good for a dog to eat. He sniffed at the cartridge twice, and was just taking a third cautious sniff when—

It was very good blasting powder, a new brand that Dave had recently got up from Sydney; and the cartridge had been excellently well made. Andy was very patient and painstaking in all he did, and nearly as handy as the average sailor with needles, twine, canvas, and rope.

Bushmen say that that kitchen jumped off its piles and on again. When the smoke and dust cleared away, the remains of the nasty yellow dog were lying against the paling fence of the yard, looking as if he had been kicked into a fire by a horse and afterwards rolled in the dust under a barrow, and finally thrown against the fence from a distance. Several saddle-horses, which had been 'hanging-up' round the verandah, were galloping wildly down the road in clouds of dust, with broken bridle-reins flying; and from a circle round the outskirts, from every point of the compass in the scrub, came the yelping of dogs. Two of them went home, to the place where they were born, thirty miles away, and reached it the same night and stayed there; it was not till towards evening that the rest came back cautiously to make inquiries. One was trying to walk on two legs, and most of 'em looked more or less singed; and a little, singed, stumpy-tailed dog, who had been in the habit of hopping the back half of him along on one leg, had reason to be glad that he'd saved up the other leg all those years, for he needed it now. There was one old one-eyed cattle-dog round that shanty for years afterwards, who couldn't stand the smell of a gun being cleaned. He it was who had taken an interest, only second to that of the yellow dog, in the cartridge. Bushmen said that it was amusing to slip up on his blind side and stick a dirty ramrod under his nose: he wouldn't wait to bring his solitary eye to bear, he'd take to the Bush and stay out all night.

For half an hour or so after the explosion there were several Bushmen round behind the stable who crouched, doubled up, against the wall, or rolled gently on the dust, trying to laugh without shrieking. There were two white women in hysterics at the house, and a half-caste rushing aimlessly round with a dipper of cold water. The publican was holding his wife tight and begging her between her squawks, to 'hold up for my sake, Mary, or I'll lam the life out of ye'.

Dave decided to apologise later on, 'when things had settled a bit', and went back to camp. And the dog that had done it all, 'Tommy', the great, idiotic mongrel retriever, came slobbering round Dave and lashing his legs with his tail, and trotted home after him, smiling his broadest, longest, and reddest smile of amiability, and apparently satisfied for one afternoon with the fun he'd had.

Andy chained the dog up securely, and cooked some more chops, while Dave went to help Jim out of the hole.

And most of this is why, for years afterwards, lanky, easy-going Bushmen, riding lazily past Dave's camp, would cry, in a lazy drawl and with just a hint of the nasal twang—

''El-lo, Da-a-ve! How's the fishin' getting on, Da-a-ve?'

THE BLACKOUT BABIES

There is a strange surge in the number of babies born around the same time in a particular region. The explanation for this is that there was a power blackout nine months earlier. This meant that people were not able to spend the night in front of the 'telly' and so had to amuse themselves in more traditional ways.

This story has been circulating in Australia since at least the 1960s. It was not new then and, in one version or another, has been recorded throughout Australia and around the world.

Instead of a power blackout, the reason for the nocturnal hijinks is often the regular and noisy arrival of the night train.

Folklorist Bill Scott has a superb version of this given to him in 1978. His version had an appropriate bureaucratic setting:

> The Census Office was puzzling over the figures of the recent Census in relation to the north coast NSW town of Kyogle. They couldn't work out why this place had a birth rate three times the national average. They sent an officer to investigate. He found the school crammed with kids and even a special new wing added to the maternity hospital. After a few days, the officer worked it out.
>
> The Kyogle Mail used to pass through town about 4.30 every morning, blowing its whistle first at the level crossing on the north side of town and waking everyone up. Just as they were dozing off again the train would cross the crossing on the south side of town and blow its whistle again. By then just about everyone in town was wide-awake. It was too early to get up, but . . .

Folklorists in Britain, America and Australia have turned up many other versions of the same tale. In South Africa the story is so well known in one particular town that the local offspring are known far and wide as 'train babies'. That train also ran through Michigan during the 1950s, through the New York City blackout of 1965 and the 1990 San Francisco Bay Area earthquake. It is still running somewhere.

THE MOST BEAUTIFUL LIES

Samuel Langhorne Clemens was born in Missouri in 1835. After looking out for himself from the age of twelve, he eventually became the great American writer and humorist known as 'Mark Twain'. His pen name derived from his days as a riverboat pilot where the cry 'mark twain' was the pilot's call to indicate a depth of two fathoms beneath a boat. By the early 1890s, Twain had made and lost a couple of fortunes and was repairing his finances through a world speaking tour. When the great American man visited Australia in 1895, he left a flurry of witty remarks and quips in his wake. Many of them are as revealing and funny now as they were back then. On arriving in Sydney, Twain was interviewed by a local journalist and declared:

> My greatest efforts are directed towards doing the world with as little hard work as possible. I frankly admit that in regard to most things I am phenomenally lazy. I have travelled from the Rocky Mountains to Jerusalem in order to escape hard work, and I have come to Australia with the same idea.

He praised the harbour as 'superbly beautiful' and described his arrival:

> We entered and cast anchor, and in the morning went oh-ing and ah-ing in admiration up through the crooks and turns of the spacious and beautiful harbor—a harbor which is the darling of Sydney and the wonder of the world. It is not surprising that the people are proud of it, nor that they put their enthusiasm into eloquent words. A returning citizen asked me what I thought of it, and I testified with a cordiality which I judged would be up to the market rate. I said it was beautiful—superbly beautiful. Then by a natural impulse I gave God the praise. The citizen did not seem altogether satisfied. He said:
> 'It is beautiful, of course it's beautiful—the Harbor; but that isn't all of it, it's only half of it; Sydney's the other half, and it takes both of them together to ring the supremacy-bell. God made the Harbor, and that's all right; but Satan made Sydney.'
> Of course I made an apology; and asked him to convey it to his friend. He was right about Sydney being half of it. It would be beautiful without Sydney, but not above half as beautiful as it is now, with Sydney added.

But travelling by train across the New South Wales–Victoria border, Twain was stunned to discover that he and all the passengers needed to change trains due to the different gauge tracks in each colony. His much-quoted comment was, 'Think of the paralysis of intellect that gave that idea birth.'

He was happier in Melbourne, especially at the Melbourne Cup:

> The Melbourne Cup is the Australasian National Day. It would be difficult to overstate its importance. It overshadows all other holidays and specialized days of whatever sort in that congeries of colonies. Overshadows them? I might almost say it blots them out. Each of them gets attention, but not everybody's; each of them evokes interest, but not everybody's; each of them rouses enthusiasm, but not everybody's; in each case a part of the attention, interest, and enthusiasm is a matter of habit and custom, and another part of it is official and perfunctory. Cup Day, and Cup Day only, commands an attention, an interest, and an enthusiasm which are universal—and spontaneous, not perfunctory. Cup Day is supreme—it has no rival. I can call to mind no specialized annual day, in any country, which can be named by that large name—Supreme. I can call to mind no specialized annual day, in any country, whose approach fires the whole land with a conflagration of conversation and preparation and anticipation and jubilation. No day save this one; but this one does it.

With a writer's ear for everyday speech, Twain gently sent up the Australian accent, reporting his hotel chambermaid's morning greeting: 'The tyble is set, and here is the piper [paper]; and if the lydy is ready I'll tell the wyter to bring up the breakfast.'

He was also fascinated by the term 'My word', seemingly in vogue at the time: 'The first time I heard an Australian say it, it was positively thrilling,' he wrote, and suggested that Americans import it for their own use.

In Adelaide, Twain was impressed by the number and variety of faiths and the various churches, temples and chapels in which they worshipped:

> She has a population, as per the latest census, of only 320,000-odd, and yet her varieties of religion indicate the presence within her borders of samples of people from pretty nearly every part of the globe you can think of. Tabulated, these varieties of religion make a remarkable show. One would have to go far to find its match.

After a table of statistics recording the numbers of the various faiths professed in Adelaide, Twain arrived at a total of just over 320,000, including 1719 'Other Religions', which included:

> Agnostics, Atheists, Believers in Christ, Buddhists, Calvinists, Christadelphians, Christians, Christ's Chapel, Christian Israelites, Christian Socialists, Church of God, Cosmopolitans, Deists, Evangelists, Exclusive Brethren, Free Church, Free Methodists, Freethinkers, Followers of Christ, Gospel Meetings, Greek Church, Infidels, Maronites, Memnonists, Moravians, Mormons, Naturalists, Orthodox, Others (indefinite), Pagans, Pantheists, Plymouth Brethren, Rationalists, Reformers, Secularists, Seventh-day Adventists, Shakers, Shintoists, Spiritualists, Theosophists, Town (City) Mission, Welsh Church, Huguenot, Hussite, Zoroastrians, Zwinglian.
>
> About 64 roads to the other world. You see how healthy the religious atmosphere is. Anything can live in it. Agnostics, Atheists, Freethinkers, Infidels, Mormons, Pagans, Indefinites, they are all there. And all the big sects of the world can do more than merely live in it: they can spread, flourish, prosper. All except the Spiritualists and the Theosophists. That is the most curious feature of this curious table. What is the matter with the specter? Why do they puff him away? He is a welcome toy everywhere else in the world.

Twain visited the goldfields of Victoria and in Ballarat he thought the Eureka Stockade 'the finest thing in Australasian history. It was a revolution—small in size; but great politically; it was a strike for liberty, a struggle for a principle, a stand against injustice and oppression' and 'another instance of a victory won by a lost battle'.

And Hobart:

Hobart has a peculiarity—it is the neatest town that the sun shines on; and I incline to believe that it is also the cleanest. However that may be, its supremacy in neatness is not to be questioned. There cannot be another town in the world that has no shabby exteriors; no rickety gates and fences, no neglected houses crumbling to ruin, no crazy and unsightly sheds, no weed-grown front-yards of the poor, no back-yards littered with tin cans and old boots and empty bottles, no rubbish in the gutters, no clutter on the sidewalks, no outer-borders fraying out into dirty lanes and tin-patched huts. No, in Hobart all the aspects are tidy, and all a comfort to the eye; the modestest cottage looks combed and brushed, and has its vines, its flowers, its neat fence, its neat gate, its comely cat asleep on the window ledge.

He concluded with a perceptive summary of the Australian experience:

Australian history is almost always picturesque; indeed, it is so curious and strange, that it is itself the chiefest novelty the country has to offer, and so it pushes the other novelties into second and third place. It does not read like history, but like the most beautiful of lies. And all of a fresh new sort, no mouldy old stale ones. It is full of surprises, and adventures, and incongruities, and contradictions, and incredibilities; but they are all true, they all happened.

Of course they did, Mark!

THE POMMIES AND THE YANKS

Rivalry between Australians, the British and the Americans has long been treated for laughs and there is a never-ending array of yarns and jokes on this theme. Here are just a few:

Two Aussies on leave from France were occupying a first-class non-smoking compartment of an English train, when an irascible old bloke blew in. The old killjoy got nasty because one of the Aussies was smoking, and without any preliminary diplomatic negotiations handed the cigar-puffer an ultimatum that he would have him removed from the compartment if he didn't stop smoking. This annoyed the Aussie, and he counter-attacked behind a strong smoke barrage. At the next station Mr Killjoy called a porter and read out the Aussie's crime sheet:

'This man is smoking in a non-smoking compartment.' He demanded that the Aussie should be removed. The porter told the Aussie that he would either have to stop smoking or stop travelling in a non-smoker.

'Well, I plead guilty to smoking in a non-smoker,' said the Aussie, 'but this old nark has no kick coming against me. He's travelling first on a second-class ticket!'

The porter demanded old Killjoy's ticket and found that the Aussie's statement was correct. Exit old Killjoy.

'How did you know he was travelling wrong class?' asked the second Aussie later.

'Oh, I saw the ticket sticking out of his vest pocket,' replied the other, between puffs, 'and it was the same colour as my own.'

Sometimes these yarns involved the ability to understand, or not, the 'great Australian slanguage':

THE YANK: 'Say, Guy, how far to battle?'

AUSSIE: 'Well, sonny, I guess it's about five kilos. Just "pencil and chalk" straight along this "frog and toad" till you come to the "romp and ramp" on the "Johnny Horner". Then dive across that "bog orange" field till you run into a barrage. That lobs you right there. D'ye compree?'

Being able to speak the right lingo could mean the difference between life and death, as highlighted in an Australian yarn:

The weary pongo was wending his way frigidly along the duckboards when he encountered a sentry.

'Halt! password?' The weary one carefully searched his thought-box, but couldn't recall the required word. He remembered, however, that it was the name of a place in Australia, so he began to run through all the places he knew, in the hope of striking it: 'Bondi, Woolloomooloo, Budgaree, Warangatta, Cootamundra, Murrumbidgee, Wagga Wagga, We Wa.'

'Pass on, Digger,' interrupted the sentry, 'you've got the dinkum talk!'

The dialogue between the American and the Australian was a popular form of Digger humour. Possibly because the Australian always tops the exaggerations of the American. This one was already old when it was first published in 1917:

A Yankee and an Aussie were having a quiet drink in the canteen. After a while the conversation came around to the subject of wildlife. 'Your dingo is nowhere near as savage as our coyote', the American claimed. 'And our cougars can outdo any of your wild beasts.'

'Is that right?' said the Aussie.

'Yeah. Take our rattlesnake. It bites you and you die in under two minutes.'

'Oh, that's nothing,' replied the Aussie. 'Our taipans come at you so fast you're dead two minutes before they bite you.'

It was not only the wildlife that featured in tall tales of this type:

It was at a military hospital in England, and the convalescents were sitting in the garden chatting. The topic was cold weather. The American had the floor.

'Wal, I reckon it was a bit cold in those French trenches this winter. But shucks! It was a heat wave compared with some of the cold snaps we get in America. Why, look here, children; I remember one day over'n New York it got so darned cold, kinder suddent like, that everybody's whiskers freezed, and the people had ter shave themselves with dynamite. Of course the explosions shook up ther old city a trifle, but, by George Washington, some whickers got shifted! Another day a cold jerk put in without notice and freezed up all the whisky. The bartenders had to go about with axes chippin' nobblers off the whisky blocks. Some cold, I reckon!'

An Australian scratched his right ear with a crutch, and put in:

'Dunno much about cold in Australia, but I ken talk heat a bit. It does warm up over there. Now, once I was humpin' me bluey in ther bush. A heat wave came up. You could see it comin' in the distance by ther kangaroos 'oppin' about with their tails on fire. I picked up a bit of old fencin' wire and lit me pipe with it. That was a sure sign too. In a few minutes that wave struck me, dealt with me, and then passed on, leavin' me with only me pocket knife and a quart pot to go on with. Of course I was new to the bush, or I couldn't have felt it so much. I met another bloke soon after. He was eatin' a baked goanna he'd picked up. I sez 'Warm, mate, eh?' He sez, 'Oh, it's been just nice to-day. Reckon it'll be fairly 'ot to-morrow.'

It was on again in World War II as well:

Overheard on Townsville beach one night in 1944—a Yank calls to an Aussie: 'Hey, Buddy, break down the language!

I'd like you to know I have a lady with me here!'

The Aussie calls back to the Yank: 'And what the hell d'ya think I have here—a ruddy seagull?'

AUSSIE EFFICIENCY

The casual Aussie dryly undercutting the pretensions of other nationalities—especially Americans—is a strong theme in our humour. This version has been around for a while; it was circulated in an internet version in America. Most of the people who commented on it didn't get the joke, an indication of the differences between what Australians and Americans find funny. What's the matter with them?

An American, a Frenchman and an Australian were sharing a drink in a bar overlooking Sydney Harbour. 'Do you know why America is the wealthiest country in the world?' asked the American. 'It's because we build big and we build fast. We put up the Empire State Building in just six weeks.'

'Six weeks, *mon Dieu*, so long!' said the Frenchman. 'Ze Eiffel Tower we erect in one month, *exactement*.' He turned to the Australian quietly contemplating his beer and asked: 'And what has Australia done to match that?'

'Ah, nuthin' that I know of, mate,' replied the Aussie.

The American pointed out the window to the Harbour Bridge. 'Well, what about that?'

The Australian looked casually over his shoulder. 'Dunno mate, wasn't there yesterday.'

Old mates at Lilydale pub, Victoria, circa 1883.

2

CHARACTERS

Mum: Dave's gone and broke his leg, Dad!
Dad: D'yer think we ought to shoot 'im?

Dad and Dave

THE DRONGO

Numbskulls—less kindly, fools—are to be found in the traditions of most cultural groups around the world. So stupid are these individuals and groups that their statements and actions take on a heroic aura. The Australian version of this folk tradition includes a number of characters, the most stupid of which is the 'Drongo'.

The Drongo is a congenitally naive figure, usually found in a bush setting, who interprets literally whatever he is told. When the boss tells him to 'hang a new gate', the Drongo takes the gate out to the nearest tree and hangs it in a noose. Asked to dig some turnips about the size of his head, the Drongo is found pulling up the entire turnip patch and trying his hat on each uprooted turnip for size. When the boss asks him to put the horse in the dray, meaning to hitch it to the front of the vehicle, the Drongo tries to lift the horse into the dray itself.

In one slightly more elaborate story, the Drongo goes fishing but has no luck. He asks another fisherman who is catching plenty what he uses for bait. The fisherman tells the Drongo he is using magpie. The Drongo gets his gun, shoots a magpie and returns to the riverside. He begins to pluck the bird but changes his mind and simply hooks the bird to his line and casts it into the water. But still he has no luck. The other fisherman cannot understand it and asks to have a look at the Drongo's line. He reels it in, revealing a sodden mess of feathers. 'You didn't pluck the bird!' exclaims the successful fisherman. The Drongo replies that he was going to pluck it but thought that if he did the fish would not be able to tell if it was a magpie or a peewee.

The Drongo was working for a farmer when the boss decided it was time to build another windmill and he needed the Drongo to help him. The Drongo agreed but then asked the farmer if he thought it really made much sense to have two windmills. The farmer asked the Drongo what he meant and he replied that as there seemed to be barely enough wind to operate the windmill the farmer already had, he doubted that there would be enough wind to work two windmills.

The name 'Drongo' is said to derive from the name of an Australian racehorse of the 1920s, famous for losing races. The name is still heard in the slanguage as an insult, as in 'Don't be a bloody Drongo' and similar idioms.

COUSIN JACKS

Another stupid character appearing in Australian folklore is 'Cousin Jack'. This term is applied to people of Cornish extraction, mainly in South Australia, where there were—and still are—significant communities of Cornish and Cornish-descended people associated especially with tin mining around the Moonta Peninsula. The lore of Cousin Jacks is of another worldwide type that concentrates on demeaning 'others' on the peripheries of the most powerful group. The English and Australian view of the Irish is one example of this. Another is the view that Canadian mainlanders have about Newfoundlanders, itself very similar to the view that many Australians have of Tasmanians. While Cousin Jacks are not considered to be inbred like Taswegians, in folklore they display a species of stupidity that citysiders have long associated with 'yokels'. Many Cousin Jack yarns poke fun at the Cornish speech style and what are portrayed in the tales as gaucheries of language.

A Cornish, or 'Cousin Jack', miner in South Australia's tin mines, enraged at the boss who has fired him, says: 'ee be nothin' but a damned rogue an' blackguard . . . an' I've darn good mind to tell ee so, too.'

Another Cousin Jack yarn tells of a Cornishman who has settled near Ballarat employing a carpenter from the same part of the world to erect a fence. When the employing Cousin Jack checks the work, he complains that the fence is a bit crooked in the middle. 'It be near enough,' says the carpenter.

'Near enough be not good enough. He must be 'zact.'

'Well, he be 'zact,' replies the carpenter.

'Oh well, if he be 'zact, he be near enough,' says the Cousin Jack employer, walking away satisfied.

TOM DOYLE

Tom Doyle is said to have been an old-time publican and mayor of the goldfields town of Kanowna in Western Australia. Tom was an Irishman whose unusual interpretations of words and phrases unfamiliar to him provide the humour of the many yarns told about him.

In one of these *faux pas*, the newly married Tom takes his bride to the city of Melbourne to honeymoon in a grand hotel. The manager of the hotel asks the wealthy but unsophisticated Tom if he would like the bridal chamber. Tom replies that while his wife may require it, he will be happy to piss out the window.

Other Tom Doyle stories concentrate on his embarrassing public outbursts, such as the occasion he attended a function for a visiting dignitary. For the first time in his life, Tom was confronted with olives. He gingerly picked one up and was concerned to discover that it was moist. Just as the dignitary rose to speak, Tom jumped up and cried out that someone had pissed on the gooseberries.

Before becoming mayor, Tom was a member of the local council. At one meeting where an extension to the local dam was under debate, Tom stood up and said that the existing dam was so small that he could piss halfway across it. Another councillor told Tom that he was out of order. 'Yes,' replied Tom, 'and if I was in order I could piss right across it.'

Tom was also noted for his sometimes unusual expressions. In response to a local dispute over whether the town cemetery should be fenced or not, Tom is rumoured to have replied: 'Why worry? Them that's in don't want to get out, and them that's out don't want to get in.' Another time he is said to have described prospectors as 'people who go into the wilderness with a shovel in one hand, a waterbag in the other and their life in their other hand'.

THE WIDOW REILLY'S PIG

The Irish influence on Australian folklore is long, wide and deep, with Irish tunes playing a large role in folk music and song. The Irish themselves, as in English lore, also appear in a great many yarns, almost always portrayed as fools, albeit often with a redeeming flash of wit. A story known as 'The Widow Reilly's Pig' was probably old by the time Daniel Healey ('Whaks Li Kell') treated it in verse form in the 1890s. There are variations on the yarn but it goes like this:

The Widow Reilly had eight children. She lived next door to Patrick and struggled to provide for her large family with some cows and some pigs.

One day a sow gave birth to ten piglets. As the piglets grew Widow Reilly's neighbour, Patrick, would admire them as he passed by on the way to work.

But one morning the Widow Reilly discovered one of the precious piglets was missing. She informed the local priest who, based on Widow Reilly's suspicions, went to see Patrick. He asked him whether he had seen the pig. Very shiftily, Pat said that he had not. The priest then reminded Patrick that on Judgment Day when all believers stand before the Good Lord that someone would have to answer for the stealing of Widow Reilly's pig.

Pat thought for a moment and asked the priest whether the Widow Reilly would be there on the Judgment Day as well. The priest assured him that she would be, along with the missing pig. 'What would you have to say then, Pat?' he asked.

Pat replied brightly, 'I would say to Mrs Reilly, "Here is your pig back, and thanks very much for the lend of it".'

THE CONVICT'S TOUR TO HELL

Arriving in Sydney in 1832 for the crime of breaking a shop window and stealing a 'piece of worsted plaid', Francis MacNamara, known as 'Frank the Poet', was one of the convict period's greatest characters. Like many of his Irish fellow convicts, he had a passionate hatred of the English and the convict system. Unlike most, he also had the ability to express his antagonism in witty and satirical verse. MacNamara's work was often more ambitious than the usual doggerel of the street ballads and included a parody of the literary versions of the mythic descent into the underworld theme, notable in the work of Dante and Swift. 'The Convict's Tour to Hell' is a small masterpiece in which Frank dreams that he has died and, like Dante, must journey through the underworld to find his true resting place for all eternity. He visits purgatory, which he finds full of priests and popes 'weeping wailing gnashing' and suffering the 'torments of the newest fashion'. He journeys on to Hell:

And having found the gloomy gate
Frank rapped aloud to know his fate
He louder knocked and louder still
When the Devil came, pray what's your will?
Alas cried the Poet I've come to dwell
With you and share your fate in Hell
Says Satan that can't be, I'm sure
For I detest and hate the poor
And none shall in my kingdom stand
Except the grandees of the land.
But Frank I think you are going astray
For convicts never come this way
But soar to Heaven in droves and legions
A place so called in the upper regions.

In Hell, Frank finds the overseers, floggers and jailers of the convict system writhing in perpetual torture for the crimes they committed against poor convicts while alive on earth. Captain Cook 'who discovered New South Wales' is here, along with dukes, mayors and lawyers. They are not alone:

Here I beheld legions of traitors
Hangmen gaolers and flagellators
Commandants, Constables and Spies
Informers and Overseers likewise
In flames of brimstone they were toiling
And lakes of sulphur round them boiling
Hell did resound with their fierce yelling
Alas how dismal was their dwelling.

One particular unfortunate seems to be suffering special torments, so Frank asks:

Who is that Sir in yonder blaze
Who on fire and brimstone seems to graze?

Satan tells him that it is 'Captain Logan of Moreton Bay'.

While Frank witnesses this dreadful scene, there is suddenly a great commotion in Hell. Drums are beaten, flags waved:

> And all the inhabitants of Hell
> With one consent rang the great bell
> Which never was heard to sound or ring
> Since Judas sold our Heavenly King
> Drums were beating flags were hoisting
> There never before was such rejoicing
> Dancing singing joy or mirth
> In Heaven above or on the earth
> Straightway to Lucifer I went
> To know what these rejoicings meant

Satan is senseless with joy as the chief tormentor of all the convicts in New South Wales enters Hell—Governor Darling. Satan's assistants have already chained him and prepared the brimstone in which he will writhe forever. Satisfied to have witnessed this wonderful sight, Frank travels on to 'that happy place/Where all the woes of mortals cease'. He knocks at the pearly gate and is met by St Peter, who asks him who in Heaven he might know. Frank answers by naming bushrangers:

> Well I know Brave Donohue
> Young Troy and Jenkins too
> And many others whom floggers mangled
> And lastly were by Jack Ketch strangled.

Then:

> 'Peter', says Jesus, 'let Frank in
> For he is thoroughly purged from sin
> And although in convict's habit dressed
> Here he shall be a welcome guest.'

A great celebration is then made by all the hosts in Heaven, 'Since Frank the Poet has come at last.' The poem ends with the lines:

Thro' Heaven's Concave their rejoicings range
And hymns of praise to God they sang
And as they praised his glorious name
I woke and found 'twas but a dream.

MAKE IT HOURS INSTEAD OF DAYS

With a story like this, it is no surprise that Frank the Poet was still remembered into the twentieth century. In 1902 a rural newspaper published a memoir of Frank's life and times. The historical details are often wrong (Frank never actually met Captain Logan), but the spirit of the story and the respect for Frank's abilities is clear:

Francis MacNamara was a man who came out to Botany Bay in the early days for the benefit of his country and the good of himself. He was one of those mixed up in the political intrigues of the 'Young Ireland Party,' and for the part he took in such with Smith O'Brien, and others he was 'transported beyond the seas.' He was well educated, and gifted with a quick perception and ready wit. His aptitude in rhyming gained for him the appellation of 'Frank the Poet,' and many stories used to be told by old hands of his smartness in getting out of a difficulty.

During a time that he was under Captain Logan at Moreton Bay he was frequently in trouble. On one occasion he was called to account for some misdeed, and asked why he should not be imprisoned for fourteen days. He answered promptly—
'Captain Logan, if you plaze,
Make it hours instead of days.'
And the Captain did.

On another occasion he was brought before Logan for inciting the other inmates of his hut to refuse a bullock's head that was being served to them as rations. Captain Logan, in a severe tone, asked him what he meant by generating a mutinous feeling among his fellows.

'Please, sir. I didn't,' said Frank. 'I only advised my mates not to accept it as rations because there was no meat on it.' 'Well MacNamara,' said the Captain, 'I am determined to check this insubordinate tendency in a way that I hope will be effective. At the same time, I am willing to hear anything you may have to say in defence before passing sentence on you.'

'Sure, Captain,' said Frank, 'I know you are just, and merciful as well. Kindly let the head be brought in, and you will see yourself that it is nothing but skin and bone, and ain't got enough flesh on it to make a feed for one man. I only said we won't be satisfied with it for our ration.' The Captain ordered the head to be brought, and when it was placed on the table he turned to Frank and said, 'There's the head. Now what about it?'

Frank advanced to the table, picked up a paper-cutter, and said to the Captain and those with him, 'Listen, your honours, to the "honey" ring it has,' and, tapping it with the paper knife, recited in a loud tone the following lines:—

'Oh, bullock, oh, bullock, thou wast brought here,
After working in a team for many a year,
Subjected to the lash, foul language and abuse
And now portioned as food for poor convicts' use.'

'Get out of my sight, you scoundrel,' roared Logan, 'and if you come before me again I'll send you to the triangle.' It is needless to say that Frank was quickly out of the room, chuckling to himself at his good luck. Some time after he was assigned to a squatter in New South Wales, and as was his wont, always in hot water. He was at last given a letter to take to the chief constable in the adjoining town.

Frank suspected the purport of the letter to be a punishment for himself, so he raked his brain in devising a means of escape. Having writing materials, and being an efficient penman, he addressed a couple of envelopes, and, putting them with the one he had received to give the officer, he started. On the outskirts of the town, he met a former acquaintance, who was on 'a ticket of leave,' and a stranger to the district. Frank had known him elsewhere and remembered him as a flogger: and on one occasion he had dropped the lash on himself.

Here was what Frank styled a heaven-sent chance, and it would be a sort of revenge for a past infliction if he succeeded in getting this fellow to deliver the letter. So he sat down and chatted for a while, and pulling out the three envelopes, regretted that they could not have a drink together. If his business was finished, they could; but his master, he said was a Tartar, and it wouldn't be safe to neglect it. So he would have to deliver the letters first. 'Perhaps I might be able to help you,' said the other. 'Blest if I know,' answered Frank, 'it would be all right so long as the cove didn't find it out.' 'Oh, chance it,' said the other, 'and we can have another hour together.'

Frank thought for a while, turning the letters about in his hands, and at last made up his mind to let the other assist him, so handed him the letter addressed to 'Mr. Snipe. Concordium.' They went on into town, and Frank, directing the ex-flogger, turned into a shop. Sneaking on a few minutes after, he heard enough to satisfy him that his surmise was correct, and he left.

On his return to the station, he was asked by the squatter if he had received any reply to the letter. 'Oh, yes,' answered he: 'a feeling reply, that I am likely to remember.' While having tea he appeared in such excellent humour that one of his mates asked the cause. 'Oh, nothing much,' said Frank, 'only circumstances to-day enabled me to pay a debt that I have owed for some years: and I am glad about it.'

The newspaper also published another recollection of Frank's doings, this time in Sydney town with the forerunners of the larrikin 'pushes' or gangs who often terrorised the streets later in the nineteenth century:

> Frank had a great down on a 'push' in Sydney known as the 'Cabbage-tree Mob,' their symbol being the wearing of a cabbage-tree hat. Well, on one occasion they bailed up poor Frank, and asked him what he had to say that they should not inflict condign punishment on him. 'Well, boys,' he said,
>
> 'Here's three cheers for the Cabbage-tree Mob—
> Too lazy to work; too frightened to rob.'
>
> They made for Frank, but just then came along a policeman known as the 'Native Dog'; so Frank escaped that time.

WHO WAS BILLY BARLOW?

With migrants arriving in more or less steady streams in the colonial period, 'new chums' became a popular stereotype. Colonial folksong and literature is full of disparaging references to newcomers who were not properly dressed or equipped or emotionally prepared for the rigours of pioneer life. It was even suggested that they should be shipped back to where they came from when they failed to measure up:

> When shearing comes lay down your drums,
> And step to the board, you brand new chums,
> With a row-dum, row-dum, rubba-dub-dub,
> We'll send 'em home in a limejuice tub.

The song makes fun of the unskilled and unhardened British recruits to the backbreaking shearer's trade and profoundly masculine lifestyle. It ends by suggesting that the new chum would be better off going back home in a 'limejuice tub', a British sailing ship—than 'humping your drum in this country'. Eventually the new chums either went home with their tails between their legs or became 'old hands' themselves, adopting the attitudes of their detractors and subjecting newcomers to the same treatment in their turn. So prevalent was the new chum that he came to be represented by a mythical figure named 'Billy Barlow', ridiculed in song and on stages across the country.

The earliest reference to Billy Barlow pops up in the 1840s, though the earliest song seems to date from an American minstrel song of a decade or so earlier. The newspaper review of an amateur theatrical production in 1843 noted that 'Several songs were sung, and Billy Barlow In Australia, was written expressly for the occasion by a gentleman in Maitland, and was received with unbounded applause.'

In this version of the story, poor Billy is left a thousand pounds by his old aunt and decides to further his fortunes in Australia. By the second verse, he has already been taken down:

When to Sydney I got, there a merchant I met,
Who said he would teach me a fortune to get;
He'd cattle and sheep past the colony's bounds,
Which he sold with the station for my thousand pounds.
Oh dear, lackaday, oh,
He gammon'd the cash out of Billy Barlow.

Things go from bad to worse as Billy goes 'up the country' where he is bailed up by bushrangers, tied to a tree and left for dead. Eventually freeing himself, he is arrested because his belongings have been stolen and so cannot identify himself. Taken to Sydney, he is eventually identified and released but on returning to his station discovers his cattle have been speared by Aborigines. Even nature conspires against the hapless new chum:

And for nine months before no rain there had been,
So the devil a blade of grass could be seen;
And one-third of my wethers the scab they had got,

And the other two-thirds had just died of the rot.
Oh dear, lackaday, oh,
'I shall soon be a settler,' said Billy Barlow.

Deep in debt, Billy is reduced to poverty and hunger—'as thin as a lath got poor Billy Barlow'. He is arrested and imprisoned for debt back in Sydney again and listed as an insolvent, or bankrupt:

Then once more I got free, but in poverty's toil;
I've no 'cattle for salting,' no 'sheep for to boil;'
I can't get a job though to any I'd stoop,
If it was only the making of 'portable soup'.
Oh dear, lackaday, oh,
Pray give some employment to Billy Barlow.

Despite his tragi-comic trials, Billy Barlow is not totally ground down and still contemplates repairing his fortunes in the final verse:

But there's still a 'spec' left may set me on my stumps,
If a wife I could get with a few of the dumps;
So if any lass here has 'ten thousand' or so,
She can just drop a line addressed 'Mr. Barlow'
Oh dear, lackaday, oh
The dear angel shall be 'Mrs. William Barlow.'

So popular and pervasive was the contempt for the new chum, that Billy Barlow became a stock character of popular entertainment for decades. He assumed all sorts of guises, including rat catcher, London street clown, butcher, clerk, gold digger, as well as the know-nothing tenderfoot of Australian tradition. Although he is now long forgotten, we still don't know who Billy Barlow was, or if he ever existed outside ballads and the popular theatre of Britain, Canada, America, South Africa and colonial Australia.

JACKY BINDI-I

Where Aboriginal people appear at all in white Australian folklore, they are typically tricksters or villains. Our earliest mingling of Indigenous and settler traditions is, revealingly, in the creation of monsters, such as the bunyip. In Aboriginal tradition the roles of settler heroes and villains are reversed. The heroic discoverer Cook becomes an oppressor and the often-demonised Kelly is a hero; in some traditions he even becomes Jesus Christ. These differences suggest the immensity of the cultural divide that separated Indigenous and European culture from colonisation. The folk figure of the Aboriginal (not, in this case, including Torres Strait Islanders) is a faint but contradictory one uneasily inhabiting the margins of narratives focused on other matters, flitting through the trickster-like tales.

However, the stories are not all of unhappiness and dispossession. Indigenous culture has more than its share of humour and a number of folktales have developed that show Aboriginal and white Australians in interestingly ambivalent interactions. A cycle of such tales centres around the sharply clever retorts of an Aboriginal man often called Jacky, Jacky-Jacky or Jacky Bindi-i.

In one such story, a white man does not know the way to a particular location. He addresses a nearby Aboriginal man by the name used for all male Aborigines by whites, saying:

'Jacky, do you know the way to Gulargambone?'
The Aboriginal man says, 'How you know my name, boss?'
'Just guessed,' says the white man sarcastically.
'Well, you can just guess the bloody way then,' the Aboriginal man replies.

Jacky Bindi-i is usually a stockman, sometimes a station roustabout, sometimes a layabout, who appears in a number of bush yarns common in the north of Australia. In some of his stories, Jacky is depicted as being more of a numbskull than a trickster and his exaggerated stupidity usually has the effect of undercutting the assumed superiority of white authority figures, including the boss, policemen and magistrates.

One day Jacky and the boss needed to cross a flooded river but the only boat was on the far bank. The boss told Jacky to swim across and bring the boat back. Jacky protested, saying that there may be crocodiles in the river. The boss said that he need not worry as crocodiles never touch blackfellas. Jacky replied that the crocodiles might be colour blind and that it would better to wait until the flood subsided.

On another occasion when Jacky was in a distant part of the property minding a mob of sheep, he needed his rations and other necessities delivered to him by the boss each week. One week the boss forgot to bring Jacky's food. Jacky was not too happy and told the boss that he only had a bone left from last week's rations and that it would be another week before any more meat came. The boss laughed and told him not to worry, saying, 'The nearer the bone the sweeter the meat.' When the boss returned the next week, the sheep were in a terrible condition as Jacky had kept them where there was no grass to eat. The boss turned on Jacky and angrily asked him what he thought he was doing. Jacky just laughed and said, 'The nearer the ground, the sweeter the grass.'

Jacky Bindi-i's other main activity is stealing sheep or cows, for which he is frequently brought before the courts. At one of his hearings, the judge gave Jacky three years in prison and asked him if he had anything to say. 'Yes,' said Jacky angrily. 'You're bloody free with other people's time.'

In another court hearing, this time for being drunk and disorderly, Jacky was fined and given twenty days in prison by the magistrate. 'I'll tell you what I'll do, boss,' said Jacky. 'I'll toss you—forty days or nothing.'

Jacky is caught red-handed by a trooper policeman one day as he butchers a stolen bullock. Jacky is tied to his horse and the trooper leads the way on his horse on the lengthy journey back to town. As they ride, Jacky asks the trooper how he had tracked him down. 'I smelled you out,' replies the policemen proudly.

They ride on and as darkness falls, so does the rain and it is not too long before the trooper loses his way. 'Do you know the way to town, Jacky?' he asks his prisoner at last.

Jacky is ready with his answer: 'Why don't you smell the way back to town the same as you smelled out Jacky?'

This form of humorous passive resistance is found in the traditions of many other occupied or colonised groups. The American 'Marster John' stories feature a slave named John who uses the white stereotype of the slave to outwit the master. In the Australian variations, it is revealing that Jacky, or his equivalent, is frequently portrayed defying or outsmarting white authority figures of the boss and the magistrate, a point of connection with the anti-authoritarianism so prevalent in Australian national identity.

In the Australian context, the folklorist John Meredith also pointed to the related Jacky-Jacky series of tales he had encountered in his extensive collecting activities. These stories deal with sexual relationships between white men and Aboriginal women:

> There are literally dozens of these stories, all concerned with situations involving Jacky-Jacky, his lubra Mary, black sheep, white sheep, the white boss and his station-hands and his wife. In this series of folk-tales, 'Jacky-Jacky' generally but not always, comes out on top, scoring a victory over the white boss.

Jacky-Jacky also features in a modern Aboriginal song which has many versions around the country:

> Jacky Jacky was a smart young fellow
> Full of fun and energy.
> He was thinkin' of gettin' married

But the lubra run away you see.
Cricketah boobelah will-de-mah
Billa na ja jingeree wah.

Jacky used to chase the emu
With his spears and his waddy too.
He's the only man that can tell you
What the emu told a kangaroo.
Cricketah boobelah will-de-mah
Billa na ja jingeree wah.

Hunting food was Jacky's business
Til the white man come along.
Put his fences across the country
Now the hunting days are gone.
Cricketah boobelah will-de-mah
Billa na ja jingeree wah.

White fella he now pay all taxes
Keep Jacky Jacky in clothes and food.
He don't care what become of the country
White fella tucker him very good.
Cricketah boobelah will-de-mah
Billa na ja jingeree wah.

Now Australia's short of money
Jacky Jacky sit, he laugh all day.
White fella want to give it back to Jacky
No fear Jacky won't have it that way.
Cricketah boobelah will-de-mah
Billa na ja jingeree wah.

Other examples of this form of intercultural humour are not hard to find, such as this first-person account from Albert Calvert's Western Australian experiences in the late nineteenth century:

A well-known explorer, worn out with fatigue, and weak from privations, flung himself by the fire to rest, having almost reached Perth on his return journey. His wretched and woebegone appearance attracted the attention of the native who accompanied him. He had some knowledge of English, and thus addressed his master: 'What for do you who have plenty to eat, and much money, walk so far away in the bush?'

The explorer, tired to death, and rather annoyed at this conundrum, made no answer. The black went on: 'You are thin, your shanks are long, your belly is small—you had plenty to eat at home, why did you not stop there?' It is hard to make these simple folk understand the love of enterprise and adventure, so the traveller had to say: 'Oh, you don't understand; you know nothing.'

'I know nothing!' he exclaimed, with a laugh, 'I know how to keep myself fat, the young women look at me and say, "he very nice, he fat". They look at you and say, "No good, he too thin, legs too long, he walk too far in the bush".'

Calvert concluded this story against himself: 'It cannot be denied that the Englishman had the worst of the argument.'

JIMMY AH FOO

Tales told of the one-time Chinese publican of Barcaldine and Longreach, Jimmy Ah Foo, often show him outwitting those who might otherwise do him harm. Jimmy's great skill was to identify with everyone and to generally make himself as agreeable as possible to his customers. In the process of doing this, he always seemed to manage to benefit himself or come out on top in some way.

During the shearer's strikes of the 1890s, there were serious outbreaks of anti-Chinese violence, the shearers fearing that the Chinese would be brought in as cheap labour strike-breakers. There was considerable pressure to have Chinese workers, including those working as cooks, removed from their jobs. A deputation of shearers visited Jimmy's pub and requested that he sack the Chinese cook he employed and they would be returning next day for his answer. When the shearers came back and asked Jimmy if he had sacked the cook, he replied that he had done as they requested and that he would now be cooking for them.

SNUFFLER OLDFIELD

Another figure of Queensland tradition is the stockman, Snuffler Oldfield. Snuffler Oldfield tales have a strong trickster element to them, and many are associated with another Queensland character named Galloping Jones. There are said to be 'thousands' of Snuffler Oldfield and Galloping Jones stories. Here's one:

> Snuffler Oldfield was droving one time. He found that he was always the one having to round up the cattle that rushed each night, while the boss and the jackaroos took it easy or slept back at the camp.
>
> One night the cattle rushed again, this time stampeding through the camp and forcing the drovers to rapidly climb into trees to save themselves from being crushed. Thinking that Snuffler Oldfield must, as usual, be somewhere out in the middle of the cattle, the boss called out for him from the tree into which he had scrambled: 'Where are you, Snuffler?'
>
> From just above the boss's head came Snuffler's voice: 'One limb above you.'

On another occasion, when Snuffler's wife was giving birth, the nurse came out to the waiting room to tell Snuffler that he had a child. She returned to the birthing room but came back a short while later saying that he now had a second baby. 'Christ, nurse,' said Snuffler, 'don't touch her again, she must be full of them!'

CORNY KENNA

Cornelius Kenna is the legendary acid-tongued wit of Victoria's Western District who always has a ready retort in his numerous yarns. The stories revolve around both his trickster-like cleverness and his ability to use the language to good effect.

In one of these, 'Corny', as he is generally called, is in the local pub where he is served an under-measure whisky. As he looks disapprovingly at the glass, the barmaid indignantly points out that the whisky is thirty years old. Kenna replies that the whisky is very small for its age.

In another Corny Kenna yarn, he is taking a lady through the bush in a timber jinker. A storm approaches so Corny whips up the horses to an unsafe speed and hits a tree stump on the rough bush track, overturning the jinker. Fortunately, no one is injured but the lady is understandably annoyed and says to Corny, 'I knew this would happen.' Corny looks at her wonderingly and asks, 'Why the devil didn't you tell me?'

A man borrows a horse from Corny Kenna, promising to return it next day. Nearly two weeks later, the horse has still not been returned and Corny meets the man who borrowed it at a local auction. The embarrassed neighbour apologises, saying he had meant to bring the horse back a dozen times. 'Once will be enough,' Corny retorts.

THE HODJA

The Australian contact with Turkish culture at Gallipoli involved not only armed conflict but a limited degree of inter-cultural communication. *The Anzac Book*, a compilation of stories, poems and other contributions from Australian and New Zealand soldiers, includes a story about the Turkish trickster known as the Hodja. It was contributed by 'APM' and published under the title 'The Tales That Abdul Tells':

One of the chief pastimes of the Turks who live behind the black and white sandbags opposite (writes an officer who knows them intimately) is that of listening to stories told by the storytellers in the cafés of the Asia Minor villages. The hero of these stories is very often a certain Nastradi Hodja (who really existed at one time, and made a reputation for his wit, as well as through his stupidity). Here is an example of the sort of story about Nastradi which especially pleases the Turk:

Nastradi Hodja's wife woke up one night through hearing a noise. She got up, and going out on to the landing on the upper floor, outside her bedroom, called out:

'Nastradi, what was that noise?'

Nastradi's voice came up from below. 'Don't pay any attention to it', he said. 'It was only my shirt that tumbled down the stairs'.

'Does a shirt make so much noise?', she asked.

'No', was the reply; 'but I was in it'.

DAD MAKES A BLUE

Perhaps the best-known forms of Australian yokel lore are the 'Dad and Dave' yarns. Probably an original literary invention of Australian author 'Steele Rudd' (Arthur Hoey Davis, 1868–1935), Dad, Mum and their foolish son, Dave, first appeared in the *Bulletin* magazine in 1895. Four years later, the sketches appeared in book form under the title *On Our Selection*, with various subsequent editions and sequels. In this yarn from Rudd's follow-up book, *Our New Selection,* Dad's scheming goes badly wrong:

A summer's night. Inside—close, suffocating, outside—calm, tranquil, not a sound, not a sign of life.

The bush silent, restful. Dad on the veranda, in his easy chair, thinking; Dave, Joe and Bill stretched on the grass near the steps, dreamily watching the clustering stars.

Close to the house the eerie note of a night bird suddenly rang out. Joe and Bill turned over to locate it. Dad and Dave took no notice. The moon came slowly over the range, weird shadows fell before her and crept over the earth, and Budgee plain was a dim expanse in the hazy, languid light.

Dad spoke.

'Whose stock's on Lawson's selection now?' he asked.

'Everyone's,' Dave said. 'Carey's, mostly.'

'Well, turn everything out t'-morrow that isn't ours.'

Dave sat up and chuckled.

'And the Careys 'll run 'em all back,' Joe joined in, 'an' put ours where we'll never see 'em again.'

'If they do I'll make it warm for them,' Dad said.

Bill laughed.

'You wasp, get inside and don't be grinnin' like a d—d cat at everythin' y' hear!'

Bill whined and said he wasn't grinning.

'Well, hold y'r noise then!' Dad shouted. Then he dragged his chair nearer the steps and spoke softly. 'T'-morrow that selection's mine,' he said. 'Lawson's thrown 't up.'

Dave mounted the steps. 'What, after fencin'!'

'After fencin'!' Dad chuckled and sat back, and no more was said.

Next morning Dad repeated his instructions to Dave to turn all stock off Lawson's selection, and started for town in the sulky.

At the Lands office he was told that Lawson's selection was in the Ipswich district, and late in the day he left for home, intending to take the train to Ipswich the following morning.

Dad pulled up at a wayside pub. Several men were leaning on the bar, their empty glasses before them. Dad invited them all to drink. They drank.

Dad lingered awhile and chatted sociably and grew very enthusiastic about dairy farming. He exaggerated his interest and spoke of Saddletop as though he owned it all. The men became interested, one in particular. He was a Carey, and Dad in his exuberance failed to recognize him. Carey's horse had got away and he was walking home. He had twelve miles yet to tramp, and when Dad asked the company if any of them wanted work, Carey said he did. Carey knew Dad.

Dad invited them all to drink.

'Jump into the trap, then,' Dad said, 'an' I'll drive y' out.'

Carey climbed in, and Dad drove off. All the way along he boasted of his possessions and prospects. Carey was an attentive listener and encouraged Dad to talk. Dad took a fancy to his companion, and in a lowered voice, in case some of the trees or fences concealed a pair of ears, became confidential. He revealed all he knew of Lawson's selection and his intentions regarding it, and, approaching Carey's own place, he whispered, hoarsely, 'Nice set of scoundrels live there!' His companion never flinched.

'Whose place is it?' he asked.

'Carey's,' Dad said—'a bad lot!' And Dad shook his head in the moonlight.

Dad pulled up at the gate.

'You camp in the barn there,' he said, indicating the building with a sweep of his hand, 'an' tackle the milkin' in the morning with the boys.' Then Dad unharnessed the mare and went inside. The 'man' went home chuckling.

Next morning Dave and Joe and Cranky Jack were in the yard milking. Dad came out.

'Where's thet feller I brought out last night—not up yet?' he asked.

Dave didn't understand. Dad explained and hobbled off to the barn. The man wasn't there. Dad returned to the yard, swearing.

'That cove wouldn't be after work,' Dave drawled. 'He had y'; he only wanted a lift. Plenty of his sort about.'

Bill, bailing up, stood and laughed. Bill's hilarity always annoyed Dad. He chased Bill out of the yard, then roared to him to come in again. Bill slunk back.

'Go in there!'—Dad pointed the way through the rails. Bill hesitated sullenly. He dropped his head and turned the whites of his eyes on Dad.

'Y' hear?'

Bill moved sideways to the rails, then judged his distance and dived. But he miscalculated. His head struck the bottom rail and he rebounded, and Dad got in his kick and grinned, and forgave the man who had taken him in the night before.

Dad reached Ipswich at night and strolled about till he found a place to put up. Then he went into the streets again and gaped at things. But he didn't see many sights. There was a large store with the shutters up. The pallid light of a few flickering gas-jets revealed the outline of an old, weird weather-worn fountain, around which 'the Army' crouched and yelled for the salvation of souls—and a church fence—and a policeman, motionless. At regular intervals a huge clock broke the silence. It had a sad, unhealthy note, and seemed to toll a requiem for the dead. Dad stared up at it and wondered.

Morning again. Dad halted at the foot of the Lands office steps and stared in surprise. Old Carey was feeling his way down them with a stick. Carey saw Dad and grinned. Dad went into the office and came out breathing heavily. He went down the street and searched for Grey till he missed the train.

'How's it y' didn't get it?' Dave said in an unhappy kind of voice.

Dad gave no reason. He sat down and thought, and we all stood round waiting as if something was going to happen.

'They've got it all right,' Dad groaned at last. Then Dave's opportunity came.

'Yairs,' he said, 'an' they've got all our cattle—pounded every one o' them, an' ten shillings a head damages on them.'

Sarah rushed out, so did Bill and Barty; but Dave and Joe held Dad down and saved the furniture.

DAD, DAVE AND MABEL

The books were bestsellers, also having stage, film and radio adaptations, and appear to have inspired the numerous humorous folktales and jokes told about Dad and Dave. These concentrate on portraying Dad, Dave and the family as country hicks:

> Mum: Dave's gone and broke his leg, Dad!
> Dad: D'yer think we ought to shoot 'im?

The other important aspect of Dad and Dave yarns is the portrayal of Dave as a gormless fool, very much in the tradition of the 'numbskull' stories. In one typical exchange, Dave is leaving home to join the army. Mum, worried about her son in the big city, prevails on Dad to give him a fatherly lecture about the perils of drink, gambling and women. Dave is anxiously and honestly at pains to let Dad know that he never has any truck with such things. Dad returns to Mum and says: 'You needn't worry. I don't think the army will take him anyway, the boy's a half-wit!'

In another such tale, Dave gets a job driving a truck in the big city. On the first day the boss asks him to deliver three Malayan bears to the zoo. Hearing nothing from Dave for a very long time, the boss decides to find out what has happened to him. He drives along the route that Dave would have taken and sees him buying tickets to the cinema for himself and the bears.

'I told you to take those bears to the zoo,' the angry boss yells at Dave. 'What are you doing at the cinema with them?'

Unperturbed, Dave slowly replies that the truck broke down and as he couldn't take the bears to the zoo he decided to take them to the 'pitchers' instead.

Many Dad and Dave yarns involve Dad, son Dave and Dave's mother, but there are also generational extensions involving Dave and his sweetheart, Mabel:

When Dave and Mabel finally got married, Dave asked Dad for a quiet word before the newlyweds left for their honeymoon. 'Could you do me a favour, Dad?' he asked.

'Of course, Dave,' Dad replied, 'what is it?'

'Would you mind going on the honeymoon for me, you know a lot more about that sort of thing than I do.'

Dave comes into a bit of extra money and decides to buy Mabel a present. He goes into the dining room, picks up the dining table and carries it down the street on his head. On the way he meets a mate who asks him if he is moving house. 'Oh no,' Dave replies cheerfully, 'I'm just going out to buy Mabel a new tablecloth.'

The theme of yokel stupidity that lies at the heart of the Dave character continues in a number of stories about Dave and Mabel's escapades in the hospitality business.

Dave and Mabel decide to make some money in the tourism business by opening an outback roadhouse. The locals and truckies were quite happy with Mabel's basic but sustaining cooking. Eventually the tourists did arrive, the first being an American. Dave sat him down and asked him what he would like to eat. The tourist looked around and noticed a truckie demolishing a meal of steak, salad, chips and eggs. 'I'll have what he's eating, but eliminate the eggs.'

Dave bustled back to the kitchen to deliver the order but after a few minutes' discussion with Mabel, he returned to the American tourist's table. 'Uhh, sorry, but we've had an accident in the kitchen and the 'liminator's broke. Would you like your eggs fried like the other bloke?'

In another story from the sequence, Dave and Mabel open a bed and breakfast. The conditions are pretty rough and ready but they eventually get a couple from the city to stay the night. When they arrive, they complain that there is no toilet. Dave reassures them that this is just the way things are in the bush and provides them with a bucket if they need to relieve themselves during the night.

Next morning Dave knocks on the door of the shack and asks what the couple would like for breakfast. They order a full bush breakfast and coffee. Dave whisks off but is back in a minute asking if they would like milk in their coffee. 'Yes, please,' chorus the couple.

'Alright,' says Dave, 'but could you give us the bucket back so's the missus can milk the cow?'

Oral Dad and Dave stories are mostly in this style, though there is a considerable body of such stories that rarely appear in print due to their sexual nature. By modern standards, this bawdy element is quite mild, though older Australians often consider such tales unsuitable for telling in public or in mixed company. Folklorists may still have the odd 'blue' yarn whispered into their ear, though the oral tradition of the Dad and Dave tales is probably almost over.

But Dad and Dave are alive and well in the small Queensland town of Nobby. Here is 'Dad and Dave Country', where visitors can find 'Rudd's Pub' after the name of the author of *On Our Selection*, who allegedly wrote there. His literarified yarns are still being told by at least one local storyteller.

ANZAC CHARACTERS

They come in all shapes and sizes, but the one thing they have in common is that they can raise an often much needed laugh:

Our prize Section Dope was trying to put the hard word on the Quarter Bloke for a tin of butter.

'But I gave you a large tin of butter the day before yesterday,' said the QM testily.

'You didn't give me a large tin of butter, it was a small tin.'

'You dopey cow, I gave you a large tin of butter and a small tin of axle grease.'

'Cripes! Then I've eaten the ruddy axle grease and put the butter on the axles!'

'Dopey' in our unit didn't seem to have any liking for soldiering, so one day I asked him why he had joined up.

'Well, you see, a cobber stole five pounds from me and ran away with my wife. There was nothing else to do but enlist.'

'That was certainly tough luck,' I sympathised.

'Yair, it was every penny I had.'

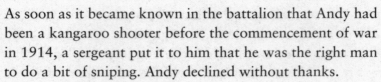

As soon as it became known in the battalion that Andy had been a kangaroo shooter before the commencement of war in 1914, a sergeant put it to him that he was the right man to do a bit of sniping. Andy declined without thanks.

'Why?' snarled the sergeant.

'I just don't like it, that's why. I've shot kangaroos, wallabies, dingoes and brumbies, an' I ain't goin' to finish up with men—at least, not sniped men, anyhow.'

The sergeant seethed, but Andy was adamant. Sniping a kangaroo, he maintained, was a different thing from sniping a man.

'Well,' said the sergeant, 'if you're THAT finicky, I'll go over and ask Fritz to hop!'

They called him Happy Henry. He was one of those grim humorous Australians who could no more resist joking about anything than he could resist accepting a cigarette. A friend remarked that his dial was hard enough to dent a railway pie at half a mile.

Happy Henry was well into the Somme scrap, and got out of it with a lump on each side of his head like young coconuts. He could hang his tin hat on either. He told the boys about it in the camp afterwards. He said: 'I'd just sent a Hun over the Never Never with the sunning end of me bayonet, when another Fritz weighin' about 'alf a ton swung the butt of his rifle against me block. Me head gave out a musical G. sharp, and as I made a smack at 'im I sez, "If yer do that agen, cobber, I'll be rude." I missed him, and he swung agen and got me a clout on the other side of the block. His rifle smashed to pieces and of course I fixed 'im then. Y'see that was where 'e made the mistake.'

'How mistake?' asked somebody.

'Well, he should 'ave lobbed me on the same place twice!'

Sandy was attached to our unit, 1 Div., 1st AIF. Like most diggers from the outback he had unorthodox ways of doing things. One day we were on parade for inspection by the Colonel. Sandy was in the front rank and was highly conspicuous by having several buttons of his tunic undone. When the Colonel reached him he stopped, bug-eyed, his pink face rapidly taking on a purplish hue. His hand shot out to point to the buttons left undone, Sandy seized the Colonel by the hand and nearly shook it off. The old boy glared at him. 'I don't know you, my man,' he roared.

'Sorry, mate,' said Sandy, 'I thought you was an old shearer bloke I knew out the back of bloody Bourke.'

The Australian platoon was under heavy Japanese frontal attack. The commander yelled out, 'Fire at will!'

'Cripes,' growled Chiller, 'if you can pick Will outa that mob, you're a better man than I am!'

'Yes, Nugget, I tell you it was cold,' said one of the 'Diamond Dinks', trying to impress an open-eyed 'reinstoushment' with his experiences of the winter on the Somme, 'as cold as the gaze of the Quarter Bloke when yer put the hard word on him for a new Aussie tunic! Struth! I tell you at Bazentin it freezed so hard that you couldn't blow a candle out! Y'ad ter knock the flame off with a stick!'

HOW HE WORKED HIS NUT

The World War I military career of a certain 'Pat' of the 3rd Battalion AIF is told in 'How He Worked His Nut', a contemporary expression for manipulating and outsmarting the system. This story is an example of the many that circulated on this theme, the trickster hero using his wits to scrounge the necessities of survival for himself and his mates. While Pat and his anonymous chronicler are long gone, they are firmly within the tradition of the character, as heard by word of mouth and read in print:

There are still many old hands left in the Battalion who remember P.F. It is over three years since he went, but his memory is still green in my mind, and his ingenuity still haunts me.

Early on Anzac he turned down Sergeant's stripes (this fact is not in official records!) and became a batman. As such we speak of him here.

At this time our rations were pure, unadulterated bully beef, hard biscuits, tea and rice; but we had P.F. and his wonderful brains.

The proximity of battleships and hospital ships riding outside Anzac Cove instantly fire his genius. On the former he knew there would be poultry pens; on the latter an ample supply of good provisions. The problem was how to procure them.

A sailor's costume and a few bandages solved the difficulty.

For the rest, he always had plenty of money. Where it came from one cannot say. Perhaps some digger who felt like floating a war loan, ten minutes after pay, can make a shrewd guess.

He has been seen on a lighter in sailor's clothes—hence eggs; and on two occasions live poultry arrived in the 3rd Battalion trenches.

He was probably evacuated through the Beach Clearing Station more than any other man on Anzac.

It is thought that he rather overdid it the day he was evacuated twice on to the same ship, and was, unfortunately, recognised by the M.O. on the gangway. However, he had the cunning of the Scarlet Pimpernel, and got away—his duty nobly done; hence fresh bread and milk in the mess that night.

He would see a fatigue party unloading flour—off with his coat and to work with them for an hour or so. One bag would, sooner or later be over-carried, and find its way to our dug-out. One day, not content with the flour, he also 'lifted' a mule from a mule train, and arrived at the trenches, mule and flour in good order.

To wait in the queue for water was a waste of time to Pat's inventive mind. Woe betides the new-chum he saw with two full tins of water. A conversation for five minutes or so and Pat had the full tins. 'So long mate, I had better get my water'—and he was out of sight. The new-chum had the two empty tins and another two or three hours' wait in the queue to fill up again.

Goodness knows what would have become of him had not the General Staff decided [to attack] Lone Pine. I saw him that day, as full of life as ever—I have not seen him since. Two days later after Lone Pine I saw a neat little bundle marked 'Killed in action'. Contents; one pay-book, one pocket-book, and photos, and one identity disc marked P.F., D. Coy., 3rd Bn. So poor Pat was dead! I believe I shed a genuine tear. The next I heard, he was inspecting one of the military hospitals as a Padre, and tipping the wink to a 3rd Battalion man who recognised him.

How he got away I never heard definitely, but I can imagine someone with a bloodstained bandage round one arm staggering into the clearing station and handing in the dead body on the way down—and P.F., alias Tom Jones was evacuated to the hospital ship. On arrival there I cannot imagine what he would do, but it is quite likely he became a steward or an A.M.C orderly, or he even may have thrown the skipper of the boat overboard and taken charge.

If ever I want a 'tenner' and P.F. is about, I'll look him up. I know, even if he has not got it—which is not likely— he will know where it is to be got!

TOM 'N' OPLAS

Tom is the central character of a number of tales collected in Sydney during the early to mid-1980s, but he is an Australian version of a folktale figure found throughout the world—the trickster. Here is a verbatim telling of a Tom 'n' Oplas tale in which the teller also acted out the various antics described:

Bank manager is sitting at his desk, round about lunchtime, when the assistant manager comes in and says, 'Look, he's done it again. Tom 'n' Oplas—he's put a thousand dollars in the bank. I can't work it out.'

And the manager says, 'Well, what should we do? You know. Do we have a responsibility to put this guy in? Is he getting his money legally, or . . .? What do you think?'

The assistant manager said, 'Well, why don't we call him in and find out?'

So come next Monday Tom 'n' Oplas arrives, puts a thousand dollars in the bank. And the assistant manager says, 'Mr Tom 'n' Oplas, the manager would like to see you.'

He goes into the office. The manager sits him down, says, 'Mr Tom 'n' Oplas, you've been one of our best customers for the last three years, but what I can't work out is every Monday morning you come in, you put a thousand dollars in the bank.'

Tom 'n' Oplas laughed. He says, 'Oh yes. Well, I'm a gambler.'

The manager says, 'What do you mean, you're a gambler? Is it something you can let me in on? Like a thousand dollars a week. That's fifty grand a year. I could retire on that.'

Tom says, 'Well, I tell you what I'll do. I'll bet you a thousand dollars that this time next week you'll have hair growing all over your back.'

And the manager thought, 'Ha, ha, ha. Obviously this fellow's gone off the rails a little bit under a bit of pressure from the bank manager.' He said, 'Mr Tom 'n' Oplas, that's a bet.'

So comes Tuesday the bank manager can't work it out how he's going to do it because he's done it every day for the last three years, and he's laughing and telling him he's just made a thousand dollars. So easy. He checks over his back. No hair. This is wonderful. He goes to bed Tuesday night. He sleeps on his back so to be sure that if any hair does grow he's got something organized. He sleeps on his back so it won't grow because he puts pressure on it.

Wednesday. He comes to the bank. He's got an overcoat, jumper because he thinks the only way Tom 'n' Oplas can get him is to tape something on his back, or put something on his shirt, or whatever. Even though it's the middle of summer. All the bank thinks he's a little bit crazy, but coming in he thinks 'a thousand dollars'.

Thursday, he works out he must be trying to get to his washing or his shirts, so what he does on Thursday is he doesn't wear a shirt. He wears just a jumper. He's a bank manager going into one of the biggest city banks with just a jumper on.

Friday he's getting a little bit toey.

Saturday and Sunday he just locks himself away in the house.

Monday morning arrives. He's still checking his back. He's got a mirror over behind his back, and he just can't see anything. There's nothing there. He's won a thousand dollars. He's beat Tom 'n' Oplas!

Tom 'n' Oplas arrives at the bank and he's got a Japanese fellow with him. The manager says, 'Mr Tom 'n' Oplas, in this way.'

And he says to the manager, 'I thought you'd be wanting to see me. I suppose you think you've won your bet.' So as soon as they get into the office the manager whips his shirt off and turns around—and the Japanese fellow faints. He says, 'Look, look, no hair, except . . . what's happened to your mate?'

Tom says, 'Oh, that's simple, I bet him two thousand dollars that within thirty seconds of being in here I'd have the shirt off your back.'

Trickster Tom 'n' Oplas is streetwise and, like tricksters the world over, ultimately ridicules social institutions, in this case a bank, never a very popular institution in Australia.

THREE BLOKES AT A PUB

Tricksters are not necessarily named individuals, real or fictional. One of the largest groups of Australian yarns concerns 'a bloke' or 'a couple of blokes'. In this case, it is three of them.

Three blokes walk into a busy pub. The first one orders a beer at the bar but the barman is too busy to take his money right away and serves another customer. He then returns to the bloke and asks for the money. 'But I already paid yer,' says the bloke. 'You went and served someone else, came back for my money, took it and put it in the till with the other money you had.'

Still busy, the barman decides that he must have forgotten and says, 'Okay.' The bloke finished his drink and left.

Then the second bloke came to the bar and ordered a beer. The barman served him without taking the money, then served another customer, coming back again to ask for the money. The second bloke made the same claim as the first, leaving the barman no choice but to agree that he must have taken the payment.

The second bloke drinks up and leaves just as the third bloke gets to the bar and orders. Now deeply suspicious that he has been rooked, the barman tells the third bloke that two blokes had just claimed they had paid for their beers while all along he was sure they had not. He reached under the bar and pulled out a heavy metal pipe, saying that he would be using this on the next bloke who tried anything funny like that.

'Look mate,' said the third bloke, 'I'm sorry for your troubles. All I want is me change, and I'll be out of here.'

Russian Jack, also known as 'Wheelbarrow Jack', is a legendary figure from the late nineteenth-century goldrushes of Western Australia, circa 1900.

3

HARD CASES

'How would I be? How would I bloody well be!'

The World's Greatest Whinger

THE COCKY

Cocky farmers are a stock feature of Australian folksong, verse and story. Of fabulous miserliness and dourness, they are among the hardest cases of Australian characters, their tight-fisted actions and attitudes featuring in many yarns. In the song 'The Cockies of Bungaree', for instance, the notoriously stingy small farmers of the Victorian town of Bungaree are portrayed as hard task-masters who get their workers up before dawn and make them work until after sunset and then they have to sleep with the animals.

We used to go to bed, you know, a little bit after dark,
The room we used to sleep in was just like Noah's Ark.
There was mice and rats and dogs and cats and pigs and
    poulter-ee,
I'll never forget the work we did down on Bungaree.

As in the ballad, many cocky stories involve the relationship between the farmer and his labourers.

In a characteristic cocky yarn, a labourer is hired on the basis that he stops work at sunset. When the sun goes down, he says to the cocky that it's about time they called it a day. The cocky replies by telling him that the sun hasn't set yet and that you can still see it if you climb up on top of the fence.

In another fable, the worker succeeds in getting the upper hand when the farmer wakes up his new labourer well before sunrise and says he needs a hand getting in the oats.

> 'Are they wild oats?' asks the sleepy labourer.
> 'No,' says the cocky, taken aback.
> 'Then why do we have to sneak up on 'em in the dark!'

As for having a day off, here's a typical cocky response. The new labourer asked the boss when he would have a day off. The cocky told him that he would have every fourth Sunday free. The labourer then wanted to know what there was to do in the area on his Sundays off. The cocky reeled off a long list, including cutting the week's firewood, mending the harnesses, tending the vegetables and washing the horses. 'After that, you can do whatever you like.'

The notorious tight-fistedness of the cocky farmer is also highlighted in many tales:

> One night in the pub a local congratulated a cocky on the upcoming marriage of his daughter. 'That will be the fourth wedding in your family during the last few years, won't it?'
> 'Yes,' replied the cocky, 'and the confetti is starting to get awful dirty.'

Other cocky yarns suggest the hardships and discomforts of his lifestyle:

> The drought had been on for so long that when a raindrop fell on the local cocky, he fainted clean away. They had to

throw two buckets-full of dust into his face to bring him back to consciousness.

Times were so hard that all the cocky had to eat was rabbits. He had them for every meal, week in, week out. He had them stewed, he had them fried, he had them boiled, he had them braised. Eventually, his diet got the better of him and his stomach began to revolt and he decided to give himself a solid dose of Epsom salts.

But this was no help. So he went to the local doctor, who asked him what he had been eating. The cocky told him that he'd had nothing but rabbits for months. The doctor asked him if he had taken anything for his sickness and the cocky told him about the Epsom salts. 'You don't need Epsom salts,' laughed the doctor, 'you need ferrets.'

Three cocky farmers were yarning over a beer about their respective properties and how many head they could run. The first cocky came from the Riverina and said he could run three head to an acre all year long.

The second cocky from central New South Wales said that he could get two head to an acre.

The third cocky was from Bourke way and said that although it was very dry where he was, he could run 95 head to an acre.

The first two cockies expressed their disbelief in a colourful and emphatic manner, but the third cocky held his ground. 'It's true,' he insisted, 'I run one head of sheep and 94 rabbits to an acre.'

'HUNGRY' TYSON

James Tyson (1819–98) was a highly successful pastoralist, or 'squatter', who made a fortune in acquiring rural land during the mid to late nineteenth century. Despite his wealth he lived simply, neither smoking, drinking nor swearing, probably something of a novelty for his time and geography.

In folklore, Tyson was renowned for his stinginess and
known universally as 'Hungry' Tyson. His Scrooge-like character was even memorialised in folk speech through the saying
'mean as Hungry Tyson'.

Sayings and yarns about Tyson echo his legendary meanness.
It was said that he would travel second-class on a train only
because there was no third-class carriage. He is rumoured to
have once claimed that he hadn't got rich by 'striking matches
when there was a fire to get a light by'.

Once, Hungry Tyson needed to get across to the other side of
the Murrumbidgee. The cost of being ferried across in the punt
was one shilling. To save having to pay the money, the tight-
fisted grazier swam across.

In contrast to his miserly image, Tyson was also said to be
an anonymous doer of good deeds, as A.B. 'Banjo' Paterson
suggests in his poem 'T.Y.S.O.N':

Across the Queensland border line
The mobs of cattle go;
They travel down in sun and shine
On dusty stage, and slow.
The drovers, riding slowly on
To let the cattle spread,
Will say: 'Here's one old landmark gone,
For old man Tyson's dead.'

What tales there'll be in every camp
By men that Tyson knew;
The swagmen, meeting on the tramp,
Will yarn the long day through,
And tell of how he passed as 'Brown',
And fooled the local men:
'But not for me—I struck the town,
And passed the message further down;
That's T.Y.S.O.N!'

There stands a little country town
Beyond the border line,
Where dusty roads go up and down,
And banks with pubs combine.
A stranger came to cash a cheque—
Few were the words he said—
A handkerchief about his neck,
An old hat on his head.

A long grey stranger, eagle-eyed—
'Know me? Of course you do?'
'It's not my work,' the boss replied,
'To know such tramps as you.'
'Well, look here, Mister, don't be flash,'
Replied the stranger then,
'I never care to make a splash,
I'm simple—but I've got the cash,
I'm T.Y.S.O.N.'

But in that last great drafting-yard,
Where Peter keeps the gate,
And souls of sinners find it barred,
And go to meet their fate,
There's one who ought to enter in,
For good deeds done on earth;
Such deeds as merit ought to win,
Kind deeds of sterling worth.

Not by the strait and narrow gate,
Reserved for wealthy men,
But through the big gate, opened wide,
The grizzled figure, eagle-eyed,
Will travel through—and then
Old Peter'll say: 'We pass him through;
There's many a thing he used to do,
Good-hearted things that no one knew;
That's T.Y.S.O.N.'

At his death, Tyson's estate was worth two million pounds, a fact that gave further force to an apparently existing outback folk belief that the money was cursed, as a literary-minded contemporary wrote shortly after the pastoralist died:

> Tyson died alone in the night in his lonely bush station, with thousands of stock on it, but with no hand to give him even a drink of water, and no voice to soothe or to console him in his last struggle with death. He was hurriedly buried. No requiem was sung at his grave. He died, and was forgotten. Only his millions, which Bacon called 'muck', and Shakespeare 'rascally counters', remained for his shoal of relatives to fight for through the law courts. Some of them were but struggling for an overdose of mortal poison, as the gold proved to be to some persons at least.
>
> There is a strange legend regarding this man's money. The old hands out back will tell you that every coin of it is cursed, and if we follow the havoc some of the money has caused, there is much food for the superstitious mind.

Tyson's folktale image is similar to that of another wealthy pastoralist of a slightly later era, Sidney (later Sir) Kidman (1857–1935). Many tales of miserliness are told of both men.

NINETY THE GLUTTON

A character featuring in a number of Tasmanian folktales is usually known as 'Ninety the Glutton'. As his name suggests, Ninety was notorious for his appetite and the large amounts of food he could consume.

Tradition has it that Ninety got his unusual name when he was looking after a mob of sheep in Tasmania's Lake Country for a period of three months. When he brought in the mob for shearing, it was found that he was 90 sheep short. On being questioned about the fate of the sheep, a surprised Ninety simply said that he had eaten one each day for his rations.

Ninety was said to have been a wanderer who turned up at various places in Tasmania in search of work—and food. Any wise property owner was usually happy to give him one large feed and send him on his way. But on one occasion Ninety came to the Malahide Estate and asked the owner for a meal. As he had a crate of apples that were about to go bad, the owner said that Ninety could eat them. About an hour later, he saw Ninety sitting amid a pile of apple cores. He looked up and asked, 'What time's dinner, Boss?'

There are numerous other Ninety tales, as well as stories about a similar Queensland character known as 'Tom the Glutton' who was able to consume a crate of bananas, sometimes including the skins, in just ten minutes.

GALLOPING JONES

Galloping Jones is usually said to have been a historical figure of Northern Queensland folklore, and to have died in 1960. Jones was a bush fighter, a drinker, a stock-stealer and a bank robber. His antics included stealing stock, selling it and stealing it back again the very same night.

Once Galloping Jones was arrested by a policeman and an Aboriginal tracker for illegally slaughtering a cow. The evidence was the cow's hide, prominently marked with someone else's brand. On the way back to town, Jones and his captors camped. Jones managed to get the policeman and his assistant drunk and when they fell asleep, he rode off into the night. However, instead of escaping, he returned a few hours later with a fresh cow hide which he substituted for the evidence carried by the policeman. Next day the party arrived in town, where Jones was tried for his crime. When they pulled the evidence from the bag, they found the hide bore Jones's brand and the case was dismissed.

In another story, Jones was again captured by a young policeman who he fooled into letting him go behind a bush to relieve himself. Of course, Jones escaped and the policeman had to

return to town without his captive. When he got to town to
report his failure to the sergeant, who was in his usual 'office',
the pub, there was Jones, washed and shaved and having a
beer. The embarrassed policeman threatened to shoot Jones,
but the trickster just said that he felt the need for a clean-up
and a drink and that he would now be happy to stroll down
to the lock-up.

Galloping Jones traditions are very much in the mould of
the larger-than-life pioneer heroes of the American west, with
more than a touch of the trickster. Many stories concerning
Galloping Jones are also told of the Queensland trickster,
Snuffler Oldfield.

CHRISTY PALMERSTON

Christy (also Christie) Palmerston (c. 1850?–97) was a historical character of Northern Queensland in the 1870s and 80s
around whom a good many yarns have developed. Most of
these centre on his alleged origins as the bastard son of the
British Prime Minister, Lord Palmerston, his ability to terrify
Aboriginal and Chinese people, his toughness and ability to live
off the land, and his shady, sometimes lethally criminal, activities including murdering Aborigines. He is also said to have
hidden caches of gold in various places and to have narrowly
escaped death on numerous occasions.

The historical Christy Palmerston was probably Cristofero
Palmerston Carandini, who seems to have arrived in Northern
Queensland in the early to mid 1870s. Probably attracted
like many others by the prospect of finding gold, Palmerston
established a reputation as a wayfinder, pioneering several
routes to and from various points, including Port Douglas,
later Darwin. In the late 1870s Palmerston conducted a questionable enterprise with several hundred Chinese diggers,
effectively imprisoning them on the Russell River goldfield,
exploiting them for labour and as customers of his monopoly
supply business. He married shortly after this, briefly ran a

pub in Townsville then worked in Borneo and Malaya. He died of fever in Malaya in 1897 at a relatively young age, though tradition has it that he died in New Guinea, as it was then known, at a ripe old age.

Like quite a few folk heroes around the world, Palmerston is a composite character with both good and bad attributes. He is commemorated in both Queensland folklore and official place-names.

In the 1960s and 70s the folklorist Ron Edwards collected a number of Christy Palmerston yarns in Queensland. In one of these stories, it is said that Palmerston and his Aboriginal co-workers murdered a dozen other Aborigines who were attempting to steal from his Russell River enterprise. He took to the bush for five years, successfully evading capture by the police. According to this story, if he undertook to survey the Millaa Millaa to Innisfail route, he would be pardoned for his crime.

MOONDYNE JOE

Welshman Joseph Bolitho Johns (1827?–1900) was transported from England to Western Australia in 1853. He absconded, was captured and escaped repeatedly throughout the late 1880s, becoming a celebrated identity in the Swan River colony, later Western Australia, under the folk name 'Moondyne Joe'. Joe's ability to escape was so frequently displayed that he became a local hero. While the only song extant about Joe is a parody of the nursery rhyme 'Pop Goes the Weasel', in its brevity can be detected that set of tensions and conflicts between unpopular authority and those suffering beneath it that typically underlie outlaw heroes:

The Governor's son has got the pip
The governor's got the measles
Moondyne Joe has give 'em the slip,
Pop! goes the weasel.

Joe was able to survive so well in the bush due to a network of friends and sympathisers. Folk traditions about Moondyne Joe include his many escapes, his cleverness and his buried gold. As well as featuring as the hero of folksong and verse, Joe still leads a lively folkloric existence as the central character of a group of folktales.

Many of these stories concern Joe's legendary escaping abilities. Arrested for unlawfully killing a horse that had supposedly eaten the oats Joe had lovingly provided for his favourite pony, he was imprisoned in Toodyay (then Newcastle) lock-up. Because he did not consider that he had done anything wrong, Joe promptly escaped, taking the warder's pistol with him for good measure.

Another of Joe's escapes is said to have occurred at the Mahogany Inn on the Great Eastern Highway. This was supposed to be one of Joe's many hide-outs. The police found out about it and, just as they arrived, Joe escaped through an upstairs window, jumping down onto a police horse, which he galloped away to freedom.

There are also stories about Joe escaping from gaols in Perth, York and Fremantle. According to one story, the escape from Fremantle Prison, in March 1867, involved Joe crossing the new Fremantle Bridge before it could be officially opened by Governor Hampton, so thumbing his nose at officialdom once again.

Apart from escape stories, one of the most commonly heard Moondyne Joe yarns has the bushranger being caught in the cellars of a local winery—which winery is disputed—dead drunk. Although this has been authoritatively refuted on a number of occasions, it is a persistent belief in and around Perth, helped along by the local tourism industry.

Released from prison in 1871, Joe made a fresh start as an honest worker, and later married. He received some literary romanticisation in the novel *Moondyne* by John Boyle O'Reilly (1887). Joseph Johns ended his days as an almost forgotten ex-convict pauper in the Fremantle Asylum, where he died in 1900.

THE EULO QUEEN

A relatively well-developed heroine tradition concerns 'The Eulo Queen'. She is at once a named individual about whom tales are told and also a representative type common in Australian folklore and popular culture, the barmaid, and, it is strongly suggested in her legend, the gold-digging prostitute.

The Eulo Queen—sometimes 'Eulo Belle'—is thought to have been a woman named Isabel Gray. She was variously said to have been born in England or Mauritius probably in 1851 and to have been the illegitimate daughter of a British army captain. She was apparently sent to Australia around 1868, marrying the first of three husbands. From the mid-1880s she was the publican of the Eulo Hotel (or Hall), as well as a number of other drinking and commercial establishments in the small Queensland opal-mining town of that name, about 70 kilometres west of Cunnamulla. Eulo was on the legendary Paroo Track, a notoriously hot, dry and dusty way described unattractively in Henry Lawson's poem 'The Paroo':

It was a week from Christmas-time,
    As near as I remember,
And half a year since in the rear
    We'd left the Darling Timber.
The track was hot and more than drear;
    The long day seemed forever;
Put now we knew that we were near
    Our camp—the Paroo River.

With blighted eyes and blistered feet,
    With stomachs out of order,
Half mad with flies and dust and heat
    We'd crossed the Queensland Border.
I longed to hear a stream go by
    And see the circles quiver;

> I longed to lay me down and die
> > That night on Paroo River.
>
> 'Tis said the land out West is grand—
> > I do not care who says it—
> It isn't even decent scrub,
> > Nor yet an honest desert;
> It's plagued with flies, and broiling hot,
> > A curse is on it ever;
> I really think that God forgot
> > The country round that river.

The Eulo Queen was a noted beauty and, with little competition in that part of the country, attracted many admirers, growing wealthy on the gifts they bestowed upon her. These enabled her to pursue a flamboyant lifestyle, further adding to her legend. It is said that she gained her name when ejecting a drunken patron from her establishment, yelling at him: 'I'm the Eulo queen—now get out!' She was thereafter known by this name, to which she is said to have made no objections.

After World War I the town declined as a centre for opals and transport and the Eulo Queen, estranged from her third husband, fell on hard times. She died in a Toowoomba psychiatric hospital in 1929, reputedly in her nineties and with only thirty pounds to her name.

WHEELBARROW JACK

Also known as 'Russian Jack', 'Wheelbarrow Jack' was a 22-year-old Russian Finn who arrived in Western Australia in the late 1880s to follow the goldrushes in the Kimberley region. He was thought to be two metres tall, had an abnormally large chest and extraordinary strength. Like many other heroic characters of Australian tradition, Jack flits continually between historical fact and folklore.

A popular method for travelling across the desert to the

remote Kimberley goldfields was to use wooden wheelbarrows. Jack built one to carry his goods overland to the diggings. It was unusually large, matching his strength, and with it he was said to be able to carry loads of 50 kilograms or more. He left Derby for the Kimberley in company with another hopeful who became sick along the way. Jack loaded the man's goods and, after he became too sick to walk, the man himself onto his barrow and wheeled him far along the track until the ailing passenger died.

There are numerous stories of other such incidents in which Jack used his strength, stamina and his barrow to rescue exhausted prospectors in the desert and carry them to safety. When Daisy Bates, herself a colourful figure, came across Jack outside the Peak Hill goldfield in 1907, he was working as a groom and as a market gardener, an occupation that suited his legendary appetite. According to Bates, he was still lending a helping hand to those in need.

These acts of charity became legendary in the West—and further afield—as an exemplar of mateship. Around these mostly documented good deeds was woven a web of less reliable tales that nevertheless reflect the esteem in which Jack's deeds were held in the frontier country of the north-west.

Jack went hunting kangaroo with a mate who had an accident and broke his leg. Jack loaded him onto his barrow and wheeled him into town. The townsfolk gathered round to admire yet another of Jack's great feats of endurance. Jack boasted that he had pushed his mate over many miles of hard country. Still lying on the wheelbarrow, his mate piped up to say that Jack had managed to hit every rock along the way.

When Jack worked at the Mount Morgan goldmine, he fell down a shaft. Badly injured, he lay there for three days until they found him. His only concern was said to be that he had missed his shift at the mine.

Some yarns tell of Jack's great strength. Once, while working for a station owner, he was given the sack. In his anger, Jack bent a thick crowbar across his knees.

Jack's only real failing was his love for the grog. It was said that a coach driver stopped near Jack's lodgings and offered him a swig of whisky. At first, Jack declined, saying he was off the grog. Prevailed upon to have a small drink, he swallowed half the bottle of whisky at once. Ruefully looking at his now-empty bottle, the driver said that if that was Jack not drinking, he would hate to see him when he was.

In another incident, said to have taken place in the gold town of Cue, Jack's love of alcohol almost got the better of him. After a few beers too many, he loaded up his barrow to make the trek back to his camp a few miles out of town. On top he carelessly threw a box of firing caps for the dynamite he also carried on his barrow. Seeing Jack weave unsteadily down the street, the local policeman decided to escort him out of town for everyone's safety. Along the way the policeman spotted the firing caps and decided to arrest Jack. As Wheelbarrow Jack was an extremely powerful man, as well as extremely drunk, this presented the policeman with a difficult situation. The policeman managed to steer the merrily singing Jack towards the police tents, where a number of other policemen offered Jack a cup of tea while they repacked his wheelbarrow to make it safe.

Jack dozed off and the police handcuffed him to a very large log outside the police tents. They then went to attend to matters elsewhere, leaving Jack asleep at the log. When they returned they were astonished to find that Jack and the log had disappeared. They followed the marks in the sand to the local pub, finding Jack drinking a beer with his unchained hand. The other one was still chained to the log propped up on the bar. Jack had woken in the night with a terrible thirst. He had casually lifted the log and gone in search of a waterbag. He found one in the police tent, drained it and went back to sleep until the fierce sun woke him the next morning. Now thirstier than ever, Jack simply threw the log onto his shoulder and made for the pub. 'Have a drink with me and I'll go back to gaol,' said Jack. But rather than drink on duty, the policeman followed Jack, still shouldering the giant log, back to the police tents where they shared a billy of tea. A now-sober Jack made off for his diggings with a safe load.

Wheelbarrow Jack died in Fremantle in 1904. During his life on the north-western Australian goldfields, he was the subject of considerable journalistic interest and attracted the attention of Mary Durack and Ernestine Hill, among many others. After his death, his life was recalled in several newspapers:

> An old identity, John Fredericks—but a hundred times better known as 'Russian Jack'—died a few days ago. His death came as a surprise for no one could imagine death in the prime of life to one of such Herculean strength. He was, so far as physical manhood is concerned, a picture, but he combined the strength of a lion with the tenderness of a woman. Though he had a loud-sounding sonorous voice that seemed to come out of his boots, there was no more harm in it than the chirp of a bird. Many instances are known of his uniform good nature, but his extraordinary kindness, some years ago, to a complete stranger—that he picked up on the track in the Kimberley gold rush—exemplified his mateship. The stranger had a wheelbarrow and some food, and the burly Russian picked the stranger up, placed him on his own large wheelbarrow, together with his meagre possessions, and wheeled him nearly 300 miles (480 kms) to a haven of refuge.

It was the travel writer and journalist Ernestine Hill who first suggested a statue be raised to commemorate Jack's deeds and legend. This initiative was carried forward by many others and led eventually to the erection of the statue of the outback hero at Hall's Creek in 1979. The statue depicts the hero in his Good Samaritan role carrying a sick digger a great distance through the desert in his wooden wheelbarrow.

Wheelbarrow Jack is a Western Australian version of a folktale type known as 'German Charlie' stories. While the heroes of such tales are not always called 'German Charlie', they are usually nicknamed in a way that draws attention to their national or ethnic origins. The characteristics of these stories are that they bring some special, unusual or exaggerated skill or attribute to an Australian community. Using that skill in helpful, often humorous, sometimes absurd ways, German Charlies become accepted members of their communities and feature in commonly told tales of their real and fancied exploits. Jack's wheelbarrow, his assistance to the needy, his strength and his prodigious boozing all combine to make him another example of a type of hard case found all around Australia.

LONG JACK

Another hard case named Jack came into being on the Western Front in World War I. He was said to have been a member of the 3rd Battalion and stood out from the crowd because of a chronic stutter and the speed with which he retorted— verbally or physically—to any perceived slight. Long Jack's exploits were recorded by an anonymous contributor to the *Third Battalion Magazine*, sometime around 1917:

> There are certain characters, which pass through our Battalion life, which are more than worth perpetuating. Such a one was long Jack Dean. In regard to his figure he was an outsider, as he was 6½ feet tall and as slender as a whippet. As a wit he stood alone. A man needed more than ordinary morale to meet him on this ground, and many who purposely or inadvertently engaged him have cause to be sorry for themselves, but glad that they were a party to adding another witty victory to Jack's account. The quickness and smartness of his retorts took the sting from them, and there was no more popular man in the unit than he. This sketch aims at reproducing some stories which came from him, and through which the man himself may be seen.
>
> At the outbreak of war, or soon afterwards he presented himself before the Recruiting Officers, but his physique was

against him. His keenness, however, was proof against his setback, and he came again and again, only to meet with the same result. At last, he asked with his inimitable stutter; 'If you c-c-can't t-take me as a s-s-soldier—s-s-send me-me as a m-m-mascot!'

The Recruiting Officer had become used to his applications, and, recognising the keenness of the man he was dealing with, answered: 'I'll tell you what I shall do. Bring me twelve receipts, and I shall accept you'. 'Done!' said Jack. 'It's a bargain'. He turned up with seventeen fit men and was taken on strength. One can imagine him taking his place among the other recruits at the training depot. His 'length without breadth' immediately singled him out as a butt and one misguided youth was foolish enough to say as he passed him; 'Smell the gum-leaves'. 'Yes', said Jack; 'feel the branches'. And his long, wiry right shot out with good effect.

He must have been the despair of all that tried to make a smart soldier out of him. Working on the coal face does not keep a long man supple; but in due time he arrived in France, and joined the Battalion—just in time to face the second time 'in' on the Somme. He quickly made himself at home, and in a very short time was known to everybody in the Battalion. It is said that Colonel Howell Price asked him if he had any brothers. 'Y-yes, sir,' he answered: 'one—he's t-t-taller than me, b-but n-not n-n-nearly so well developed'.

Being thin made him appear taller than he actually was, and his height was always the point in question to those who were not used to it. A Tommy saw him ambling along the road very much the worse for wear as a result of a tour in the line and in the mud. 'Reach me down a star, choom,' said the Tommy. 'Take your pick out of these, sonny,' was Jack's answer, together with a very forceful uppercut to the chin. Our late Brigadier never failed to talk to Jack when he met him.

'Good-day, Jack,' was his invariable greeting. 'G-g-g-good day, Brig.,' was always Jack's reply, and it never failed to amuse Brigadier Leslie.

There is one other story which illustrates J.D.'s democratic soul. The Brigadier stopped to have a word with him, and remarked that he wasn't getting any fatter. 'How the hell can a man get fat on 8 to a loaf?' was the response.

Jack's feet were always his worst enemy, and they were the cause of him falling to the rear on one occasion, during a rather stiff route march. He was getting along as best he could when he came up with the Brigadier. 'What Jack! You out!' said the latter. 'Me blanky p-p-p-paddles h-have gone on me, Brig,' replied Jack.

It is only possible to write this sketch because the subject is no longer with us. We hope he is now on his way to Australia as he has done his bit well, and had come to that stage when he could not effectively carry on. While waiting for the Board which was to examine and determine his future, one of the Sisters like all who saw him for the first time, said; 'What a lot of disadvantages there must be for such a tall man'. 'Yes,' said Jack. 'The greatest trouble I have is with the rum issue; it dries up before it hits my stomach'.

Jack will remain in our memories and we are grateful to him for these and many other sayings of his which have amused us at all times when we needed the lift of genuine amusement.

DIABOLICAL DICK

The Western Australian cray (lobster) fishing industry has long been a tough and colourful way to earn a living. The industry and its workers have generated extensive folktale traditions, including stories about a folk hero known as 'Diabolical Dick'. In the manner of all occupational heroes, Dick has larger than life encounters with outsize crays, giant waves and 'occkies' (octopus) who get their tentacles caught in his steel-bottomed craypots and clank around the seafloor all night, disturbing humans and wildlife along the Geraldton coast. He finally dissuades them by encircling his craypots with barbed wire.

On one occasion, Dick sailed so far off the Western Australian coast that he was just about in Africa, returning to port with a couple of assegais and arrows embedded in the wheelhouse.

On another cray trip, Dick laid his pots in a wave so big that when it crashed one of the pots was propelled so far inland, it was halfway to the Warburton Ranges, where it felled a passing 'roo. The tale continues in like vein: 'This is, however, not a common occurrence, as few pots land east of Meekatharra in these circumstances, though they are listed as air navigational hazards by MMA pilots.'

PUPPY PIE AND DOG'S DINNER

A popular cook yarn involved a Chinese cook who was managing to serve up delicious food for some weeks. Suddenly, the delectable pies and stews ceased. The shearers asked the cook why he was no longer serving up his greatly anticipated dishes. He shrugged his shoulders and said, 'No more puppy, no more pie.'

This oft-told story has been treated in literature by Brunton Stephens in his 'My Other Chinese Cook' in the late 1880s and its central motif, the European suspicion that Chinese food is largely cats and dogs, also appears in modern urban legends.

Whenever a pet cat or dog goes missing in Australia, it is inevitably suggested by someone that the distressed owner check the local Chinese restaurant. This relatively light-hearted prejudice is also the pivot of a popular modern legend, often known as 'The Chinese Restaurant', though the version below, collected in Perth in 1987, is called 'Dog's Dinner', for reasons that will be obvious:

I read in the paper that this well-to-do French couple went to Hong Kong or China or somewhere and they went to this local restaurant with their pet poodle for a meal. They asked the waiters for a meal for their dog, as well as for themselves, but there was a bit of a language barrier. But anyway they got it sorted out at last and the waiters took their dog out to the kitchen to look after it. Later on their meal was brought out to them, and when they took the covers off the dishes they found their meal was their dog!

The Chinese restaurant story is well known and heard in all sorts of places. It is also set in all sorts of places. Frequently it is overseas, especially Hong Kong, Singapore or Malaysia. It was reported in Zurich by Reuters news service as early as 1971. A Scandinavian version is set in Paris—with a rat in the dinner instead of a dog. A version collected in Queensland in 1988 locates the restaurant in not-very-exotic Adelaide and identifies the dog as a chihuahua.

According to the story, a couple visited a restaurant with their pet dog, usually a chihuahua or one of the smaller breeds, and asked for a meal. The waiter had trouble understanding them but eventually picked up the pet dog and took it to the kitchen, where the couple assumed the man was going to feed it. After some time he returned with a covered plate. Upon taking off the lid, the couple found their pet dog, cooked and served with bamboo shoots and other garnishes, sometimes on a bed of rice, sometimes with an apple or orange in its mouth. The couple usually suffer a nervous breakdown and return home immediately.

There is still a widespread belief that Chinese, Vietnamese and other 'Asian' restaurants cook dogs and cats, usually scoured from the local neighbourhood. Such expressions do not seem to stop Australians from frequently dining at these restaurants. The 'poodle with noodles' legend, as it has also been dubbed, refuses to go away and is still leading a more than healthy life on the internet and in emails.

THE WORLD'S GREATEST WHINGER

Sometimes said to be as old as the Boer War (1899–1902), the elaborate anecdote usually known as 'The World's Greatest

Whinger' probably dates only from World War II. It lives mainly in print and is given here in one of many such versions, but draws on the venerable tradition of unusually developed attributes to achieve its widely appreciated effect:

> I struck him first on a shearing station in outback Queensland. He was knocking the fleeces from a four-year-old wether when I asked him the innocent question: 'How are you?'
>
> He didn't answer immediately, but waited till he had carved the last bit of wool from the sheep, allowing it to regain its feet. Kicking it through the door, dropping the shears and spitting a stream of what looked like molten metal about three yards. Then he fixed me with a pair of malevolent eyes in which fires of a deep hatred seemed to burn, and he pierced me with them as he said:
>
> 'How would I be? How would you bloody well expect me to be? Get a load of me, will you? Dags on every inch of me bloody hide; drinking me own bloody sweat; swallowing dirt with every breath I breathe; shearing sheep which should have been dogs' meat years ago; working for the lousiest bastard in Australia; and frightened to leave because the old woman has got some bloody hound looking for me with a bloody maintenance order.
>
> 'How would I be? I haven't tasted a beer for weeks, and the last glass I had was knocked over by some clumsy bastard before I'd finished it.'
>
> The next time I saw him was in Sydney. He had just joined the A.I.F. He was trying to get into a set of webbing and almost ruptured himself in the process. I said to him: 'How would you be, Dig?'
>
> He almost choked before replying. 'How would I be? How *would* I bloody well be? Take a gander at me, will you? Get a load of this bloody outfit—look at me bloody hat, size nine and a half and I take six and a half. Get a bloody eyeful of these strides! Why, you could hide a bloody brewery horse

in the seat of them and still have room for me! Get on this shirt—just get on the bloody thing, will you? Get on these bloody boots; why, there's enough leather in the bastard to make a full set of harness. And some know-all bastard told me this was a men's outfit!

'How would I be? How would I bloody well be!'

I saw him next in Tobruk. He was seated on an upturned box, tin hat over one eye, cigarette butt hanging from his bottom lip, rifle leaning against one knee, and he was engaged in trying to clean his nails with the tip of his bayonet. I should have known better, but I asked him: 'How would you be, Dig?'

He swallowed the butt and fixed me a really mad look. 'How would I be? How would I bloody well be! How would you expect me to be? Six months in this bloody place, being shot at by every Fritz in Africa; eating bloody sand with every meal; flies in me hair and eyes; frightened to sleep a bloody wink expecting to die in this bloody place; and copping the bloody crow whenever there's a handout by anybody.

'How would I be? How would I bloody well be!'

The last time I saw him was in Paradise, and his answer to my question was: 'How would I be? How would I bloody well be! Get an eyeful of this bloody nightgown, will you? A man trips over the bloody thing fifty times a day, and it takes a man ten minutes to lift the bloody thing when he wants to scratch his shin!

'Get a gander at this bloody right wing—feathers missing everywhere. A man must be bloody well moulting!

'Get an eyeful of this bloody halo! Only me bloody ears keep the rotten thing on me skull—and look at the bloody dents on the bloody thing!

'How would I be? Cast your eyes on this bloody harp. Five bloody strings missing, and there's a band practice in five minutes!

'How would I be, you ask. How would you expect a bloody man to bloody well be?'

THE CAPTAIN OF THE PUSH

The street gangs of Sydney and Melbourne are almost as old as the cities themselves. In Sydney, the 'Cabbage Tree Mob' was frequently mentioned in negative terms in the local press: 'There are to be found all round the doors of the Sydney Theatre a sort of loafer known as the Cabbage-Tree Mob. The Cabbage-Tree Mob are always up for a "spree" and some of their pastimes are so rough an order as to deserve to be repaid with bloody coxcombs.'

Probably not a coherent gang or 'push' so much as an occasional assembly of young working-class men, the mob was distinguished by the kind of headgear they favoured, a hat made from cabbage tree fronds. Whatever their exact nature, the cabbage tree mob hung around theatres, race grounds and markets, and specialised in cat-calling and otherwise harassing the respectable middle classes. Some of them were ex-convicts, some were descended from convict stock.

By the 1870s, groups of this sort were being called 'larrikins'. Their favoured pastimes were a development of the earlier troublemakers and included disrupting Salvation Army meetings with volleys of rotten vegetables, rocks and the odd dead cat. The larrikins were also noted for dancing with young women friends, events often portrayed by journalists as 'orgies'. By the 1880s observers began to speak of larrikin 'pushes' or gangs, also sometimes referred to as the 'talent'. These were usually associated with particular suburbs or areas. In Sydney there were the 'Haymarket Bummers', the 'Rocks Push', the 'Cow Lane Push' and the 'Woolloomooloo Push'. In Melbourne, it was the 'Fitzroy Forties' and the 'Stephen Street Push', as well as the surely ironic 'Flying Angels', among others. The pushes were mostly male, young and with a strong loyalty ethic, each supporting the others when needed.

The larrikins revelled in fighting with police, resisting arrest, and there were notable pitched battles between them and large groups of police in the last decades of the nineteenth century. Despite, or because of, their criminality and anti-social behaviour, the crudely colourful larrikins soon became the objects of literary interest. Henry Lawson's 'The Captain of the Push' was an early rendering of the larrikin culture.

Based loosely on real events, 'The Captain of the Push' (also unprintably parodied as 'The Bastard from the Bush') begins:

> As the night was falling slowly down on city, town and bush,
> From a slum in Jones's Alley sloped the Captain of the Push;
> And he scowled towards the North, and he scowled
>   towards the South,
> As he hooked his little finger in the corners of his mouth.
> Then his whistle, loud and shrill, woke the echoes of the
>   'Rocks',
> And a dozen ghouls came sloping round the corners of the
>   blocks.

The ghouls, called the 'Gory Bleeders', 'spoke the gutter language' of the slums and brothels and swore fearsomely and fulsomely with every breath. Their 'captain' is:

> . . . bottle-shouldered, pale and thin,
> For he was the beau-ideal of a Sydney larrikin;
> E'en his hat was most suggestive of the city where we live,
> With a gallows-tilt that no one, save a larrikin, can give.

He wears the larrikin outfit of tight bell-bottom trousers, elaborate boots, uncollared shirt and necktie. The gang encounters a stranger in the street who turns out to be a man from the bush who wants to join the gang. He has read of their exploits in the 'Weekly Gasbag', and sitting alone in his bush humpy decided that he:

> 'Longed to share the dangers and the pleasures of the push!
> 'Gosh! I hate the swells and good 'uns—I could burn 'em
>   in their beds;

'I am with you, if you'll have me, and I'll break their
    blazing heads.'

The larrikins demand to know if the bushman would match
them in perfidy and violence. Would he punish an informer
who breaks the code of loyalty? 'Would you lay him out and
kick him to a jelly on the ground?' Would he 'smash a bleedin'
bobbie', 'break a swell or Chinkie' and 'have a moll to keep
yer'? To all of which the stranger answers, 'My Kerlonial oath,
I would!' They test him practically by asking him to smash a
window. The stranger is sworn in and becomes an exemplary
larrikin, if a little over-zealous even for the Gory Bleeders. One
morning the captain wakes and finds the stranger gone:

Quickly going through the pockets of his 'blooming' bags,
    he learned
That the stranger had been through him for the stuff his
    'moll' had earned;
And the language that he muttered I should scarcely like to
    tell.
(Stars! and notes of exclamation!! blank and dash will do
    as well).

The rest of the bleeders soon forget the bloke who briefly joined
them and robbed their leader. But the captain: 'Still is laying
round in ballast, for the nameless from the bush.'

Louis Stone's flawed masterpiece, *Jonah* (1911), presented a
more realistic picture of the Sydney slum lifestyle that produced
and nourished the larrikins. Its eponymous hero makes his
own fortune by hard work and astute business sense, though
forfeits his working-class roots, loses in love and fails as a
decent human being in the process.

Probably taking his lead from this approach, C.J. Dennis
began writing the verse that would eventually become the
much-loved characters of *The Songs of a Sentimental Bloke*
and *The Moods of Ginger Mick*. Soft Bill, 'the Bloke', his love

Doreen and his friend the street rabbit-seller, Ginger Mick, together with others who hung around Melbourne's 'Little Lon', were highly romanticised and bore almost no resemblance to the realities of the street. But the verse novellas chronicling their imaginary doings sold in very great numbers, making Dennis a wealthy man and establishing the 'rough diamond' with a soft centre stereotype of the larrikin, recycled for decades in stage shows and the early Australian cinema. The image lives on still.

THE SOUVENIR KING

The Anzacs were not the only troops to souvenir all manner of items from the field of battle, but they were noted exponents of the art, as suggested in a couple of Digger yarns:

> On the Western Front, a sergeant halted the enormous Private Smith, who was wearing a spiked German helmet.
>
> 'Who gave you permission to wear German issue?' he asked.
>
> 'Please, sergeant,' said Private Smith, 'don't make me give this lid up; I had to kill seven Germans to get my size.'
>
> The sergeant looked at Private Smith's feet. 'If you ever lose your boots,' he said, 'the flamin' *war's over.*'

And one about the enthusiastic war photographer:

> It is well known to most front line Diggers that the Aussie official photographer was one of the gamest men in the war. One day he was taking the usual risks, oblivious of all considerations but that of getting a good picture. A purposeful Digger was seen stalking him from shell-hole to shell-hole.
>
> 'What in th'll yer doing, Ginger?' yelled a cobber.
>
> 'Oh, it's all right. I'm just waiting for this photo bloke to get knocked. I want to souvenir his camera!'

The story of the colourful character who became known as 'The Souvenir King' is full of folklore as much as fact. John Hines, known as 'Barney', was born in Liverpool in 1873. After many years of roughing it around the world, he ended up in Australia, enlisting in the AIF in 1915 and becoming a member of the 45th Battalion. On the Western Front he proved to be, like so many other 'bad characters', as good at soldiering as he was bad at staying sober, obeying orders and otherwise knuckling down to military discipline. In addition to his apparent fearlessness and talent for taking large numbers of prisoners, Barney had a very special ability with souvenirs.

Souveniring—also known as 'ratting'—was a popular pastime of Australian troops. It involved obtaining items of enemy equipment—clothing, weaponry, medals or anything else that might be worth a few bob. Whether these items were obtained from Germans after they no longer had a need for them or if they were 'liberated' from prisoners was of no consequence. Possession, as they say, was nine points of the law. So efficient was Barney at obtaining his trophies that he was dubbed 'The Souvenir King' and generally recognised as the finest exponent of the art. It was not only the number and range of items that Barney managed to filch from enemy sources, or elsewhere, but also their occasional oddity or extravagance. On one occasion he souvenired a grandfather clock. Another time saw a full barrel of English beer added to his stocks.

To be fair, Barney was far from being the only collector of questionable mementos in the AIF or any other army. It was the publication of an evocative photograph taken by Frank Hurley of Barney sitting with a pile of his keepsakes that provided him with a raffish celebrity around which grew quite a few legends. The most widespread of these is the most unlikely tale that when the German head of state, Kaiser Wilhelm, heard of Barney's looting he placed a price on his head, encouraging German troops to hunt The Souvenir King down. His notorious reputation for unhappy dealings with authority also generated the story that he was once arrested by British Military Police but caused so much trouble to them that he was soon handed back to his unit. His battlefield bravery led to the folk belief that he had killed more German soldiers than any other member of the AIF.

Barney was wounded on several occasions and was given a medical discharge in 1916. But he re-enlisted and went back to fight and souvenir for another year or so until he was again discharged for health reasons in 1918. He returned to Australia, where he set up house in a humpy on the fringes of Sydney, eking out a living with various forms of manual and itinerant labour and, of course, selling souvenirs. It is said that he took the train into the suburbs each week to deliver a sack of vegetables to ex-soldiers in the repatriation hospital. Occasional republication of the famous photograph briefly revived his notoriety from time to time. When war again began in 1939, Barney tried to enlist but was rejected due to his age. He died in 1958.

MRS DELANEY

The possibly historical Mrs Delaney is a character well known in railway lore and legend. Said to hail from Tasmania and to have lived sometime before World War I (1914–18), she was a fruit-seller with a quick wit and a sharp tongue. Her stories are also frequently ribald, though the story of her encounter with another legend, the wealthy politician King O'Malley, focuses on her ability to answer back and to take no nonsense.

According to the story, O'Malley was travelling on the Hobart train and noticed that the well-known figure of the fruit-seller had become rather plump since his last journey. Ungallantly, he prodded her ample behind and asked what she intended to call the baby. Mrs Delaney is said to have replied that if it was a boy, he would be called after Saint Patrick. If it was a girl, she would be Brigid after her mother. 'But if it is what I think it is, all piss and wind, I'll call it after you.'

DOPES

The racetrack has long been the stamping ground of hard cases of all types. This tale of the turf involves the practice of 'doping' a horse in order to make it—usually—run faster. There are many ways to do this, most of them more folkloric than scientific:

A not very sophisticated trainer makes up some dope and absorbs it into a sugar cube. While he is slipping the cube to his horse before the race begins, the Chief Steward of the track, or 'stipe', catches him. 'What are you feeding that horse?' he demands to know.

The trainer replies that it is just a treat for the horse before the race to calm the horse down in the starting gate. Seeing that the 'stipe' is still suspicious, the trainer seeks to reassure him by eating one of the cubes himself. The 'stipe' then demands to try one as well, but apparently finds nothing wrong with it and continues on his way, leaving the trainer free to saddle his horse for the race. While doing this, the trainer whispers to the jockey to let the doped horse simply run the race: 'Give him his head and don't use the whip.'

'But what if someone starts coming at me in the straight?' asks the jockey.

'Don't worry,' replies the trainer, 'it will only be me or the bloody stipe.'

TAKEN FOR A RIDE

An oft-told tale of the turf involves a city bookie taking his horse from the city to a country race meeting. He decides to get the jockey to run the horse 'dead', meaning that it will lose the race even though it is a good horse. He inflates the odds to 2–1.

A punter then approaches the bookie to make a bet on a three-horse race. Depending on which version of the story is being told, either the punter or the bookie pumps up the odds on the favourite to the point where the punter has laid out a lot of money. The race begins and the favourite, despite being held back by the jockey, still somehow wins against the other two unbelievably slow local horses. At this point the bookie, facing a very large pay-out, snarls at the punter and says something like, 'Hey, mate, you think you're pretty bloody clever, don't you? But you didn't know I owned the favourite.'

The punter laughs and says, 'I know, but I own the other two.'

BEA MILES

Bea (sometimes 'Bee' or just 'B') Miles was one of Sydney's great eccentrics. Born in 1902, she had a difficult relationship with her middle-class family from an early age. At Abbottsleigh school, she made political comments and wrote essays criticising the conduct of World War I, which was then raging. An inheritance allowed her to become financially independent but conflicts with her father over what was then considered her immoral Bohemian lifestyle continued. After a brief enrolment at Sydney University, Bea contracted encephalitis. The disease reportedly sharpened her independent outlook and what some considered her anti-social behaviour, allowing her father to commit her to the insane asylum at Gladesville in 1923.

Bea remained in the asylum until 1925, when an article about her plight titled 'Mad House Mystery of Beautiful Sydney Girl' on the front page of the *Smith's Weekly* newspaper led to her eventual release. Bea then became a notorious ratbag about town, sleeping rough, jumping into stationary cars with a demand to be given a lift and reciting Shakespeare on street corners to anyone who would pay. But her main pastime was boarding taxis and refusing to pay the fare. She became the scourge of the Sydney taxi industry, with most drivers dreading her presence. Three racegoers encountered Bea in the mid-1950s:

The lady was large, very vocal; and she wore a worse-for-wear tennis shade rakishly tilted over one eye. She sat beside the worried-looking taximan piloting yours, etc., and a couple more males to try our luck at the races. She offered to bet us a couple of bob each that the taxi wouldn't pass more than 39 cars on our way from Ashfield to Canterbury. Recovering, we declined politely. Foiled, the lady went to work on the driver, issuing loud commands on the route to be taken. The driver, not so politely, said 'nertz'.

Outside the racecourse, we three mere males alighted, but the large, vocal lady with the tipped-over eye shade refused to budge. 'Stone the crows,' moaned the taximan, giving us an anguished look as we left him stranded with— Bea Miles.

Bea was known to sometimes leave a cab after being abused by the driver, bending the passenger door right back on its hinges to show her dissatisfaction. She had a few friends in the taxi business, though, and they were happy to drive her on some legendary journeys. John Beynon took Bea from Sydney to Hobart, Adelaide and the long way to Melbourne through Broken Hill. But Bea's greatest trip needed two taxi drivers— Beynon and Mrs Sylvia Markham. The two drivers secured the greatest fare of their lives when Bea booked them to drive her to Perth—and back again.

The details of this epic of public transport have become muddied over the years but it seems that Beynon, Markham and Bea left Sydney early in January 1955. They made it to Perth in around seven days of very hot travelling in the age before automobile air conditioning. Bea spent four days there, apparently behaving herself, and then they set off back to Sydney.

Bea was paying one shilling a mile for the trip. That worked out to be around 300 pounds one-way across the Nullarbor. Every 100 miles, Bea handed over a five-pound note to her driver. It all added up to a lot of money at the time.

On the way back, Bea spoke with a journalist in Perth on the telephone from Eucla, explaining the reason for her unusual journey:

> Primarily I undertook the trip to collect flowers for the Sydney herbarium but the weather has been so blazing hot—up to 108 dig [degrees] at Madura—I've not seen a flower worth collecting along [the] Eyre-highway. However, we are having a lot of fun and the open-air life suits me fine.

The journalist also spoke with Sylvia Markham, who said: 'I got a bit of a shock when asked to drive across Australia and back, but I'm glad I agreed.'

Sleeping outside each night, as they had on the way, the intrepid three expected to be in Adelaide about 24 January and back in Sydney a few days later. All up, the cab fare for the round trip was 600 pounds.

Bea continued her wayward life. She claimed to have been convicted of various charges 195 times, 100 of them fairly. As she aged, Bea's antics became evermore irritating and she wore out the already thin welcome she had at places like the Public Library, where she was in the habit of spending the day reading. She was banned from the library in the late 1950s. Old and ill, she was taken in by the Little Sisters of the Poor at Randwick in 1964. One of the many colourful quotes attributed to her comes from this period: 'I have no allergies that I know of, one complex, no delusions, two inhibitions, no neuroses, three phobias, no superstitions and no frustrations.'

Gems like this, together with Bea's utter irreverence towards authority, the police, the law and respectability in general, made her a folk hero to Sydneysiders. In 1961 her portrait was entered in the Archibald Prize by artist Alex Robertson.

Even at the end, Bea went out in outrageous style. When she died in 1973, her coffin was covered in Australian wildflowers and a jazz band played 'Waltzing Matilda', 'Tie Me Kangaroo Down, Sport' and 'Advance Australia Fair'.

Bea's larrikin life has featured in a musical, a poem by Les Murray, and in Kate Grenville's 1985 novel *Lillian's Story* and the subsequent film of the same name. Now mostly forgotten, her legend is kept alive through the occasional media article and in the B Miles Women's Foundation.

DOING BUSINESS WITH REG

One of Australia's prominent businessmen was the founder of the airline he characteristically named after himself. Reg Ansett was very much the self-made man. He finished school at fourteen and worked as an axeman in the Northern Territory to earn enough to buy a Studebaker to start a road transport company. This allowed him to buy a Gypsy Moth airplane and in 1938 he started Ansett Airways. He was then just 28 years old. He continued to display his legendary stubbornness and business acumen through the rest of his life, branching into car hire and other mostly successful businesses. He was a colourful character with a considerable public profile in his day, eventually being knighted for his achievements.

Reg Ansett entered Australian folklore in various ways, but particularly in a story often told about him by friend and foe alike:

A young man was keen to make a name for himself in business, just like the then-ageing but incredibly eminent Reg Ansett. The young bloke couldn't believe his luck when he was in a restaurant for a meeting with an important client and he spotted Reg at a table full of other prominent business people. And obviously settled in for a long session.

Screwing up his courage, he approached the table and nervously addressed the great man, asking for a moment of his time and for a bit of a leg up the slippery ladder of business. Magnanimously, Reg condescended to help out and asked what he could do.

'Well, Mr Ansett,' said the young man, 'I have a very important client coming to lunch with me today. I need to impress this person with my business ideas and also with my contacts. Would you be kind enough to pretend that you know me?'

'Sure,' agreed Reg, mildly amused at the effrontery of the young man and probably reminded of his own early days.

'Thank you so much,' gushed the young man. 'When I leave the restaurant with my client I'll come past your table. Would you be good enough to stand up and greet me as if I were a valued business colleague?'

Reg was a bit taken aback, but he was in a good mood over his latest business deal. 'Okay, young fella,' he replied condescendingly, 'always happy to give a newcomer a helping hand.'

Reg went back to his celebrations and the young man returned to his table to meet his client.

When the meal was over, Reg and his mates were still hard at it. The young man paid the bill and carefully manoeuvered himself and his client to pass right next to Reg's table. Reg couldn't miss them and remembered that he had agreed to take part in the harmless deception. He got to his feet and enthusiastically held out his hand to the young man, saying 'Good to see you again, how's business?'

The young man stopped, looked coldly at the great man and said, 'Piss off, Reg, you can see I'm busy.'

AN UNWELCOME MIRACLE

One of many examples of the 'Australian, Irishman and Englishman' jokes:

An Australian, an Irishman and an Englishman are sitting in a bar. The only other person in the bar is a man.

The three men keep looking at this other man, for he

seems terribly familiar. They stare and stare, wondering where they have seen him before, when suddenly the Irishman cries out 'My God, I know who that man is. It's Jesus!'

The others look again and, sure enough, it is Jesus himself, sitting alone at a table.

The Irishman calls out, 'Hey, you!!! Are you Jesus?'

The man looks over at him, smiles a small smile and nods his head. 'Yes, I am Jesus,' he says.

The Irishman calls the bartender over and says to him 'I'd like you to give Jesus over there a pint of Guinness from me.'

So, the bartender pours Jesus a Guinness and takes it over to his table. Jesus looks over, raises his glass, smiles a 'thank you' and drinks.

The Englishman then calls out, 'Errr, excuse me Sir, but would you be Jesus?'

Jesus smiles and says, 'Yes, I am Jesus.'

The Englishman beckons the bartender and tells him to send over a pint of Newcastle Brown Ale for Jesus, which the bartender duly does. As before, Jesus accepts the drink and smiles over at the men.

Then the Australian calls out, 'Oi, you! D'ya reckon you're Jesus, or what?'

Jesus nods and says, 'Yes, I am Jesus.'

The Australian is mightily impressed and has the bartender send over a stubbie of Victoria Bitter for Jesus, which he accepts with pleasure.

Some time later, after finishing the drinks, Jesus leaves his seat and approaches the three men. He reaches for the hand of the Irishman and shakes it, thanking him for the Guinness. When he lets go, the Irishman gives a cry of amazement, 'Oh God, the arthritis is gone,' he says. 'The arthritis I've had for years is gone. It's a miracle!'

Jesus then shakes the hand of the Englishman, thanking him for the Newcastle Brown Ale. Upon letting go, the

Englishman's eyes widen in shock. 'By Jove', he exclaims, 'the migraine I've had for over 40 years is completely gone. It's a miracle!'

Smiling beatifically, Jesus then approaches the Australian, who has a terrified look on his face. As Jesus reaches for his hand, the Aussie whispers . . . 'Piss off mate, I'm on Worker's Comp!'

Hard tack lives up to its name with army biscuits,
WWII, Victoria, circa 1942.

4

DIGGEROSITIES

*'They made that much fuss, you'd have thought I'd won a
medal in the Olympic Games.'*

Digger to his mate after being presented
with the Victoria Cross

A MILLION CAT-CALLS

In the 1914–18 war, the Anzacs were notorious among British
troops for indiscipline and a casual attitude towards the
military in general. They tended to address officers by their
first names and, of course, rarely saluted. This was beyond the
understanding of the disciplinarian British army and led to
many sometimes serious, sometimes amusing confrontations.
This one took place in Belgium at a place called Strazeele. The
Australians were camped across the road from the 10th Battalion Royal Fusiliers, as recounted by Fusilier Private C. Miles:

The Colonel decided that he would have a full dress parade
of the guard mounting. Well, the Aussies looked over at
us amazed. The band was playing, we were all smartened

115

up, spit and polish, on parade, and that happened every morning. We marched up and down, up and down.

The Aussies couldn't get over it, and when we were off duty we naturally used to talk to them, go over and have a smoke with them, or meet them when we were hanging about the road or having a stroll. They kept asking us: 'Do you like this sort of thing? All these parades, do you want to do it?' Of course we said, 'No, of course we don't. We're supposed to be on rest, and all the time we've got goes to posh up and turn out on parade.' So they looked at us a bit strangely and said, 'OK, cobbers, we'll soon alter that for you.'

The Australians didn't approve of it because they never polished or did anything. They had a band, but their brass instruments were all filthy. Still, they knew how to play them.

The next evening, our Sergeant-Major was taking the parade. Sergeant-Major Rowbotham, a nice man, but a stickler for discipline. He was just getting ready to bawl us all out when the Australians started with their band. They marched up and down the road outside the field, playing any old thing. There was no tune you could recognise, they were just blowing as loud as they could on their instruments. It sounded like a million cat-calls.

And poor old Sergeant Rowbotham, he couldn't make his voice heard. It was an absolute fiasco. They never tried to mount another parade, because they could see the Aussies watching us from across the road, just ready to step in and sabotage the whole thing. So they decided that parades for mounting the guards should be washed out, and after that they just posted the guards in the ordinary way as if we were in the line.

RELIGION

Religion was another point of difference and potential sectarian dissension within the ranks. Personal experience stories featured frequently in the trench canon. These were sometimes simple accounts of unusual and/or humorous experiences, at other times they were retellings of traditional yarns and tall stories. Often they were in all likelihood apocryphal, though nonetheless revealing for that, as in this handwritten slice of sectarian rivalry under the title 'We'll Have That Moment Again':

> An R.C. Padre was tripping gaily along somewhere near supports, when he noticed a burying party just putting the finishing touches to the graves of four of their comrades. He pulled up, and finding that three of them were of his creed, asked who had read the service. 'Some Tommy C of E, Padre, Sir,' was the reply. The R.C. Chaplain asked nothing more but walked straight to the graves, and, in a voice like a sergeant-major, gave the order, 'Numbers 2, 3 and 4—As you were!'—Then proceeded to re-read the burial service.

Many years after the end of World War II, Mr R.F. Young of Tasmania remembered an incident that typified the predominant Digger attitude to formal religious affiliations:

> When I was joining the A.I.F. back in 1940, a big bushman ahead of me in the line was being asked by the Recruiting Depot Lieutenant about his name, age, and so on. When it came to his religious denomination he drawled, 'Aw, I'm not fussy. What are you short of?'

MONOCLES

This anecdote is from the Boer War and suggests that the attitudes of the Diggers were already in formation a long time before 1915:

> It was during the Boer War. He was walking down the street in a city in South Africa when he noticed a very polished and obviously very new British Army lieutenant complete with monocle and swagger stick, walking across the road.

About to cross the road from the other side was a very dirty and obviously very experienced Australian Light Horseman, complete with slouch hat, the inevitable 'makings' hanging from his lower lip, and a saddle over one arm.

The young lieutenant halted the Aussie, apparently with the intention of asking him what he meant by appearing in the streets in such an untidy get-up. He demanded to know what regiment the Aussie belonged to.

The Aussie spat his cigarette onto the road and eyed the young officer up and down. 'The Queensland Bushrangers,' he answered casually. Then he lifted a saddle stirrup to one eye in imitation of the monocle, and said with a forced accent, 'And you, my good man—what bloody regiment, may I ask, do you belong to?'

The Diggers of the Great War didn't have it all their own way when it came to British officers and monocles:

One Australian unit had a posh-talking officer who wore a monocle. One morning when the men came out to parade before the officer, they all lined up with a coin in one eye. The British officer looked at them, then tossed his head upwards sending his monocle spinning into the air, catching it in his other eye.

'Now, which one of you bastards can do that?' he asked in an impeccable English accent.

It is said that the Diggers were so impressed they all wanted to buy the officer a drink.

FOOD AND DRINK

If troops are not properly fed, they cannot fight well due both to physical and psychological decline. Sometimes it becomes necessary to resort to deception to improve the menu, as recounted in this tale from Gallipoli:

The ration problem on Gallipoli was at times a very real one, but probably the most trying part of it, to the troops at any rate, was that the only commodity in the 'sweets' line of business was apricot jam. Australians often wondered why that particular form of preserve seemed to be unlimited. The explanation is that in 1914 the English crop of 'cots was one of the heaviest on record. Thousands of tons of the fruit were jammed and canned, and some makers (can any of us ever forget Tickler, with his picture on the label?) made fortunes, though all of them didn't deserve to. Naturally the troops, and especially the Australians, got sick of the sight of the stuff.

One dark night in November, '15, it fell to my lot to take a fatigue party of 20 men down from 'Q Pip' [Quinn's Post] to the beach. None of us knew the route we had been ordered to follow, and we got helplessly bushed until I espied a light in what turned out to be an ASC sub-depot. 'I've been lookin' for you,' said a voice. 'You'll be the party for the stuff for the Jocks [Scottish Horse].' Scenting something good, I took the risk and said that we were. Darkness aided in hiding the Aussie uniform and silence did the rest. We afterwards discovered that we had got away with over 200 jars of Deiller's Dundee marmalade, among the best of Scotia's products. I have often wondered what happened to the wight [person] who issued the stuff without a murmur. But in those days one could do a lot and get away with it.

Alcohol has always featured heavily in the life and lore of soldiers. During the Great War rum and other forms of alcohol were often issued to troops when at the front line—and greatly appreciated it was, as reflected in this World War I ditty:

The Frenchman likes his sparkling wine,
The German likes his beer,
The Tommie likes his half and half
Because it brings good cheer.

The Scotsman likes his whisky,
And Paddy likes his pot,
But the Digger has no national drink,
So he drinks the blanky lot.

Many yarns were spun around the subject of grog. This one allegedly took place in the French town of Le Havre immediately after the war's end on 11 November 1918. The reference to the 'eight horses and forty men', in French, was a favourite World War I Digger term for the very basic rail carriages in which they were often transported. As this story tells it, four days of this form of travel put the Diggers in the mood for a drink:

> After the Armistice the troops were sent to Le Havre in a car de-luxe of the '8 chevaux ou 40 hommes' brand. The weather being cold, the food crook, and the journey taking anything up to four days, the troops arrived at their destination in a somewhat peevish mood.
>
> Our crowd was reported to have busted open some railway trucks at Abbeville and helped themselves to cognac, and the O.C. No. 5 Company at the Australian delousing camp was deputed to intercept the train at Revlon and search it. He carried out his duties faithfully telling the O.C. train his orders and saying 'I shall be back in twenty minutes with my staff and I will search thoroughly. If I find any cognac, heaven help anyone found with it.'
>
> When the search was made the honour of the AIF was vindicated. Next morning the O.C. No. 5 found a bottle of cognac on his bunk.

ARMY BISCUITS

Perhaps the single most detested item of army food was the biscuit, also known as a 'tile' or 'hard tack', all names suggesting the unnatural solidity of the food. There was much to be lampooned about the biscuit, as O.E. Burton of the New

Zealand Medical Corps wrote on Gallipoli, the extravagance of his prose suggesting the depth of feeling towards the offending item:

BISCUITS! Army biscuits! What a volume of blessings and cursing have been uttered on the subject of biscuits—army biscuits!

What a part they take in our daily routine: the carrying of them, the eating of them, the cursing at them!

Could we find any substitute for biscuits? Surely not! It is easy to think of biscuits without any army, but of an army without biscuits—never.

Biscuits, like the poor, are always with us. Crawling from our earthly dens at the dim dawning of the day, we receive no portion of the dainties which once were ours in the long ago times of effete civilization: but, instead, we devour with eagerness—biscuits porridge. We eat our meat, not with thankfulness but with biscuits. We lengthen out the taste of jam—with biscuits. We pound them to powder. We boil them with bully. We fry them as fritters. We curse them with many and bitter cursings, and we bless them with few blessings.

Biscuits! Army biscuits! Consider the hardness of them. Remember the cracking of your plate, the breaking of this tooth, the splintering of that. Call to mind how your finest gold crown weakened, wobbled, and finally shriveled under the terrific strain of masticating Puntley and Chalmer's No.5's.

Think of the aching void where once grew a goodly tooth. Think of the struggler and strain, the crushing and crunching as two molars wrestled with some rocky fragment. Think of the momentary elation during the fleeting seconds when it seemed that the molars would triumphantly blast and scrunch through every stratum of the thrice-hardened rock. Call to mind the disappointment, the agony of mind and body, as the almost victorious grinder missed its footing, slipped, and snapped hard upon its mate, while the elusive biscuit rasped and scraped upon bruised and tender gums.

Biscuits! Army biscuits! Have you, reader, ever analysed with due carefulness the taste of army biscuits? It is the delicious succulency of ground granite or the savoury toothsomeness of powdered marble? Do we perceive a delicate flavouring of ferro-concrete with just a dash of scaped iron railings? Certainly, army biscuits, if they have a taste, have one which is peculiarly their own. The choicest dishes of civilized life, stewed or steamed, fried, frizzled, roasted or toasted, whether they be composed of meat or fish, fruit or vegetable, have not (thank Heaven!) any like taste to that of army biscuits. Army biscuits taste like nothing else on the Gallipoli Peninsula. It is a debatable question indeed whether or not they have the quality of taste. If it be granted that they possess this faculty of stimulating the peripheral extremities of a soldier's taste-buds, then it must also be conceded that the stimulation is on the whole of an unpleasant sort. In short, that the soldier's feeling apart from the joy, the pride, and the satisfaction at his completed achievement in transferring a whole biscuit from his outer to his inner man without undue accident or loss of teeth, is one of pain, unease and dissatisfaction.

It may seem almost incredible, wholly unbelievable indeed, but armies have marched and fought, made sieges, retired according to plan, stormed impregnable cities, toiled in weariness and painfulness, kept lonely vigils, suffered the extremes of burning heat and of freezing cold, and have, in the last extremity, bled and died, laurel-crowned and greatly triumphant, the heroes of legend and of song, all without the moral or physical, or even spiritual, aid of army biscuits.

Agamemnon and the Greeks camped for ten years on the windy plains of Troy without one box of army biscuits. When Xerxes threw his pontoon bridge across the Narrows and marched 1,000,000 men into Greece, his transport included none of Teak Green and Co.'s paving-stones for the hardening of his soldiers' hearts and the stiffening of their backs. Caesar subdues Britons, Gauls and Germans. Before the lines of Dyrrhachium, his legions lived many days on boiled grass and such-like delicacies, but they never exercised their jaws upon a rough, tough bit of army biscuit.

Biscuits! Army biscuits! They are old friends, now, and, like all old friends, they will stand much hard wear and tear. Well glazed, they would make excellent tiles or fine flagstones. After the war they will have great scarcity value as curios, as souvenirs which one can pass on from generation to generation, souvenirs which will endure while the Empire stands. If we cannot get physical strength from army biscuits, let us at least catch the great spiritual ideal of enduring hardness, which they are so magnificently fitted to proclaim.

The seasons change. Antwerp falls, Louvain is burned, the tide of battle surges back and forth: new reputations are made, the old ones pass away; Warsaw, Lemberg, Servia, the stern battles of Gallipoli, Hindenburg, Mackensen, each name catches our ear for a brief moment of time, and then gives way to another crowding it out; but army biscuits are abiding facts, always with us, patient, appealing, enduring. We can move to other theatres, we can change our clothes, our arms and our generals, but we must have our biscuits, army biscuits, else we are no longer an army.

BABBLING BROOKS

The image of the dreadful cook is a long one that stretches back to the pioneering days and features often in the lore of shearing and the bush in general. In this story, the shearers are so fed up with the appalling food their cook serves that there is an argument in which one of them calls the cook a 'bastard'. The cook complains to the boss, who comes into the men's shed to find the culprit. 'Who called the cook a bastard?' he demands to know. 'Who called the bastard a cook,' comes the rapid-fire reply.

The tradition continued into the 1st AIF where, in a variation on the theme, a Digger is being questioned by the officer in charge of his court-martial: 'Did you call the cook a bastard?'

'No,' the Digger answers, 'but I could kiss the bastard who did!'

And in another incident involving bad food and bad language:

I came out of my dugout one morning attracted by a terrible outburst of Aussie slanguage in the trench. The company dag was standing in about three feet of mud, holding his mess tin in front of him and gazing contemptuously at a piece of badly cooked bacon, while he made a few heated remarks concerning one known as Bolo, the babbling brook. He concluded an earnest and powerful address thus:

'An' if the _____ that cooked this bacon ever gets hung for bein' a cook, the poor _____ will be innocent.'

Cooks were usually known by their rhyming slang name as 'Babbling Brooks', or simply 'Babblers':

'What's this the Babbling Brook has given me—tea or stew?' asked the new hand perplexedly, as he contemplated the concoction in his dixie.

'It's tea,' announced his cobber.

'How can you tell?' said the new hand.

'You can always tell when you've got tea or stew by where he puts it. If he puts it in the dixie lid it's stew, but if he puts it in the dixie itself it's tea.'

Repetition of the same offering could also cause concern:

During the advance towards the outer defences of the Hindenburg Line early in September, 1918, the supply of rations got a bit disorganized, and for three solid days the cookhouse menu was stew, made of biscuits and bully-beef, with sundry dehydrated vegetable out through the mince, and boiled with a little water. Every man who came to the cookhouse made practically the same remark: 'Struth! Stoo again!' Then followed a wider range of language.

It nearly drove the cook mad. On the evening of the third day a notice was chalked up outside the cookhouse: 'It's Stew Again! But the first insulting cow who says so will be made Fresh Meat!'

Cooks were usually considered to be less than hygienic in both their trade and their personal characteristics:

Back in the First World War days there was a company cook—we'll call him Bill—who was probably the finest spoiler of Army rations in the whole A.I.F. He was also the greasiest trooper ever to don uniform.

'I learnt to cook from me old mother,' he would reminisce. 'Every Saturday she useter boil a sheep's head for Dad and us 14 kids; and she always cooked the head with the eyes in, as she reckoned it'd 'ave to see us through the week.'

Old Bill returned home after the armistice, sound in wind and limb, his nearest approach to a 'Blighty' being up at Messines in '17, when a whizzbang shell struck him fair and square in the chest. But he was so greasy the shell merely glanced off him and killed two mules attached to the cooker.

The tradition, and the problem, continued into the next war:

The boys hated the new cook, and one of them filled his boots with pig-wash in the dead of night. The cook said nothing next day when the lads visited the cookhouse after dinner, and the jester said:

'Well, cookie, who filled your boots with pig-wash?'

'Dunno,' cookie said, 'but I know who ate it.'

In another place, also during World War II:

'How you liking it?' the cook said to the new recruit eating his first camp dinner.

'What is it?' the new recruit said.

'Horseflesh,' the cook said. 'How'd you feel about that, eh?'

'I don't mind horseflesh,' the new recruit said, 'but you might have taken the harness off.'

And according to Tobruk legend:

> An officer was inspecting the cooking arrangements in a darkened dugout. 'You've got too many flies in here, Cookie,' he told the individual entrusted with feeding the troops.
>
> ''Ave I sir?' came the puzzled reply—''Ow many should I 'ave?'

Historian of World War I, C.E.W. Bean, provided an insight into the dual roles of the cook in Digger culture, roles that were also at the base of the cook's bush personality. 'This individual was both a provider of sustenance and the (mostly) willing butt of humour within the military group with which he was affiliated, bearing the "oaths and good-natured sarcasm" of those who had no option but to consume his offerings, with equanimity and humorous forbearance.'

THE CASUAL DIGGER

A good many Anzac yarns play with the Digger's casual attitude to war:

> There was once an Australian VC winner who was exceptionally modest. It was only with great reluctance that he agreed to attend a ceremony at which he was to be presented with his decoration. When it was all over, a friend asked him how he felt after such a tumultuous reception.

'They got on my nerves,' said the VC winner. 'They made that much fuss, you'd have thought I'd won a medal in the Olympic Games.'

Queenslander Jim Matheson had a yarn about his war:

In France during 1917, the Eighth Brigade was moving up in open formation under intense rifle fire. My Queensland mate and I were under fire for the first time. As the bullets whizzed and spatted around us, my mate said to me, 'Didya hear that one, Jim?'

'Yes', I replied, 'twice. Once when it passed us, and once when we passed it.'

The Diggers played their favourite gambling game of two-up, regardless of the circumstances:

Recently, one of our patrols was overdue, and I was detailed as one of a search party . . . Suddenly we saw the shadows of a number of men standing silently in the darkness. 'Fritzes!' said someone, and we all ducked into shell-holes. Fritz's next flare revealed a small party, all stooping and gazing intently on the ground. Then one of them cried softly and exultantly, 'Two heads are right!' picked up the pennies and pocketed the winnings. It was the lost patrol. They were making their bets and tossing the coins in the darkness, and then waiting for the light from a Fritz flare to see the result.

This one was reported in the British *Evening News* and reprinted in the *Australian Corps News Sheet* in 1918 under the title 'Taking the war calmly':

An Australian told me this:—We were advancing, and had been going about an hour, and my platoon numbered about fifteen men. Going over a ridge we saw a pill-box. We poured machine-gun fire at it, and threw grenades too. No reply came, and we congratulated ourselves that we had no casualties.

All the time we could see smoke coming from the aperture; this worried us so we decided to charge it. We had our charge, with whoops and yells. I got to the door-way, and was met with, 'Say, Digger, what the —— is all the noise about?'

There stood an Australian, with a frying-pan in his hand, cooking bully beef over a fire which the Huns had left.

And, in Digger lore at least, even the British Tommies recognised the bravery of their Anzac allies:

Tommy (to Australian): 'That was a rare plucky thing you did this morning, to bring your mate in under that heavy fire.'

Australian: 'Yairs, the blasted cow, he had all me b—— tobacco with him.'

OFFICERS

In his *Bad Characters: Sex, Crime, Mutiny, Murder and the Australian Imperial Force*, Peter Stanley recounts an incident in which a very proper British officer addresses a group of Australians in what was the normal British army style. The Anzacs found this unacceptable and proceeded to count him out, a practice relatively common in the AIF though unthinkable in the British army. The 300 soldiers each sang out their number, ending at 300. The conclusion was the chorus 'Out you Tommy Woodbine bastard'. The men then dispersed, some reportedly playing two-up, and leaving the outraged British officer to complain that this was an act of mutiny. But a staff sergeant, more experienced with the ways of the AIF, told him that such things were nothing remarkable and that no one in authority in the Australian hierarchy would take such an accusation seriously.

True or not, the many yarns about officers, usually highlighting the anti-authoritarian aspect of the Digger's worldview,

were legion in both world wars, as in this anecdote from the
first war:

> A Digger is travelling on a train with two English officers.
> The officers are discussing their family backgrounds, rela-
> tionships and pedigrees. After listening to this conversation
> for a while, the Digger introduces himself to the officers as
> 'Bluey' Johnson . . . not married, two sons—both majors in
> the British army.

Identity is the theme of another yarn from the 1914–18 war:

> Two Diggers on leave in London fail to salute a passing
> British officer. The outraged officer demands of the Diggers:
> 'Do you know who I am?' One Digger turns to the other
> and says, casually: 'Did you hear that, Dig? He doesn't even
> know who he is.'

The theme persisted into World War II:

> A couple of Diggers were on leave in Damascus. They visited
> a number of drinking establishments, sampling the local spirit
> known as 'arrack', a strong and fiery brew. Not surprisingly,
> they became lost. Unable to speak Arabic, they couldn't get any
> help from the locals. Fortunately, a British general suddenly
> appeared in full dress uniform. 'Hey mate,' one of the tipsy
> Australians called out, 'can you tell us where we are?'
>
> The general stiffened with indignation at being addressed
> in such an insubordinate manner and replied frostily, 'Do
> you men know who I am?'
>
> 'Cripes Bill,' said the Digger turning to his mate, 'this
> bloke's worse off than us. We mightn't know where we are
> but the poor bugger doesn't know who he is!'

This one is said to have taken place on a footpath in Tel Aviv
during October 1942:

An older English colonel and a younger American major were deep in discussion about the war. Four young Australian soldiers, fairly intoxicated, came along towards them, divided into pairs, passed the officers and went unsteadily on their way.

'Who the blazes are that gol-darned rabble?' asked the American major.

'They're Orstralians,' replied the English colonel.

'And whose side are they on?'

'Ours, Major, they are our allies,' said the colonel.

'But dammit, they didn't salute us,' bleated the major.

The colonel admitted that this was so: 'But at least they had the decency to walk around us. If it had been their fathers from the last war, they would have walked right over us.'

The same egalitarian theme is heard in many other Digger yarns, such as the two Diggers who walk backwards into camp, fooling the sentry into believing that they are leaving rather than returning late. Often these are tinged with anti-British sentiment:

Saw a Digger on leave in London walk past a young officer without slinging a salute. On being pulled up and asked didn't he know whom he had passed, Dig said that the face was familiar but that he could not place him.

'I'm an officer in His Majesty's Imperial Army,' exploded the Sir, 'and entitled to a salute!'

'Oh, garn, you little b——!' says the Dig, and walked on.

Coming across an Aussie sergeant shortly afterwards, the officer unfolded his tale, repeating the Digger's last blessing.

'But you're not one, are you?' mildly asks the sergeant.

'Certainly not!' exploded the officer.

'Well, go back and tell him that he's a blinking liar,' drawled the sergeant.

It was not only British or American officers who were the butt of Digger yarns, as in this one from the Western Front:

Digger Jones (of the 1st Div. ASC) was washing down his two donks, in a shell hole at Fleureaux, about fifty yards from the old duckboard track, where the mud and slush was about two feet deep, in 1916. Having cleaned and groomed one down, he led him back and stood him on the duckboard track. A Staff Officer dressed in white corduroys, glittering spurs and polished leggings wending his way to battalion headquarters, was annoyed to find a mule blocking his pathway. Approaching the mule he gave it a heavy shove, forcing it back into the slush, much to the annoyance of Digger Jones. 'Here, what the h—— do you think you're doing?' he yelled indignantly.

'What do you mean by blocking the track with your confounded mule?' said the officer. 'I'll have you arrested for this. What is your name and number?'

Digger Jones surveyed the ground between them, and then replied: 'You come over and get it.'

On another occasion:

General Braithwaite, known more or less affectionately to New Zealanders as 'Bill the Bight', was taking his brigade up into the line when one of those inevitable hold-ups occurred at a crossroad. This caused a halt of the brigade alongside an Aussie battery wagon line. Bill rode up on his charger as natural as ever (that is, he was fuming!), and roared out, 'De-lay, de-lay! What is the meaning of this de-lay?' To which the Aussies' greasy cook took it upon himself to answer, 'It's French for milk, you silly old basket.'

And the soldier who took the sergeant major's suggestion too seriously:

Sergeant major to a private who has missed eleven shots out of twelve: 'What, eleven misses; good heavens, man, go around the corner and shoot yourself.'

Hearing a shot around the corner, the sergeant major rushes around, to be confronted by the bad shot—

'Sorry, Sir, another miss,' the private murmurs.

Very rarely, the officer might get one up on the Digger, as in this example from World War II:

In Whitehall recently an English major general stopped a non-saluting Aussie, and demanded to know who he was.

'I'm a kind of Aussie soldier,' was the reply.

Said the officer: 'Well, I'm a kind of major general and you owe me a salute.'

Said the Aussie: 'Okay, brother, I'll give you a kind of salute.'

And he did.

However, mostly the Digger is irreverent, especially to the many British army protocols. A sergeant major is calling the roll at parade:

'Johnson!'

'Yair,' drawled Johnson.

'Simpson!'

''Ere.'

'Jackson!'

'She's sweet.'

'Smith!'

'Here, Sir.'

'Crawler!' shouted the platoon.

In the opposite form of this situation is the well-travelled tale about the officer who is expecting an inspection from the top brass. He assembles his men to brief them and when he has finished he tells them, 'And whatever you do, for Christ's sake, don't call me Alf.'

A certain Australian sergeant major during World War I gave his commands in a most unorthodox manner:

'Slope arms—you, too!'
'Present arms—you, too!'
'Forward march—you, too!'

After the parade one day, a young lieutenant approached the sar'major and asked him the reason for his unusual commands.

'Well, Sir,' he replied, 'it's like this. Those men are a tough mob. Every time I give an order I know they're going to abuse me, so I get in first.'

BIRDIE

On Gallipoli and at the Western Front, the Anzacs created a whole cycle of yarns about a character known as 'Birdie'. In reality, this was General Birdwood (nominally acting lieutenant general, later made permanent), commanding officer on Gallipoli, a leader who earned the deep respect of ordinary Australian and New Zealand soldiers. This was something particularly difficult to achieve given their problems with military authority and was based on Birdwood's concern for the wellbeing of his men and his willingness to appear at the front line when necessary. General Ian Hamilton, overall commander of the campaign and effectively Birdwood's boss, generously summed up the man's impressive reputation, calling him 'the soul of Anzac' and declaring that, 'Not for one single day has he ever quitted his post. Cheery and full of human sympathy, he has spent many hours of each twenty-four inspiring the defenders of the front trenches, and if he does not know every soldier in his force, at least every soldier in the force believes he is known to his chief.'

In the many stories about him, Birdie is portrayed as a good bloke who understands the attitudes of his men and is prepared to bend the rules to accommodate them, especially those regulations related to military rank, as in this favourite Birdie story:

General Birdwood is talking to an English staff officer outside the Australian Imperial Force headquarters in

Horseferry Road, London. The staff officer is amazed and annoyed that Australian soldiers passing by do not bother to salute the general: 'I say, why don't you make your men salute you?'

'What!' exclaims Birdwood. 'Do you think I want to start a brawl in the heart of London!'

And at Gallipoli:

Birdwood was nearing a dangerous gap in a sap when the sentry called out: 'Duck, Birdie; you'd better —— well duck!'

'What did you do?' asked the outraged generals to whom Birdwood told the story.

'Do? Why, I —— well ducked!'

As well, there is the Gallipoli reinforcement who mistakes the general for a cook, again because he is not wearing his badges of rank:

A new reinforcement was going to Rest Gully when he got away from his track and, seeing a soldier studying a paper, went up to him and said: 'Can you tell me the way to my crowd?' The reinforcement has failed to recognise General Birdwood who answers, 'You'd better go and ask the cook just there.'

'Oh, I beg your pardon,' replies the reinforcement. 'I thought you were the cook.'

Birdwood maintained his good image with the Diggers on the Western Front:

We were holding a nice, quiet sector of the line at le Touquet, when General Birdwood decided to pay our brigade a visit. To me fell the job of conducting his party. On arrival at the reserve lines, Birdy decided to pay the 'Gas Alarm post' a visit. The sentry was a reinforcement, and failed to either salute Birdie or notice the party, so the General decided to have a little yarn, and the following dialogue took place:

Birdie: 'Do you know me, son?'

Dig: 'No. Don't want to!'

Birdie: 'Been in France long?'

Dig: 'Too blanky long.'

Birdie: 'Do you know that I am General Birdwood?'

Dig (very surprised): 'Go on! I 'ave heard of you. Shake hands!'

The brass hats nearly fainted, but to Birdie's everlasting credit, let it be recorded that he shook hands heartily.

And in another classic of the same kind:

A Digger was lying in camp dead broke, so irreverently decided to write to God for a tenner. He addressed the letter 'per General Birdwood, Headquarters'. When the general got the letter, he was much amused. He took it into the officers' mess, and all the officers entered into the humour of the joke. The general said: 'We will collect amongst us and raise the tenner for this fellow.' But all he could raise was seven pounds; so he sent it to the Digger. Next day the receipt came to hand as follows:

'Dear God,—Thanks for sending me the tenner; but the next lot you send don't send it through Headquarters, as Birdie and his mob pinched three quid of it.'

THE PIECE OF PAPER

A favourite Anzac yarn of both world wars is usually known as the 'Scrap of Paper' or the 'Piece of Paper'. In its World War I version, it appeared in the *Anzac Records Gazette* of November 1915 in this form and under the title 'Anzacalities':

The Australian soldier in a well-known hospital in Egypt developed a habit of picking up every bit of paper he could find. A Medical Board decided he was harmless and might be better for a trip to Australia. On the trip to Australia he still continued the practice and on arrival there he was again boarded and the Board decided he was too eccentric for active service. On receiving his discharge he looked at it closely and remarked with a dry smile, 'Thanks! That is the piece of paper I have been looking for.'

By 1942, the story had been updated and much more elaborated, as in this version published in a number of places, an indication of its popularity:

Sandy was a popular figure in his unit, always cheerful and high-spirited. But once, when he got back from leave, he told his mates he'd met a 'beaut Sheila' and was anxious to get out of the army to marry her. As many others were similarly placed, little notice was taken of Sandy when he 'got down in the dumps' occasionally.

One evening he was out with two friends taking a stroll when he saw a piece of paper on the ground ahead of him. He ran forward, picked it up, scrutinized it carefully, and threw it away again, sadly shaking his head. His mates asked him whether he'd expected to find a fiver, but he only said, 'It isn't what I'm looking for.'

As time went on Sandy became the talk of the section. Every time he saw a piece of paper, he picked it up and looked at it carefully; but he always shook his head and threw it away, saying sadly, 'That's not what I'm looking for.'

It began to be rumoured that Sandy was 'troppo'. The orderly sergeant thought he might need a break from his usual routine, so he placed him on pioneer fatigue. But one of Sandy's new jobs was to empty the orderly room waste-paper basket.

His 'disease' now really manifested itself. He closely studied each piece of paper in every basket he emptied. And, as usual, the paper wasn't what he was looking for.

Everyone was now thoroughly worried about Sandy.

The climax came when the section was on parade for an inspection by some visiting brass. The colonel was highly pleased with his tour and was just about to compliment the major when Sandy stepped forward three paces, picked up a piece of paper that had floated down to the ground in front of him, looked at it sadly and then returned smartly to his place in the ranks.

Later, Sandy was paraded before the major, who, nonplussed at his behaviour, told the orderly sergeant to take him to the medical officer.

In the M.O.'s tent Sandy's first action was to pick up a couple of sheets of paper from the table and examine them, putting them back down with a shake of his head. The M.O. couldn't get much out of Sandy. All he would say was that he hadn't found what he was looking for.

'Acute neurosis.' Was the M.O.'s verdict. He recommended that Sandy be sent down to have his case examined by a medical board. This was arranged and Sandy went south.

In due course, the board considered his case. Obviously acute neurosis. It was agreed that Sandy should be discharged medically unfit.

As the officer at the G.D.D. handed Sandy his discharge certificate, he remarked with a grin, for he'd heard all about Sandy's case, 'Hang on to THAT bit of paper, won't you!'

'By cripes I will!' said Sandy, laughing as he folded up the form and put it in his pocket. 'That's the bit of paper I've been looking for!'

PARABLES OF ANZAC

While many Diggers were notoriously reticent about their experiences, there were others willing to speak for them. Principle among these was Charles Bean, whose multiple roles as official war correspondent, editor of trench newspapers and

The Anzac Book, as well as editor and principal author of the *Official History of Australia in the Great War*, allowed him to express and embed his view of the Australian fighting man. Bean had written extensively before the war about the ideal bushman. When he joined the troops as correspondent and chronicler of the Diggers, he interpreted their actions and attitudes through eyes already full of the bush hero. In his many dispatches home and other writings throughout the war, Bean rarely failed to extol the Anzac virtues and the magnificence of the Digger.

At the end of the Dardanelles campaign, Bean edited *The Anzac Book*, a compilation of verse, prose and art by Gallipoli troops that was a bestseller, with many Australian homes having a copy on otherwise sparsely populated bookshelves. It selectively portrayed the Anzac troops, who would later be named 'Diggers', largely in their own words and images. Under the heading 'Parables of Anzac', a couple of yarns gave a glimpse of casual Digger humour:

From Shell Green

From a Correspondent in Australian Field Artillery, 'Sea View,' Bolton's Knoll, near Shell Green.

I was looking out front the entrance of my dug-out, thinking how peaceful everything was, when Johnny Turk opened on our trenches. Shells were bursting, and fragments scattered all about Shell Green. Just at this time some new reinforcements were eagerly collecting spent fuses and shells as mementoes. While this fusillade was on, men were walking about the Green just as usual, when one was hit by a falling fuse. Out rushed one of the reinforcement chaps, and when he saw that the man was not hurt, he asked: 'Want the fuse, mate?'

The other looked at him calmly. 'What do you think I stopped it for?' he asked.

Another parable highlights the potential perils of using the crude periscopes the Anzacs invented to safely observe the enemy from below the parapet of the trench:

Bill Blankson was a real hard case, happy-go-lucky, regardless of danger. Bill was out on sapping for over a fortnight, and at the end of that time had a growth of stubble that would have brought a flush of pride to his dirty face if he had seen it. But he hadn't seen it—one does not carry a looking-glass when sapping.

At the end of the fortnight he was taken off sapping and put on observing. Anyone who has used a periscope knows that unless the periscope is held well up before the eyes, instead of the landscape, one sees only one's own visage reflected in the lower glass.

Bill did not hold the periscope up far enough, and what he saw in it was a dark, dirty face with a wild growth of black stubble glaring straight back at him. He dropped the periscope, grabbed his rifle, and scrambled up the parapet, fully intending to finish the Turk who had dared to look down the other end of his periscope.

He had mistaken his own reflection for a Turk's.

BALDY BECOME MOBILE

Those things that amused the Diggers do not necessarily amuse everyone, though this story shows how the Anzacs dealt with the impositions of officialdom in a characteristically straightforward manner:

About the end of March 1918, when the wilting flower of England's Fifth Army was doing a marathon for home and mother, pursued by the beastly Bosche, the heads broadcasted one hateful word throughout the AIF.

'Be Mobile!' was the official edict. Every five minutes, it seemed, some bird of braid-hat plumage would flutter in gasping as if he'd brought the news from Ghent. Then, he'd cast an eagle eye over the collective water-bottle and the blancoed bandolier, and swoop off to some other harassed unit twittering, 'Be Mobile!'

After the first few days the whole place became a hot-bed of mobility. Everyone from the boss to the last bandsman wore a mobile look. 'Are you mobile?' became a form of greeting. The very stew we ate seemed to have a mobile flavour. Such a positive nightmare did the word become that many a brave soldier shuddered at its sound.

After, the only living soul in our unit that couldn't be quite called mobile was Baldy, the mule, whose fairy footsteps were usually guided by Blackie Crayton. Blackie himself was sufficiently mobile to pass muster. As a combination, however, he and Baldy delayed every 'mobile' exercise, and held up every 'mobile' route march.

'Can't you make the mule more mobile, Crayton?' the sergeant major used to roar.

Late one night on the way up to Ypres Sector, Baldy, who had been respectably mobile for the greater part of the day, suddenly became immobile. Baldy just stubbed his toes, so to speak, in the pave and stopped dead. Blackie was at his wit's end. A desperately cold night, another three or four kilometers to get to the prepared billets and a hot meal, and Baldy reneging!

For nearly two hours Blackie, wet through and finished, struggled—coaxing, bullying, blaspheming and getting madder every minute. His frantic efforts proving futile—the jibbing animal never budged an inch—Blackie went absolutely berserk.

'You bald-faced atrocity!' he howled. 'I'll lay a shade of odds THIS'LL shift you, you—that's what you are!' With which solemn incantation he placed a couple of Mills beneath the noble beast, and fled. By the time he reached safety, the bombs had made their presence felt, and Baldy shifted according to forecast.

The first person the fed-up Blackie met as he trudged along wearily into the village was our dear old friend and soul-mate, the sergeant major.

'Where's that cranky mule?' he questioned. The almost hysterical Blackie stood silent for fully thirty seconds before he responded.

'Baldy?' queried Blackie in tense tones. 'Baldy? Baldy is mobile. Mobile at last. In fact, he's so blanky mobile that he'll be on the move from now till the Resurrection, pulling himself together and collecting his scattered remains. Baldy's gone to his long home. An' it's so darned long he'll never reach it. Yes! Take it from me, Baldy's more blinkin' mobile than any of us! Now, tell me where's the mobile cook-house?'

THE ROO DE KANGA

In September 1917 a correspondent for an English newspaper visited the Western Front. Australian forces had just broken the German lines at Mont St Quentin and Peronne. Three VCs were won, but the Australians suffered around 3000 casualties. The unnamed journalist closely observed the recently victorious Diggers and was struck by their casual attitude towards the business of war and their irreverent sense of humour, among other characteristics:

To test one's psychological impression of the war solely by the Australian front would be rash. For the Australian Corps is very individualistic, and, after its recent victories, very happy, so that it strikes one less as part of a tragic world contest than as a band of Elizabethan adventurers in great fettle, engaged on a high emprise of their own which they pursue with ardour, gaity, and an immense confidence. The note is well struck in PERONNE. Here and there in the cleared space between shapeless heaps of brick and mortar which is the main street of that town one may pick out the signs of five occupations. Very faint are the traces of its peaceful day . . . The German notice boards of the first occupation are commoner, with traces of the French return superimposed upon them. But in his last tenure, the enemy had plastered it all afresh . . . And suddenly one comes on the largest notice board of all. The effect is like that of a clean and merry wind blowing through a swamp. The board bears the title 'Roo de Kanga,' and it marks the Australian conquest of the ruins of Sept. 1.

And what of the 'Digger', as the Australian private is content to call himself? One could learn much of him quickly, for he has no servility and little shyness. Sometimes one had a quite uncomfortable revelation of him, as when four self-conscious civilians who arrived, not without misgivings, in the forward area met a battalion of him fresh from the trenches and were greeted with the crushing comment: 'Thank God, the Americans at last!' Or one would note him crowding, in the highest spirits, round a cageful of newly captured Germans, comparing notes in a dispassionately professional vein on the recent engagement, or offering, not without success, to exchange a tin of bully beef for an Iron Cross. In the major features of his thirty-mile push the Digger is less interested than in such sporting venture as that of a little party of Australians who pushed across the SOMME into CHIPILLY. Whence the enemy was enfilading the line, and bluffed a German force many times their size into surrender. He is delighted, too, with the mule who was set to draw a dummy tank, and did so dejectedly, for a while, but later, satisfying himself with an inquisitive sniff that the thing was vulnerable, kicked it to smithereens. He is, too, most boyishly gleeful about the colossal German gun which he came on in a peaceful glade in the course of his forward rush . . . Its great bulking carriage towers from its concrete base among the trees, a tremendous monument of man's madness. The Digger has written on it 'captured by Waacs,' and Australian names are graven all over it, from that of the Prime Minister downwards.

And everywhere he will have sport. You can see him with his brown chest and arms gleaming in the sun, defending a wicket on a pitch in a bend of the SOMME that he has just captured; or scarcely to be stopped from that super-energetic sort of rugby that is played under his code to watch the 'Archies' peppering a Boche airman; or cheering a famous Australian jockey pelting along in a mule race on a course improvised where the shell holes are fewest. In lazier moments he is regaled by one of the troops of entertainers for which his Corps is famous in a theatre he has knocked together out of nothing; or he is to be found studying with much interest, one of the large maps of the front, with which he is kept in touch with the latest news of the whole line, and deciding what he would do at this or the next place if he were Foch [commander of the French forces].

BLIGHTY

In World War I, Britain was known to all British, Canadian and Anzac troops as 'Blighty'. For the British soldiers it was home, and for the Anzacs and other empire troops it was an opportunity to be away from the fighting on leave or recuperation if they had been wounded. The time taken to sail to and fro between the Pacific and Europe meant that it was difficult for Australians or New Zealanders to return home for even fairly lengthy periods of leave. When asked by an English woman how often he had leave, an Australian soldier was rumoured to have replied, 'Once every war.'

As well as getting 'Blighty leave', many soldiers hoped to receive 'a Blighty one', meaning a wound serious enough for them to need treatment in Britain, while not serious enough to be life threatening. As the Adelaide journalist and soldier Hugh Garland DCM wrote in his *Vignettes of War*, this ditty was popular with the Australian troops at the front:

Dear Lord our ways we're wending
To toil and strife again.

Where Fritz is always sending
His shrapnel down like rain.
O, teach us, Lord, to dodge 'em
And, if you don't do that,
Please tell old Fritz to lodge 'em
For blighties neat and pat.

Sadly, Garland was not lucky enough to receive a Blighty one; he was killed in action.

If a Digger did win some time in a British hospital, there was an opportunity to spin a few yarns to the locals. Diggers were notorious in Britain during the first war for the whopping lies they frequently told gullible 'pommies' about their goanna farms and the like back home.

I've heard Aussies tell stories to the unsophisticated of many different kind of farms we have 'out there'—there's the jackeroo farm, the nulla-nulla farm, the wombat farm, etc., etc. But the boy with the flea farm is the best novelty I've struck. He was a badly wounded inmate of an English hospital. At every opportunity he would tell the nurse about his wonderful flea farm. Finally, the nurse concluded that he had gone off his block and reported the matter to the doctor.

'What do you do with this flea farm of yours?' the doctor asked him.

'Oh,' replied the Aussie, 'we make beer out of the hops.'

While recuperating from his 'blighty one', a Digger would often be visited by well-meaning citizens doing their bit for the war effort by cheering up recovering soldiers. While this was appreciated, it could often be a little wearing as the citizens, ignorant of the reality of the front line, invariably asked lots of silly questions. Anecdotes on this theme were many:

In a British hospital a lady had put more questions to a wounded Australian than an insurance agent could. 'Do you get much windy weather in Australia?' she at length asked. Then the soldier departed from the strict truth. 'Windy weather!' he exclaimed. 'Why, I should reckon. For instance, sometimes a cold south gale will come on, and blow so darned hard, that it blows the sun out. Then you've got to sit round in the dark sometimes for a week, 'til a hot, northerly sets in and lights it up again.'

And while being away from the front, even with over-inquisitive locals, was pretty good, it was 'not all beer and skittles'. A battle-scarred Gunner Millard was welcomed to England off his hospital ship by scores of girls carrying fresh fruit for the wounded. But things went downhill from there, not only for himself but also for the British people, as he wrote home from No. 4 Convalescent Camp on Salisbury Plain:

> In camp we never taste sugar or butter and get very little meat. The main ration is mostly fat at that. Things are getting fairly serious with the civilian population. The people have to wait in queues for hours to get a few ounces of margarine, butter being a thing of the past. The same applies to meat, tea, etc. Hundreds have to go away empty-handed as there is seldom enough to go around. A lot of the London butchers are now selling horse-flesh, having given up the unequal contest for other meat.

London was also the location of the Australian Army Head-quarters in the Horseferry Road. Most Australians would turn up here sooner or later if they were in London, either for some official reason or for the social facilities available there. However, it seems that the encounters they had were not always pleasant. A story about a Digger just off the boat from the trenches being upbraided for the state of his uniform by a staff member at Horseferry Road became a poem and a famous soldier song:

> He landed in London and straightaway strode
> Direct to Headquarters in Horseferry Road.
> A Buckshee Corporal said 'pardon me, please,

But there's dust on your tunic and dirt on your knees.
You look so disgraceful that people will laugh,'
Said the cold-footed coward that works on the staff.

The Aussie just gave him a murderous glance,
And said 'I've just come from the trenches in France,
Where shrapnel is falling and comforts are few,
And Aussies are fighting for cowards like you.
I wonder, old shirker, if your mother ee'er knew
That her son is a waster and afraid of the strafe,
But holds a soft snap on the Horseferry staff?'

By the time the Anzacs went home after the war, the song had
changed a bit, but the sentiments remained the same in this
version from a homeward bound troopship in 1919:

'Your hat should be turned up at the side like mine,
Your boots, I might state, are in want of a shine,
Your puttees are falling away from your calf';
Said the cold footed b******s of Horseferry staff.

The soldiers gave him a murderous glance,
'Remember I'm just home from the trenches in France.
Where shrapnel is flying and comforts are few,
Where the soldiers are fighting for b******s like you!'

So well did 'Horseferry Road' capture the attitude of Diggers
towards authority that it was also sung in various versions
in Australia's next few wars. By 1941 'Horseferry Road' had
become the famous 'Dinky-di' and had grown a chorus: 'Dinky-
di, dinky-di, "I am a Digger and I won't tell a lie . . ."'
Other versions were still being sung in the Vietnam War.

VERY IRRITATED

Civilian questions to soldiers returned home from the front
line often betrayed such ignorance of what the soldiers were

experiencing that they were parodied in Digger humour. On this occasion, the question seemed to be a sensible one, though the answer could perhaps be taken with a grain or two of salt. The 'Cheer-Up Hut' was run by a civilian society dedicated to providing soldiers with comforts, before and after their periods of active service during World War I.

'Do the Australians still keep up their cheerfulness at the front!' I asked a soldier at the Cheer-Up Hut, Adelaide, recently. He had just returned from France.

'Yes, easy,' he replied. 'I only struck one feller who didn't. He was as cheery a chap you ever seen too. 'E was all grins and jokes. 'Is smile was like a sunrise on a patch o' golden wattles. One day 'e went with 'is battalion bayonetin' Germans. It was a 'ell of a scrap. 'E was singin' "Australia will be there" all through it, and every time 'e notched a German, 'e'd yell somethin' funny. 'E got six wounds in different parts of 'is frame. When 'e was bein' carried on a stretcher to the dressin' station 'e laughed over the fight as it 'ad been a little game o' ticky touchwood. 'E was fixed up with bandages until 'e looked like a bloomin' mummy, and every time 'e moved 'is wounds stung 'im like scorpions. But 'e just laughed as merry as a baby in a bath tub. Suddent 'e lost all 'is joy, and began to swear like—like lemme see— well, like an A.S.C. [Army Services Corps] man, 'e was wild!'

'And what made him so cross?' I asked.

'Why, 'e found 'e'd lost 'is pipe in their fight.'

THINKING AHEAD

It's early one winter London evening in 1916. Two unusually well-dressed Diggers, on leave from the front line, walk into the local police station and ask to see the sergeant.

The self-important officer bustles up to the desk, looks the two smiling Diggers up and down, and asks: 'How can I help you—gentlemen?'

'Well, Sarge,' says the first Digger earnestly, 'me and me mate are going out on the town tonight and, to save any trouble later on, we thought we'd post our bail money before we start.'

The sergeant's response has been lost to history.

FINDING THE 'AWSTRALIANS'

One of many yarns about the distinctive language of the Diggers:

It was an especially dark night on the Western Front, some time in 1917. There was a 'show' on and the shells were flying thick and fast. Communications were down and the general staff at headquarters desperately needed to contact the Australian trenches, somewhere out in no-man's land. The general pointed to a young British officer and volunteered him to get out there and find the Australians.

Snapping to it, the officer headed out into the maelstrom of fire and fury to search for the Australians. He waded through mud up to his ankles until he came to a trench. He sloshed in and asked, 'I say, are you chaps the Awstralians?' It turned out to be a trench full of British Tommies. So the officer set out again, heading close to the front lines and wading through even thicker mud up to his knees.

At last he reached another trench and asked again: 'I say, are you chaps the Awstralians?' No, they turned out to be Canadians. There was nothing for it but to struggle out to the furthest front line position, where the shelling was fiercest and the mud was up to his waist.

Eventually, the officer reached the furthest trench. Tumbling in he asked once more: 'I say, are you chaps the Awstralians?' There was a momentary lull in the roar of artillery and out of the darkened trench came the shouted reply: 'Who the bloody hell wants to know?'

'Ahh,' said the British officer, greatly relieved, 'I've found the Awstralians at last.'

PLEASE LET US TAKE TOBRUK!

During the Siege of Tobruk in 1941, the 'Rats' were assailed with propaganda leaflets dropped from enemy planes. Addressed to 'Aussies', the sheets pointed out that Germany and her allies were closing in and that the 'offensive from Egypt to relieve you [is] totally smashed'. The sheet went on to claim, 'You cannot escape. Our dive bombers are waiting to sink your transports,' and finally, 'SURRENDER!'

The Diggers thought the Germans had it all wrong. After finding a hygienic use for the propaganda sheets, they wrote their own version of what the enemy should have said if they really wanted the 'Rats' to surrender:

We have been trying to get you out of your 'rat holes' for the past three months, and we're getting a bit fed up with it. Every one of your chaps we get costs us about ten, and it's getting a bit thick.

Do you think that's fair? Play the game, you cads! Come out and give yourselves up. The German beer is the best in the world, and we have millions of gallons of it here. And if you can't stand our Sauerkraut, we'll give you steak and eggs any time you want them.

We look after our prisoners very well, and every Aussie is supplied with a Batwoman; this is on the instructions of the great and farsighted Fuhrer, who hopes in time to improve the fighting quality of the German race.

Our prison camp is the most luxurious in the world—two-up schools every night, coursing every Wednesday, trots on Monday afternoons, and the gee-gees every Tuesday, Thursday and Saturday.

It's all yours, if you . . .

Please, please let us take Tobruk!

So famous were the 'Rats of Tobruk' after the siege that they became the subjects of impersonation. This ditty displays the same resilient sense of humour:

In all the Aussie papers
That have chanced to pass my way,
It seems that every Digger
Returning home must say,
That he's a gun-scarred warrior
Who went through Greece and Crete
Who saw the show in Syria,
And braved the desert's heat.
They never missed a battle,
They were always in the ruck.
And there's not a man among them
Who wasn't in Tobruk.

Well, they can have the limelight,
Though some have got it free.
But if they're the veterans of Tobruk
THEN WHO THE HELL ARE WE?

COUNT YOUR CHILDREN

Back at the home front, the country was being invaded by American troops. They were better paid, better dressed and had better teeth than Australian men, making them attractive to many young Australian women. The blokes were jealous and a number of ditties on this issue were circulated. This one, to the tune of 'The Halls of Montezuma', also used for 'The Marines' Hymn', was sung in Melbourne and, with the appropriate name changes, in Perth:

From the streets of old Perth city to Cottesloe by the sea,
The Aussie girls are showing us how silly they can be.
In the good old days before the war the Aussie girls were
  gay,
But now they've gone completely mad on the twerps from
  the USA.

With their dashing Yankee accents and their money
   flowing free,
They have stolen all the hearts but those who have used
   their eyes to see.
But when this war is over and the Yanks are no more seen,
They'll prefer an Aussie dustman to the glorious marine.

So here's to the girls who have been true to the boys of the
   southern cross,
They have helped the brave to see it through, it will never
   cost a loss.
But the girls who skinned the digger for the glamour and
   the swank,
When this war is finished it's the Aussies they'll have to
   thank.

Another, to the tune of 'Count Your Blessings', also made the
rounds:

Count your children, count them one by one,
Count your children, count them one by one,
Count your children, count them one by one,
You will be surprised at what the Yanks have done!

PARABLE OF THE KIT INSPECTION

The Vietnam War generated its fair share of Digger humour,
including this exaggerated biblical parody:

And it came to pass, that there cometh one which bore on
his shoulder, three stars, who spaketh; saying; 'Bring unto
me the Sergeant Major.'
   And there cometh one who bore on his arm a golden
crown. Then he of the three stars saith unto him of the
golden crown; 'Tomorrow at the ninth hour, parade before
me one hundred men and all that is theirs.'

And the one of the golden crown answered, saying, 'Lord it is done.'

And behold! On the morrow, at the ninth hour, there did parade before him of the three stars, one hundred men, with all that they did have, as had been promised him. Then cometh others which bore on their shoulders two stars and yet others who bore one star. These were called 'Subbies', which being translated from the Latin meaneth 'Small Fry' or 'Little Potatoes'. Then he of the golden crown, standing before the one hundred men, cried out with a loud voice, and did cause them to become pillars of stone.

And behold! There cometh one which was called 'Quartermaster.' This man held great power, for he belonged to that tribe which said; 'These men must purchase from us.' Thus did they wax fat in the land! And, passing amongst one hundred men, he did say unto this man and unto that man; 'Where is this thing,' and 'Where is that thing.'

And they all had save one which was called 'Spudus Murphy', and he lacked. Then he, the one which was called Quartermaster, saith unto him; 'Friend, where are thy drawers woollen long and thy boots ankle, pair of one?' And Spudus Murphy answered saying; 'Lord, on the third day of the week, I did thirst and had not the wherewithal to satisfy my thirst, for I had not received my reward. And I did take my drawers woollen long and my boots ankle pair of one, unto mine uncle of the tribe of "Love"', and did say unto him "How many pieces of silver for these things?" And he saith unto me, "Seven." And I saith unto him; "Give to me that I may thirst not." And he did trade with me. Then I took the pieces of silver unto the abode of him that sold wine and did say unto him; "Give me to drink that I may thirst not." And he gave me, and I knew no more until the fourth day of the week.'

Then he of the three stars waxed exceeding wrath, and calling two men, he placed one to the East, and one to the West of Spudus Murphy and, turning sharply on his left heel and right toe, he was led away and cast unto the prison.

And on the morrow, he was brought before one which

bore on his shoulder, a crown and a star, showing him to be above all men! This one was called CO, which, being translated, meaneth: 'Putter up of the wind'. And he saith unto Spudus Murphy; 'What are these things that I hear concerning thee? Sayest thou aught?'

Then Spudus Murphy related to him how that he had exchanged his drawers woollen long and his boots ankle pair of one, for silver for wine. Then he that was called CO waxed exceeding wrath, and his anger was kindled against Spudus Murphy, and he saith unto him, 'Why has thou broken the laws which I have made? Knowest not that thou has sinned? Now because thou has done this thing, thou shalt be punished. Twenty and eight days shall thou labour.'

Then was Spudus Murphy led away to a place where he would hear the tick of the clock; but could not tell the passage of time. And the name of that place was 'The House of Glass'. And he was in that place twenty and eight days.

So my friends, be not as the one, but rather as the ninety and nine. Where thou thirsteth and has not the wherewithal to satisfy thy thirst, wait until the day of reward; then shall the joy be increased a thousand fold.

And now may the blessing of that great Saint, The Regimental Paymaster, be amongst you, now and always.

THE AIR FORCE WIFE

The trials and tribulations of the long-suffering air force wife were graphically described in this bittersweet account from the Vietnam War years:

An air force wife is mainly a girl. But there are times, such as when her husband is away and she is mowing the lawn or fixing a flat tyre on a youngster's bike, that she begins to suspect she is also a boy.

She usually comes in three sizes: petite, plump or pregnant. During the early years of her marriage it is often hard to determine which size is her normal one.

She has babies all over the world and measures time in terms of places as other women do in years. 'It was at Amberley that we all had the mumps . . . in Butterworth Dan was promoted.'

At least one of her babies was born or a posting was accomplished while she was alone. This causes her to suspect a secret pact between her husband and the air force providing for a man to be overseas or on temporary duty at such times as these.

An air force wife is international. She may be a Wagga farm girl, a South Australian nurse, a Victorian typist or Queensland meter maid. When discussing service problems they all speak the same language.

She can be a great actress. To heartbroken children at parting time, she gives an Academy Award performance: 'Melbourne is going to be such fun! I hear they have Australian Rules Football and briquettes and trams!' But her heart is breaking with theirs. She wonders if this is worth the sacrifice.

An ideal air force wife has the patience of an angel, the flexibility of putty, the wisdom of a scholar and the stamina of a horse. If she dislikes money, it helps. She is sentimental, carrying her memories with her in an old footlocker.

One might say she is married to a bigamist, because she shares her husband with a demanding entity called 'duty'. When duty calls, she becomes no. 2 wife. Until she accepts this fact her life can be miserable.

She is above all a woman who married an airman who offered her the permanency of a gypsy, the miseries of loneliness, the frustration of conformity, and the security of love. Sitting on her packing boxes with squabbling children nearby, she [is] sometimes willing to chuck it all in until she hears that firm step and cheerful voice of the lug who gave her all this. Then she is happy to be . . . his air force wife.

Women dressed in men's working clothes for a laugh at The Retreat in Bardeman, NSW, circa 1920. They are Mary Regan, Flo Colls, Kath Regan and Gin Regan.

5

WORKING FOR A LAUGH

We, the Willing, led by the Unknowing
are doing the impossible for the Ungrateful.
We have done so much for so long with so little
We are now qualified to do anything at all.

Anonymous

THE GARBOS' CHRISTMAS

A characteristically Australian Christmas occupational tradition, now probably obsolete, involved the 'garbos' or garbage men. For many decades the garbos were in the habit of leaving a Christmas message, often in verse, for their clients. The message would generally wish the household well for the coming year and was also designed as a reminder of the traditional garbos' Christmas gift. Almost invariably, in New South Wales at least, this would be bottles or cans of beer left out along with the garbage bin on the last garbage collection day before the season began. Here are a couple of World War I examples of some Melbourne garbo greetings:

YOUR
SANITARY ATTENDANT
WISHES YOU
A Merry Christmas

Awake, awake, all freeborn sons,
Sound your voices loud and clear,
Wishing all a Merry Christmas
Likewise a glad New Year.

While referring to the Sewerage Scheme
As the greatest in the nation,
Until completed, I hope you'll give
Us some consideration.

The mission of our life just now,
Is to cleanse and purify,
We do our duty faithfully,
Be the weather wet or dry.

So while you're spending Xmas
In mirth and melody,
And friends to friends some present give,
Just spare a thought for me.

A MERRY CHRISTMAS

In later years this custom seems to have dwindled, with only brief messages, if any, appearing. But even as late as 1983 it was possible to receive something like the following:

CHRISTMAS GREETINGS FROM
GARBO SQUAD
(Garbologists to you)

The year from us has gone,
Now it's time to think upon
Our blessings great and small:
May they continue for us all.

Your health, we hope, like ours is fine.
May 1984 be in similar line,
And in the New Year, we pray,
We'll serve you truly every day.

To you and yours joy we wish
That Christmas be a full dish
Of gladness, content and good health,
And the New Year bring you wealth.

Brian, Neville, Wayne

A CHRISTMAS MESSAGE

Always a time for overindulgence, Christmas at the O.K. Mine back in the roaring days was celebrated with enthusiasm, by some at least:

It was Christmas Eve at O.K. in the days when the mine was in full swing and the local pub was the scene of a glorious general spree. In front of the building there lay many inches of thick red dust, also various stumps. On the following morning several booze-soaked individuals were slumbering in the layers of red powder after many hours of rolling and burrowing about. Waiting outside the pub for the breakfast bell to ring, the mine engineer was accosted by an aboriginal man named Jacky, who, after gazing thoughtfully for some time at the inebriated individuals sleeping in the dust, remarked, 'My word boss, white Australia all right today, eh?'

RECHTUB KLAT

Butchers in Australia developed a version of a secret trade jargon, or back-slang, known as 'Rechtub Klat' (pronounced 'rech-tub kay-lat')—Butcher Talk. This descended from the similar back-slang of migrating or transported butchers from London's markets, among whom back-slanging was especially rife. In Australia there was little need for trade secrets to be protected, but a secret language allowed butchers to converse while others were present, perhaps commenting on the price to be charged or admiring the physical qualities of a female customer. Another valued use of this lingo was to insult troublesome customers with impunity. A similar convolution of language was also traditionally uttered by butchers in France, where it was known as *loucherbem*, *loucher* being French for 'butcher'. Got that?

Although now spoken by very few, Rechtub Klat was once a relatively well-developed language. Today its vocabulary is fairly restricted to types of meat—*feeb* for beef, *bmal* for lamb and *gip* for pig—and crude but admiring comments such as *doog tsub* (good bust) and *doog esra* (good arse), among other such constructions crafted as required. A few other slabs of butcher talk are *kool, toh lrig* (look, hot girl), *gaf* (fag, as in cigarette) and *toor*, meaning *root*, as in the Australian vulgarism for sexual intercourse. Here are a couple more to translate:

> *Cuf ecaf*
> *On erom feeb, gip, bmal*
> *Traf*
> *Tish*

As well as commenting negatively on fussy customers and admiringly on young ladies, it could be used to let the other butchers know that a particular cut had run out. So if there were *on steltuc ni eht pohs*, they should sell something different to any customer who wanted *steltuc* (cutlets). Back in the day it was not unknown for butchers to have complete clandestine conversations among themselves, as featured in the Australian movie *The Hard Word* (2002), used by the bank-robbing main characters to securely communicate their secrets to each other.

THE WHARFIE'S REPLY

Another old favourite of city work humour is the story of the wharfie and the dockyard guard:

> At the end of his shift at the dockyard, the old wharfie would wheel his barrow out for the day. The guard's job was to search wharfies for any pilfered items that they might have on or about them. But no matter how carefully he frisked the wharfie, the guard never found any loot on the old bloke.
>
> Not too long afterwards, the wharfie retired. A few months later the guard was having a drink in a waterside pub where he came across the wharfie. 'Howya goin', mate?' said the guard and bought the wharfie a beer for old times' sake. It didn't take long for the conversation to get around to working life on the docks. After a while, the guard said to the wharfie. 'You're well out of there now mate, so why don't you tell me the truth? I knew yer were knockin' something off, but we never found anything on you. What were yer stealin'?'
>
> The wharfie smiled broadly as he answered, 'Wheel-barrows.'

THE UNION DOG

The union dog is a good example of a folktale that circulates in both oral and written versions:

> Four union members were discussing how smart their dogs were.
>
> The first was a member of the Vehicle Workers' Union, who said his dog could do maths calculations. His dog was

named T-square, and he told him to go to the blackboard and draw a square, a circle and a triangle, which the dog did with consummate ease.

The Amalgamated Metalworkers' Union member said he thought his dog, Slide-rule, was much better. He told the dog to fetch a dozen biscuits and divide them into four piles, which Slide-rule did without a problem.

The Liquor Trades' Union member admitted that both dogs were quite good, but that his could outperform them. His dog, named Measure, was told to go and fetch a stubby of beer and pour seven ounces into a ten-ounce glass. The dog did this without a flaw.

The three men turned to the Waterside Workers' Union member and said, 'What can your mongrel do?'

The Waterside Workers' member, whose dog was called Tea-break, said to his dog, 'Show these bastards what you can do, mate!'

Tea-break ate the biscuits, drank the beer, pissed on the blackboard, screwed the other three dogs, claimed he injured his back, filled out a workers' compensation form and shot through on sick leave.

WORKING ON THE RAILWAY

The Australian railways have provided a living and even a way of life for very many people and their families. Railway tradition is rich with poems, songs and yarns about the joys and irritations of keeping the trains running. Old-time railmen will tell you about boiling the billy and frying eggs on their coal shovels as they stoked the boilers of steam trains. Or regale you with yarns about having to burn the sleepers lying beside the track when the coal ran out, just to keep the 'loco' going and getting passengers to their destinations on time. Despite this level of commitment and effort, the slow train is a common feature of railway lore, with countless yarns on the same topic being lovingly retold across the decades and across the country.

On many rural and regional lines, trains were once so regularly and reliably late that passengers were resigned to very long waits. But one day on an isolated platform that shall remain nameless, the train arrived smack on time. A delighted and astounded passenger was so overcome by the experience that he ran up to the engine driver and thanked him profusely for arriving on time this once. The driver smiled faintly and replied, 'No chance, mate, this is yesterday's train.'

An anonymous poet expressed the desolate feeling of waiting for a train that may possibly never come at all:

> All around the water tank
> Waitin' for a train
> I'm a thousand miles away from home
> Just a'standin' in the rain
> I'm sittin'
> Drinkin'
> Waitin'
> Thinkin'
> Hopin' for a train.

HIGH-OCTANE TRAVEL

An old railway yarn told in many places:

A couple of mechanics worked together in the railway sheds servicing diesel trains in Brisbane. One day there is a stop-work meeting over some issue or other and the two find themselves sitting around with nothing to do. They'd like to go to the pub, of course, but they can't leave the workplace. Then one of them, let's call him Phil, has a bright idea. 'I've heard that you can get a really good kick from drinking diesel fuel. Want to give it a go?'

His mate, we'll call him Bruce, bored out of his mind, readily agrees. They pour a sizeable glass of diesel each and get stuck in. Sure enough, they have a great day.

Next morning Phil wakes up, gets out of bed and is pleasantly surprised to find that despite yesterday's diesel spree he feels pretty good. Shortly afterwards, his phone rings. It's Bruce. He asks Phil how he is feeling. 'Great mate, no hangover at all. What about you?'

'No,' agrees Bruce, 'all good.'

'That's amazing,' replies Phil. 'We should get into that diesel more often.'

'Sure mate,' says Bruce, 'but have you farted yet?'

'What?' replies Phil, a bit taken aback. 'No, I haven't.'

'Well, make sure you don't 'cause I'm in Melbourne.'

RAILWAY BIRDS

This tongue-in-cheek description of various railway occupations in the form of a bird-spotting guide is at least as old as the 1930s, and probably earlier. No prizes for guessing which occupational group originated this item:

Engine Drivers—Rare birds, dusky plumage. Generally useful. No song; but for a consideration will jump points, signals etc. Have been known to drink freely near the haunts of man—especially at isolated stations. Occasionally inter-marry with station-masters' daughters (*see* station-masters). Known colloquially by such names as 'Hell Fire Jack', 'Mad Hector', 'Speedy Steve', 'Whaler', 'Smokebox' and 'Bashes'. Great sports, often carried from their engines suffering from shock—caused by wrong information.

Cleaners—Very little is known regarding the habits of these animals. How the name originated remains a mystery.

Guards—Fairly common. Red faces. Can go a long time without water. Easily recognisable by their habit of strutting up and down. Shrill whistle, but no sense of time. Sleep between stations, hence common cry of 'Up Guards, and at 'em'. Serve no generally useful purpose, but can be trained to move light perambulators, keep an eye on unescorted females, and wave small flags.

Porters—Habits strangely variable. Sometimes seen in great numbers: sometimes not at all. Much attracted by small bright objects. No song, but have been known to hum— between trains. Naturally indolent, but will carry heavy weights if treated rightly (i.e. sufficiently). Natural enemies of passengers (*see* passengers). Treated with contempt by station-masters.

Station-masters—Lordly. Brilliant plumage. Rarely leave their nests. Ardent sitters. Most naturalists state these birds have no song, but Railway Commissioners dispute this. Have been known to eat porters (*see* porters). Female offspring occasionally intermarry with very fast Engine Drivers.

Repair Gangs—Plumage nondescript. Migratory in habit. Nests are conspicuous and usually found in clusters near railway lines. No song but passengers assert their plaintive echoing cry of 'Pa-p-er' is unmistakable.

Passengers—Very common. Varied plumage. Will stand anything as a rule, but have been known to attack porters (*see* porters). Often kept in captivity under deplorable conditions by ticket inspectors, guards etc. Will greedily and rapidly devour sandwiches and buns under certain (i.e. rotten) conditions. These birds are harmless when properly treated, and should be encouraged by all nature lovers.

TOTAL ECLIPSE OF COMMUNICATION

A favourite theme of workplace humour is communication— its failure, its absence or its distortion. One example is the shrinking memo, and the message it tried, at first, to convey.

This item begins with a memo from the top levels of authority to the next level down, let's say from the Managing Director to the Works Director. The memo begins:

> Tomorrow morning there will be a total eclipse of the sun at 9 o'clock. This is something that we cannot see happen every day, so allow the workforce to line up outside in their best clothes to watch it. To mark the occasion of this rare occurrence I will personally explain it to them. If it is raining we shall not be able to see it very well and in that case the workforce should assemble in the canteen.

The next memo conveys this message down the line from the Works Director to the General Works Manager:

> By order of the Managing Director there will be a total eclipse of the sun at 9 o'clock tomorrow morning.

> If it is raining we shall not be able to see it very well on the site in our best clothes. In that case, the disappearance of the sun will be followed through in the canteen. This is something that we cannot see happen every day.

The General Works Manager then writes to the Works Manager an even briefer version of this rapidly disintegrating communication:

> By order of the General Manager we shall follow through, in our best clothes, the disappearance of the sun in the canteen at 9 o'clock tomorrow morning.

> The Managing Director will tell us whether it is going to rain. This is something which we cannot see every day.

In turn, the Works Manager passes this on to the Foreman in another memo:

If it is raining in the canteen tomorrow morning, which is something we cannot see happening every day, our Managing Director in his best clothes, will disappear at 9 o'clock.

Finally, the Foreman posts the message, or at least a version of it, on the Shop Floor noticeboard. It reads:

Tomorrow morning at 9 o'clock our Managing Director will disappear. It is a pity that we cannot see this happen every day.

THE LAWS OF WORKING LIFE

Whatever can go wrong will go wrong. That's Murphy's Law. Even if you haven't heard of this universal truth, you'll be familiar with the general principle and the fact that whatever does go wrong at work will be at the worst possible time and in the worst possible way.

It seems things go wrong for us so often and with such devastating consequences that Murphy's Law alone cannot predict all the consequences of human error and disaster. There is a worryingly large number of similar laws, corollaries, axioms and the like. They provide advice hard won from bitter experience. You know the sort of thing. If you drop a slice of buttered bread, it will unfailingly land butter-side down.

And it's not just bread and butter, either. What about the curious fact that everything always seems to cost more than you happen to have in your pocket or bank account. Or, when you try to take out a loan, you have to prove that you don't really need it. Here are some further helpful hints:

The probability of a given event occurring is inversely proportional to its desirability.

Left to themselves, things will always go from bad to worse.

Any error in any calculation will be in the area of most harm.

A short cut is the longest distance between two points.

Work expands to fill the time available.

Mess expands to fill the space available.

If you fool around with something long enough, it will eventually break.

The most important points in any communication will be those first forgotten.

Whatever you want to do, you have to do something else first.

Nothing is as simple as it seems.

Everything takes longer than expected.

Nothing ever quite works out.

It's easier to get into a thing than to get out of it.

When all else fails, read the instructions.

Reading these little difficulties and dilemmas of work life suggests that none of us should bother getting out of bed in the morning. And, of course, not everything in life goes wrong. Sometimes you can have really great days when the sun shines, the birds sing and you feel on top of the world.

But next time you seem to be having a day like this, just remind yourself of the last law of working life:

If everything seems to be going well, you probably don't know what is going on.

SOMEBODY ELSE'S JOB

Once upon a time there were four people, named Everybody, Somebody, Anybody and Nobody.

There was an important job to be done and Everybody was sure that Somebody would do it.

Anybody could have done it, but Nobody did it.

Somebody got angry about that because it was Everybody's job.

Everybody thought Anybody could do it, but Nobody realised that Everybody didn't do it.

It ended with Everybody blaming Somebody, when really, Nobody could accuse Anybody.

THE BASIC WORK SURVIVAL GUIDE

Some old favourites in Australian workplaces:

The opulence of the front office decor varies inversely with the fundamental solvency of the company.

No project ever gets built on schedule or within budget.

A meeting is an event at which minutes are kept and hours are lost.

The first myth of management is that it exists at all.

A failure will not appear until a new product has passed its final inspection.

New systems will generate new problems.

Nothing motivates a worker more than seeing the boss put in an honest day's work.

After all is said and done, a lot more is said than done.

The friendlier the client's secretary, the greater the chance that the competition has already secured the order.

In any organisation the degree of technical competence is inversely proportional to the level of management.

The grass is brown on both sides of the fence.

No matter what stage of completion the project reaches, the cost of the remainder of the project remains the same.

Most jobs are marginally better than daytime TV.

TWELVE THINGS YOU'LL NEVER HEAR AN EMPLOYEE TELL THE BOSS

Wishful thinking is nothing new, as this list of helpful suggestions implies:

Never give me work in the morning. Always wait until 5 pm and then bring it to me. The challenge of a deadline is always refreshing.

If it's really a 'rush job', run in and interrupt me every ten minutes to inquire how it's going. That greatly aids my efficiency.

Always leave without telling anyone where you're going. It gives me a chance to be creative when someone asks where you are.

If my arms are full of papers, boxes, books or supplies, don't open the door for me. I might need to learn how to function as a paraplegic in future and opening doors is good training.

If you give me more than one job to do, don't tell me which is the priority. Let me guess.

Do your best to keep me late. I like the office and really have nowhere to go or anything to do.

If a job I do pleases you, keep it a secret. Leaks like that could get me a promotion.

If you don't like my work, tell everyone. I like my name to be popular in conversations.

If you have special instructions for a job, don't write them down. If fact, save them until the job is almost done.

Never introduce me to the people you're with. When you refer to them later, my shrewd deductions will identify them.

Be nice to me only when the job I'm doing for you could really change your life.

Tell me all your little problems. No one else has any and it's nice to know someone is less fortunate.

EXCESSIVE ABSENCE

This is one of the great classics of workplace humour. It was old when it was kicking around the old Post Master General's department in the late 1960s. Versions can still be found on the internet:

Internal Memo # 125/JCg RE : EXCESSIVE ABSENCE

TO ALL PERSONNEL.
Due to excessive absences during the past year, it has
become necessary to put the following new rules into operation immediately.

1. SICKNESS

No excuse. The Management will no longer accept your
Doctor's Certificate as proof. We believe that if you are able
to go to your doctor, you are able to attend work.

2. DEATH (YOUR OWN)

This will be accepted as an excuse. We would like two
weeks' notice however, since we feel it is your duty to train
someone else for your job.

3. DEATH (OTHER THAN YOUR OWN)

This is no excuse. There is nothing you can do for them
and henceforth no time will be allowed off for funerals.
However, in case it should cause some hardship to some of
our employees, please note that on your behalf the Management has a special scheme in conjunction with the local
council for lunchtime burials, thus ensuring that no time is
lost from work.

4. LEAVE OF ABSENCE FOR AN OPERATION

We wish to discourage any thoughts you may have of
needing an operation and henceforth no leave of absence
will be granted for hospital visits. The management
believes that as long as you are an employee here, you
will need what you already have and should not consider
having any of it removed. We engaged you for your particular job with all your parts and having anything removed
would mean that we would be getting less of you than we
bargained for.

5. VISITS TO THE TOILETS

Far too much time is spent on the practice. In future the procedure will be that all personal shall go in alphabetical order. For example:—those with the surname beginning 'A' will go from 9.30 to 9.45. 'B' will go from 9.45 to 10.00. Those of you who are unable to attend at your appropriate time will have to wait until the next day when your turn comes up.

Have a nice day.
THE MANAGEMENT

THE END OF A PERFECT DAY

Pigs do not fly, of course, but in the world of work they can—and sometimes must—be made to do so:

Another day ends . . .

All targets met
All systems in working order
All customers satisfied
All staff eager and enthusiastic
All pigs fed and ready to fly.

TOTAL QUALITY MANAGEMENT (TQM)

'Sucking up', 'brown-nosing', 'crawling to the boss' and so on are widely reviled and widely practised arts of working life. There is no shortage of occupational humour on this subject. One old favourite is the 'Total Quality Management (TQM)' flowchart, a tersely effective rendition of the frequent reality of corporate and bureaucratic survival.

TOTAL QUALITY MANAGEMENT

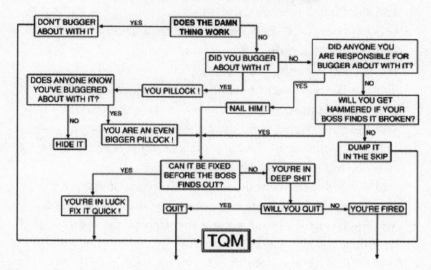

But, if you do blame someone else, just remember . . .

> The toes you step on today
> May well be attached to the legs
> That support the arse
> You need to kiss
> Tomorrow.

POLICY DEVELOPMENT

Bureaucracies of all kinds, public and private, find it necessary to develop agreed ways of doing things. These go by various names, but 'policy' is a widely used term for such arrangements. Those affected by such policies are often at a loss to understand how they came about, even when consultation has been a part of the policy development process. This biblical-sounding description provides a glimpse of policy-making in action. It is not reassuring:

> In the beginning was the Plan.
> And then came the Assumptions.

And the Assumptions were without form.

And the Plan was without substance.

And darkness was upon the face of the Workers.

And they spoke among themselves, saying,

'It is a crock of shit, and it stinks.'

And the Workers went unto their Supervisors and said,

'It is a pail of dung, and we can't live with the smell.'

And the Supervisors went unto their Managers, saying,

'It is the container of the excrements, and it is very strong, such that none may abide by it.'

And the Mangers went unto their Directors, saying,

'It is a vessel of fertiliser, and none may abide its strength.'

And the Directors spoke among themselves, saying to one another,

'It promotes growth, and it is very powerful.'

And the Vice Presidents went to the President, saying unto him,

'This new plan will actively promote the growth and vigor of the company

with very powerful effects.'

And the President looked upon the Plan and saw that it was good.

And the Plan became Policy.

And that is how shit happens.

THE BOAT RACE

The inevitable consequences of failing to be competitive fall, as this tale shows, on those at the bottom of the ladder:

A Japanese company and an American company decided to have a canoe race on the Missouri River. Both teams practiced long and hard to reach their peak performance before the race. On the big day, the Japanese won by a mile.

The Americans, very discouraged and depressed, decided to investigate the reason for the crushing defeat.

A management team made up of senior management was formed to investigate and recommend appropriate action.

Their conclusion was the Japanese had 8 people rowing and 1 person steering, while the American team had 8 people steering and 1 person rowing. So American management hired a consulting company referred to them by the US government and paid them a large amount of money for a second opinion.

The consultants advised that too many people were steering the boat, while not enough people were rowing. To prevent another loss to the Japanese, the rowing team's management structure was totally reorganised into 3 steering supervisors, 1 area steering superintendent, 1 publicity manager, 1 HR diversity coordinator, 1 union rep, and 1 rower.

They also implemented a new performance system that would give the 1 person rowing the boat greater incentive to work harder. It was called the 'Rowing Team Quality First Program', with a lunch and a free company pen for the rower. There was discussion of getting new paddles, canoes and other equipment, extra vacation days for practices and performance-tied bonuses, but that decision was held up in committee.

The next year the Japanese won by two miles.

Humiliated, the American management laid off the rower for poor performance, halted development of a new canoe, sold the paddles and cancelled all capital investments for new equipment. The money from all sales and all forecasted monies saved from further competition was distributed to the senior executives as bonuses and the next year's racing team was out-sourced to India.

The end.

PROSPECTIVE EMPLOYEE ASSESSMENT

Hopefully, you'll never have to go for a job in this place:

Subject: Prospective Employee Assessment

To: All Managers

The following guidelines shall be followed when hiring new personnel:

Take the prospective employees you are trying to place and put them in a room with only a table and two chairs. Leave them alone for two hours without any instruction. At the end of that time, go back and see what they are doing.

If they have taken the table apart in that time, put them in Engineering.

If they are counting the butts in the ashtray, assign them to Finance.

If they are screaming and waving their arms, send them off to Manufacturing.

If they are talking to the chairs, Personnel is a good place for them.

If they are sleeping, they are Management material.

If they are writing up the experience, send them to Technical Publications.

If they don't even look up when you enter the room, assign them to Security.

If they try to tell you it's not as bad as it looks, send them to Marketing.

And if they have left early, put them in Sales.

SPECIALISED HIGH-INTENSITY TRAINING (S.H.I.T.)

Another dig at office bureaucracy and official policies:

Interoffice Memo
To: All Employees

From: Management
Subject: Specialised High-Intensity Training

In order to assure the highest levels of quality work and productivity from our employees, it will be our policy to keep all employees well trained through our program of Specialised High-Intensity Training (S.H.I.T.). We aim to give our employees more S.H.I.T. than anyone else.

If you feel that you do not receive your share of S.H.I.T. on the job, please contact your supervisor. You will immediately be placed at the top of the S.H.I.T. list. Your supervisor has been specially trained to give you all the S.H.I.T. you can handle.

Employees who do not take any S.H.I.T. will be placed in the Departmental Employee Evaluation Program for Specialised High-Intensity Training (D.E.E.P.S.H.I.T.). Those who fail to complete D.E.E.P.S.H.I.T. will be sent to Employee Attitude Training for Specialised High-Intensity Training (E.A.T.S.H.I.T.). Since the supervisory staff took S.H.I.T. before their promotions, they do not have to do S.H.I.T. anymore; they are already full of S.H.I.T.

If you are already proficient in S.H.I.T., you may be interested in giving S.H.I.T. to other workers. We can add your name to the Basic Understanding Lecture List for Specialised High-Intensity Training (B.U.L.L.S.H.I.T.). Those who complete B.U.L.L.S.H.I.T. will get the S.H.I.T. jobs and can apply for promotion to Director of Intensity Programming for Specialised High-Intensity Training (D.I.P.S.H.I.T.).

If you have further questions, please direct them to:

Head of Training, Specialised High-Intensity Training (H.O.T.S.H.I.T.).

Thank you,
Business/Industrial Guidance for Specialised High-Intensity Training (B.I.G.S.H.I.T.)

P.S. If you write broken code, you will become a member of Project for Idiot Employee Continuing Education of Specialised High-Intensity Training (P.I.E.C.E. of S.H.I.T.).

EARLY RETIREMENT

One of the realities of worklife is the profound cynicism expressed by many employees at the circumstances of their employment. Dissatisfaction with pay, management, conditions, job security and so on and on are constant factors of modern worklife. A lot of occupational humour reflects these disenchantments, none perhaps more than this one, usually known as 'Early Retirement Program':

Due to the financial situation within the farming industry, the government has decided to place all farmers over the age of 60 on an early retirement scheme.

The scheme (Retire Agricultural Personnel Early) will be known as RAPE. Persons selected to be RAPED can apply for Special Help After Farm Termination or SHAFT.

Those who have been RAPED and SHAFTED will then be reviewed under the Scheme for Retired Early Workers or SCREW. Please note: You can only be RAPED once, SHAFTED twice but SCREWED as many times as the government deems appropriate.

Persons who have been RAPED can apply to get AIDS (Additional Income for Dependants) or HERPES (Half Earnings for Rural Personnel on Early Severance).

Those farmers remaining in the industry will receive as much Special High-Intensity Training or SHIT and Caring Responsive Assistance Programme or CRAP as possible.

As you are aware, the government has always prided itself on the amount of SHIT and CRAP it gives to farmers. Should you feel, however, you are not receiving enough SHIT, or that you are not responding to all the CRAP, please bring this to the attention of the Minister as he has been especially trained to give you all the SHIT and CRAP that you can handle.

DIFFERENCES BETWEEN YOU AND YOUR BOSS

There are quite a few, in case you haven't already noticed:

When you take a long time, you're slow.
When your boss takes a long time, he's thorough.
When you don't do it, you're lazy.
When your boss doesn't do it, he's too busy.
When you make a mistake, you're an idiot.
When your boss makes a mistake, he's only human.
When doing something without being told, you're overstepping your authority.
When your boss does the same thing, that's initiative.
When you take a stand, you're being pig-headed.
When your boss does it, he's being firm.
When you overlooked a rule of etiquette, you're being rude.
When your boss skips a few rules, he's being original.
When you please your boss, you're ass-kissing.
When your boss pleases his boss, he's being cooperative.
When you're out of the office, you're wandering around.
When your boss is out of the office, he's on business.
When you have a day off sick, you're always sick.
When your boss has a day off sick, he must be very ill.
When you apply for leave, you must be going for an interview.
When your boss applies for leave, it's because he's overworked.

WHAT DO THEY REALLY MEAN?

A guide to decoding the real meaning of everyday office talk:

It's a pleasure	— What a hassle.
Glad to be of help	— I'd rather be doing something else.
Have a nice day	— Drop dead, it's all the same to me.
How are you?	— Spare me the details. I really don't care.
Long time, no see	— Thank God.
Can I help you?	— Oh, please say 'No'.
That's really interesting	— What's for lunch?
Lovely outfit, is it new?	— My God, I bet they laughed you out of the shop.
Did you have a nice weekend?	— Please spare me your usual rambling account.
Can't stop, I've another appointment	— With the speaking clock.
Sorry to hear your hampster died	— Get a life.
Of course this idea will work	— Your guess is as good as mine.
I would love to be involved in this project	— I would rather scrape graffiti off walls.
No problem	— So long as I reschedule my life for the next week and work until midnight every night.

THE LITTLE RED HEN

This is another tale that turns on tensions between the boss and the workers. This long-standing element of Australian life is no less prevalent today, though it may take more modern forms than this traditional yarn.

Once upon a time there was a little red hen who scratched around and found some grains of wheat. She called upon the other animals to help her plant the wheat.

'Too busy,' said the cow.

'Wrong union,' said the horse.

'Not me,' said the goose.

'Where's the environmental impact study?' asked the duck.

So the hen planted the grain, tended it and reaped the wheat. Then she called for assistance to bake some bread.

'I'll lose my unemployment relief,' said the duck.

'I'll get more from the RED scheme,' said the sheep.

'Out of my classification, and I've already explained the union problem,' said the horse.

'At this hour?' queried the goose.

'I'm preparing a submission to the IAC,' said the cow.

So the little red hen baked five lovely loaves of bread and held them up for everyone to see.

'I want some,' said the duck and sheep together.

'I demand my share,' said the horse.

'No,' said the little red hen. 'I have done all the work. I will keep the bread and rest awhile.'

'Excess profit,' snorted the cow.

'Capitalist pig,' screamed the duck.

'Foreign multi-national,' yelled the horse.

'Where's the workers' share?' demanded the pig.

So they hurriedly painted picket signs and paraded around the hen, yelling, 'We shall overcome.' And they did, for the farmer came to see what all the commotion was about.

'You must not be greedy, little red hen,' he admonished. 'Look at the disadvantaged goose, the underprivileged pig, the less fortunate horse, the out-of-work duck. You are guilty of making second-class citizens out of them. You must learn to share.'

'But I have worked to produce my own bread,' said the little red hen.

'Exactly,' said the farmer, 'that is what free enterprise is all about these days. You are free to work as hard as you like. If you were on a communist farm, you would have to give up all the bread. Here you can share it with your needy companions.'

So they lived happily ever after. But the university research team, having obtained a large government grant to study this odd happening, wondered why the little red hen never baked any more bread.

Based, allegedly, on a folktale that has itself been published in book form since at least the nineteenth century, this photocopied satire from the 1980s still resonates today with its down-to-earth simplification of industrial politics. Like most folktales, this one has a sharp point to make.

THE AIRLINE STEWARD'S REVENGE

This urban legend nicely encapsulates the workplace fantasy of getting one's own back on an especially difficult customer:

A steward was working in First Class on a plane from South Africa to Sydney. On the flight was a very wealthy and snooty elderly couple. A little way into the flight, the steward came along the aisle to where the couple was seated. 'What would you like to drink, madam?' he asked.

There was no reply. Thinking that the woman might not have heard him, the steward asked again what she would like to drink.

Once more she ignored him. But her husband leaned over and said, 'My wife doesn't speak to the help. She would like a bottle of red.'

So the steward went off to get the wine but as he walked away the man called out, 'Boy, boy!' The steward came quickly back to the couple. 'Yes Sir, how can I help you?'

The man said, 'My wife was wondering about the situation with domestic help in Australia.'

Swiftly the steward replied, 'Oh Sir, I'm sure Madam will have no trouble at all finding a job.'

According to the union official who told this tale, the steward was sacked by the airline but later reinstated. The story simultaneously takes down the snobbishness of the first-class couple, shows the rapier-sharp wit of the worker, and chimes in well with our cherished notions of Australia as a place of equality.

THE BOSS

Despite the modernity of most of these expressions and their transmission by current technological channels, their themes are often the traditional ones of humour, satire, of catching out the unwary and with a general down-to-earth view of life at their base. One popular item of this kind is based on a fable at least as old as Aesop, continuing that venerable cautionary narrative into the modern world in ways that most of us can relate to.

When the lord made man, all the parts of the body argued over who would be the BOSS.

The BRAIN explained that since he controlled all the parts of the body, he should be the BOSS.

The LEGS argued that since they took the man wherever he wanted to go, they should be the BOSS.

The STOMACH countered with the explanation that since he digested all the food, he should be the boss.

The EYES said that without them, man would be helpless, so they should be BOSS.

Then the ARSEHOLE applied for the job.

The other parts of the body laughed so hard that the ARSEHOLE got mad and closed up.

After a few days the BRAIN went foggy, the LEGS got wobbly, the STOMACH got ill and the EYES got crossed and unable to see.

They all conceded defeat and made the ARSEHOLE the BOSS.

This proves that you don't have to be a brain to be BOSS . . .

JUST AN ARSEHOLE.

AFTER WORK . . .

This one has been popular in the social media and emails of 'seniors':

Subject: Pensioner shopping at Coles

Yesterday I was at my local Coles store buying a large bag of Chum dog food for my loyal pet and was in the checkout queue when a woman behind me asked if I had a dog.

What did she think I had, an elephant? So, since I'm retired and have little to do, on impulse I told her that no, I didn't have a dog, I was starting the Chum Diet again. I added that I probably shouldn't, because I ended up in hospital last time, but I'd lost 2 stone before I woke up in intensive care with tubes coming out of most of my orifices and IVs in both arms.

I told her that it was essentially a perfect diet and that the way that it works is to load your pockets with Chum nuggets and simply eat one or two every time you feel hungry. The food is nutritionally complete so it works well and I was going to try it again. (I have to mention here that practically everyone in the queue was now enthralled with my story.)

Horrified, she asked me if I ended up in intensive care because the dog food poisoned me. I told her no, I stepped off the kerb to sniff an Irish Setter's arse and a car hit me.

I thought the guy behind her was going to have a heart attack he was laughing so hard. I'm now banned from Coles.

Better watch what you ask retired people. They have all the time in the world to think of daft things to say.

MEETINGS

They are the bane of working life, but we must have them, as this notice suggests:

Are you lonely?
Hate having to make decisions?
Rather talk about it than do it?
Want to pass the buck?

HOLD A MEETING!

Sharpen your skills in meaningless verbal interaction.
Learn to off-load decisions.
Write volumes of meaningless rhetoric.
Feel important, impress your colleagues.
Catch up on your sleep.

AND ALL ON WORK TIME!

Meetings:
the practical alternative to work

PRAYER FOR THE STRESSED

Spiritual help for a common workplace problem:

Grant me the serenity to accept the things I cannot change.
the courage to change the things I cannot accept,

and the wisdom to hide the bodies of those I had
to kill today because they got on my nerves.
And also, help me to be careful of the toes I step on
today as they may be connected to the feet I may have
to kiss tomorrow.
Help me to always give 100% at work . . .
12% on Monday
23% on Tuesday
40% on Wednesday
20% on Thursday
5% on Friday
And help me to remember . . .
When I'm having a really bad day,
and it seems that people are trying to wind me up,
that it takes 42 muscles to frown, 28 to smile and
only 4 to extend my arm and smack someone in the mouth!

THE JOB APPLICATION

There are various versions of this send-up of the job application. It probably originated in America and usually begins with an assurance that 'This is an actual job application that a 17-year-old boy submitted at a fast-food hamburger restaurant; and they hired him because he was so honest and funny!':

NAME: Greg Bulmash

SEX: Not yet. Still waiting for the right person.

DESIRED POSITION: Company's President or Vice President. But seriously, whatever's available. If I was in a position to be picky, I wouldn't be applying here in the first place.

DESIRED SALARY: $185,000 a year plus stock options and a Michael Ovitz style severance package. If that's not possible, make an offer and we can haggle.

EDUCATION: Yes.

LAST POSITION HELD: Target for middle management hostility.

SALARY: Less than I'm worth.

MOST NOTABLE ACHIEVEMENT: My incredible collection of stolen pens and 'post-it' notes.

REASON FOR LEAVING: It sucked.

AVAILABLE FOR WORK: Of course. That's why I'm applying.

PREFERRED HOURS: 1.30–3.30 pm, Monday, Tuesday and Thursday.

DO YOU HAVE ANY SPECIAL SKILLS?: Yes, but they're better suited to a more intimate environment.

MAY WE CONTACT YOUR CURRENT EMPLOYER? If I had one, would I be here?

DO YOU HAVE ANY PHYSICAL CONDITIONS THAT WOULD PROHIBIT YOU FROM LIFTING UP TO 50 LBS? 50 lbs of what?

DO YOU HAVE A CAR? I think the appropriate question here would be 'Do you have a car that runs?'

HAVE YOU RECEIVED ANY SPECIAL AWARDS OR RECOGNITION? I may already be the winner of the Publishers Clearinghouse Sweepstakes.

DO YOU SMOKE?: On the job, no, on my breaks, yes.

WHAT WOULD YOU LIKE TO BE DOING IN FIVE YEARS? Living in the Bahamas with a fabulously wealthy dumb blonde supermodel who thinks I'm the greatest thing since sliced bread. Actually, I'd like to be doing that now.

DO YOU CERTIFY THAT THE ABOVE IS TRUE AND COMPLETE TO THE BEST OF YOUR KNOWLEDGE?: Yes. Absolutely.

SIGN HERE: Aries.

THE BOSS'S REPLY

This conversation gives the boss's point of view about you having a day off:

So, you want the day off:—
Let's take a look at what you are asking for:—
There are 365 days in the year available for work.
There are 52 weeks in the year, in which you already have two days off per week, leaving 261 days available for work.
Since you spend 16 hours each day away from work, you have used up 170 days, leaving only 91 days available.
You spend 50 minutes each day in coffee breaks which accounts for 23 days per year, leaving only 68 days available.
With a 1-hour lunch period each day, you have used up another 46 days, leaving only 22 days available for work.
You normally spend 2 days per year on sick leave.
This leaves only 20 days available for work.
We are off for 5 holidays per year, so your available working time is down to 15 days.
We generously give you 14 days vacation per year, which leaves only 1 day available for work, and I'll be damned if I'm going to let you take that day off.

ODE TO PUBLIC SERVANTS

A comment on 'downsizing', 'redeployment' and 'change management', euphemisms for getting the sack:

Ten public servants standing in a line,
One of them was downsized—then there were nine.

Nine public servants who must negotiate,
One joined the union—then there were eight.

Eight public servants thought they were in heaven,
'til one of them was redeployed—then there were seven.

Seven public servants, their jobs as safe as bricks,
But one was reclassified—then there were six.

Six public servants trying to survive,
One of them was privatised—then there were five.

Five public servants ready to give more,
But one golden handshake reduced them to four.

Four public servants full of loyalty,
Their jobs were advertised—then there were three.

Three public servants under review,
One left on secondment—then there were two.

Two public servants coping on the run,
One went out on stress leave—then there was one.

The last public servant agreed to relocate,
Replaced by ten consultants at twice the hourly rate.

JARGONING

The ability to 'speak the lingo' is an essential requirement of belonging to any human group. We need to be able to understand and to speak in the language appropriate to the people, the time, place and circumstances. Work groups are no different in this respect. The significant numbers of humorous items that deal with some aspect of occupational language suggests that this is an important element in modern worklife, a fact that makes language and its uses well worth our consideration.

The glossary or dictionary of technical terms is a standard in many professions, trades and industries. These take many forms, including engineering terms, mathematical equations, scientific formulations and so on. Usually these compilations are spoofs on the jargon of the business they represent. A relatively recent addition to these ranks is the 'Glossary of Management Terms'. This includes such delightful definitions as:

TO DELEGATE—to pass the buck
TO DELEGATE UPWARDS—to pass the buck back
URGENCY—panic
EXTREME URGENCY—blind panic
FORECAST—a guess
LONG-RANGE FORECAST—a wild guess
LEADERSHIP—having a loud voice
JOB ROTATION—determining who gets the crap jobs this
   week
INDUSTRIAL BY-PRODUCT—our waste
ENVIRONMENTAL POLLUTION—other people's waste
PILFERING—theft by employees
FRINGE BENEFITS—theft by executives
PERFORMANCE APPRAISAL—revenge
ORGANISATION—reaching the office earlier than the boss
SUPPLEMENTARY INFORMATION—bullshit

THE JARGON GENERATOR

The use of jargon to impress and obfuscate is also frequently encountered within occupational environments. Decades ago this was recognised in the anonymous creation of a device that is still common in various forms. Usually known as 'The Jargon Generator', this useful item allows the ambitious manager or professional to instantly generate impressive-sounding but safely meaningless phrases. These can be used with wild abandon at every possible opportunity, amazing colleagues and impressing clients. Simply pick a numbered word from each column, such as 0 6 9, to produce an impressive phrase of gobbledygook, in this case, 'integrated transitional contingency'.

There are many different versions of The Jargon Generator. It's especially popular in high-tech and IT occupations and, of course, your required jargon can now be accomplished online with a variety of totally automated matrixes—here's some for you!

Column 1	Column 2	Column 3
0. integrated	0. management	0. options
1. total	1. organisational	1. flexibility
2. systematised	2. monitored	2. capability
3. parallel	3. reciprocal	3. mobility
4. functional	4. digital	4. programming
5. responsive	5. logistical	5. concept
6. optimal	6. transitional	6. time-phase
7. synchronised	7. incremental	7. projection
8. compatible	8. third-generation	8. hardware
9. balanced	9. policy	9. contingency

GOVERNMENTIUM

Versions and variations of this one have been around since at least the 1980s. It is also known as 'Administratium' or 'Bureaucratium'. The joke seems to have originated in scientific research establishments, but applies to any large organisation where there is a significant bureaucracy—in other words, everywhere.

Scientists at CERN in Geneva have announced the discovery of the HEAVIEST element yet known to science.

AND yes . . . it was discovered in Australia, which is now the leading producer.

The new element is Governmentium (Gv). It has one neutron, 25 assistant neutrons, 88 deputy neutrons and 198 assistant deputy neutrons, giving it an atomic mass of 312.

These 312 particles are held together by forces called morons, which are surrounded by vast quantities of lefton-like particles called peons.

Since Governmentium has no electrons or protons, it is inert. However, it can be detected, because it impedes every reaction with which it comes in contact.

A tiny amount of Governmentium can cause a reaction normally taking less than a second to take from four days to four years to complete.

Governmentium has a normal half-life of 2–6 years. It does not decay but instead undergoes a reorganisation in which a portion of the assistant neutrons and deputy neutrons exchange places.

In fact, Governmentium's mass will actually increase over time, since each reorganisation will cause more morons to become neutrons, forming isodopes. This characteristic of moron promotion leads some scientists to believe that Governmentium is formed whenever morons reach a critical concentration. This hypothetical quantity is referred to as critical morass.

When catalysed with money, Governmentium becomes Administratium, an element that radiates just as much energy as Governmentium since it has half as many peons but twice as many morons.

All of the money is consumed.

THE SURPRISE PARTY

Relationships at work can sometimes get out of hand:

A man works in an office with a beautiful female secretary. His birthday arrives and, for no apparent reason, the secretary invites the man over to her place for a drink and dinner. Hardly able to believe his luck, the man quickly accepts and after work they drive over to the secretary's flat.

Inside, she tells the man to make himself comfortable while she goes into the other room. She says that she will be back in a minute or two. Anticipating a night of passion, the man undresses and waits naked with an enormous erection. Suddenly, the secretary opens the double doors into the lounge room to reveal the man's wife, children, friends and co-workers all chorusing 'Surprise, surprise . . . !'

Surprise and embarrassment are the joint themes of 'The Surprise Party', as it is usually known. American folklorists have made quite a study of this tale and its variations. They have found early tellings of it in the 1920s and in the March 1997 *Reader's Digest* it turned up in the guise of a true story, an incident that really happened to the ex-boss of a reader—*Reader's Digest* probably paid the contributor good money for it, too. In Australia, it is more usually told as a joke or humorous yarn—a fabrication—than as a contemporary legend or apparent 'truth'.

THE SEX LIFE OF AN ELECTRON

Authorship of this piece is often attributed to one 'Eddy Current'. It constructs a narrative that depends on occupational jargon terms to create its sexual double entendre:

One night when his charge was high, Micro Farad decided to seek out a cute coil to let him discharge. He picked up Milli Amp and took her for a ride on his mega cycle. They rode across a Wheatstone bridge, around the sine waves and stopped in a magnetic field beside a flowing current.

Micro Farad was attracted by Milli Amp's characteristic curve and soon had her fully charged and excited her resistance to a minimum. He laid her on the ground potential and raised her frequency and lowered her inductance. He pulled out his high frequency probe and inserted it into her socket, connecting them in parallel and short-circuiting her resistance shunt so as to cause surges with the utmost intensity. Then, when fully exited, Milli Amp mumbled 'OHM, OHM, OHM'. With his tube operating at a maximum and her field vibrating with current flow, it caused her to shunt over and Micro Farad rapidly discharged, drawing every electron. They fluxed all night, trying different connections and sockets until his magnet had a soft core and lost its field strength.

Afterwards, Milli Amp tried self-induction and damaged her solenoids in doing so. With his battery discharged, Micro Farad was unable to excite his field, so they spent the night reversing polarity and blowing each other's fuses.

DEATH OF EMPLOYEES

Satires on official forms, policies and regulations are especially rich on the subject of requesting leave. This one has been around since at least the 1960s:

COMMONWEALTH OF AUSTRALIA
FEDERAL GOVERNMENT
DIRECTIVE E/E/A. 5769/1 URGENT
TO: ALL employees
RE: Standard Procedure Instructions in Case of Death of Employees

It has recently been brought to the attention of this office that many employees have been dying whilst on duty, for apparently no good reason at all. Furthermore, the same employees are refusing to fall over after they are dead.

Where it can be proved that the employee is being held up by a bench, counter, desk, typewriter, or any other support which is the property of the Department, a 90 day period of grace will be granted.

The following procedure will hereforth be strictly adhered to:

If after several hours it is noticed that an employee has not moved or changed position, the Department Head will promptly investigate. Because of the highly sensitive nature of our employees and the very close resemblance between death and their natural working attitude, the investigation will be made quietly so as to prevent waking the employee if he or she is asleep. If some doubt as to his or her true condition is felt, the extending of a pay envelope is a fine test. If the employee does not grasp it, it may be reasonably assumed that he or she is dead.

NOTE: In some cases, the instinct to extend the hand for the pay envelope is so strongly developed that a spasmodic 'clutcher reflex' action may even occur after death. In all cases, a sworn statement by the dead person must be filled out in full detail on a special form provided for the purpose. Fifteen copies will be made, three copies to be sent to the Commonwealth Department, two to the State Office, and two to the deceased. The others, in accordance with usual routine, will be promptly lost in the Department's files.

WORKPLACE AGREEMENTS

The same concerns lie behind this more recent variation on the employee-death theme. Different times, same old problem:

AUSTRALIA WORKPLACE AGREEMENTS
CONSULTANTS IN EMPLOYEE RELATIONS
MANAGEMENT

Sick Days
We will no longer accept a doctor's statement as proof of sickness. If you are able to go to the doctor, you are able to come to work.

Personal Days
Each employee will receive 104 personal days a year. They are called Saturday and Sunday.

Bereavement Leave
This is no excuse for missing work. There is nothing you can do for dead friends, relatives or co-workers. Every effort should be made to have non-employees attend to the arrangements. In rare cases where employee involvement is necessary, the funeral should be scheduled in the late afternoon. We will be glad to allow you to work through your lunch hour and subsequently leave one hour early.

Toilet Use
Entirely too much time is being spent in the toilet. There is now a strict three-minute time limit in the stalls. At the end of the three minutes, an alarm will sound, the toilet paper will retract, the stall door will open, and a picture will be taken. After your second offence, your picture will be posted on the company bulletin board under the 'Chronic Offenders category'. Anyone caught smiling in the picture will be sanctioned under the company's mental health policy.

Lunch Break
Skinny people get 30 minutes for lunch, as they need to eat more, so that they can look healthy. Normal size people get 15 minutes for lunch to get a balanced meal to maintain

their average figure. Chubby people get 5 minutes for lunch, because that's all the time needed to drink a Slim-Fast.

Death Clause
Any worker found dead at their desk will be promptly fired. All deaths will need to be applied for in advance and will only be approved if you can show your death will not affect productivity.

Thank you for your loyalty to our company. We are here to provide a positive employment experience. Therefore, all questions, comments, concerns, complaints, frustrations, irritations, aggravations, insinuations, allegations, accusations, consternation and input should be directed elsewhere.

POPULATION OF AUSTRALIA

Sometimes, it feels like this, even though the population has doubled since this spoof report was circulated:

Of the many figures that have been recently released from Canberra, the following may be of interest. These, incidentally, were not released by the Commonwealth Statistician.

Population of Australia	12,000,000
People of 65 and over	2,000,000
BALANCE LEFT TO DO THE TOIL	10,000,000
People of 18 and less	5,000,000
BALANCE LEFT TO DO THE TOIL	5,000,000
People working for the Government, State and Council Offices	2,200,000
BALANCE LEFT TO DO THE TOIL	2,800,000
People in the Armed Forces	950,000

BALANCE LEFT TO DO THE TOIL   1,850,000

People in Banks, Insurance etc.   1,100,000
BALANCE LEFT TO DO THE TOIL   750,000

People in asylums, hospitals and
Engaged in Trotting & Greyhound
racing   600,000
BALANCE LEFT TO DO THE TOIL   150,000

University students & others who
won't work   125,000
BALANCE LEFT TO DO THE TOIL   25,000

People in prison   24,998
BALANCE LEFT TO DO THE TOIL   2 (you and me—
and you'd better
pull your socks
up, because I'm
sick of running
this country on
my own)

Two swaggies strike a pose! Local graziers, Jabez Nicholls and Sam Nicholls, dressed as swaggies in front of Ryans Boots and Shoes, Gundagai, NSW, late nineteenth-century.

6

A SWAG OF LAUGHS

Kind friends, pray give attention
To this, my little song.
Some rum things I will mention,
And I'll not detain you long.

A.B. 'Banjo' Paterson

THE GREAT AUSTRALIAN YARN

Usually, humorous anecdotes of bush life and legend are a staple element of Australian folklore. Such pithy anecdotes are also found in other frontier traditions but Australian yarns often have a certain dryness of wit and acerbic tone that connects them to the angularity of much Australian folk culture. Most of this material revolves around white male bush workers and reflects that particular worldview.

The swagman, or itinerant bush worker, features in a great many humorous bush folktales. Most of these depict the 'swaggie' as a taciturn, anti-authoritarian loner, as in a brief story sometimes called 'The Great Australian Yarn' and often hailed as the quintessential Australian anecdote. This story of the swaggie's reply to the squatter is known and told around the country. One Western Australian version has the incident occurring somewhere between Derby and Fitzroy Crossing:

> A swaggie is battling along the dry and dusty track in blazing heat. A solitary car comes along the track and stops by the swaggie. The driver, usually said to be a farmer, land-owner or 'squatter', leans out of the car window and asks the swaggie 'Where ya goin', mate?' The swaggie replies, 'Wyndham,' and the driver says, 'Climb in, I'll give you a lift.' The swaggie replies: 'No thanks; you can open and shut your own bloody gates.'

THE BAGMAN'S GAZETTE

The 'Bagman's Gazette' was a term for the efficient word-of-mouth network on the track. News, rumour and gossip were carried along this unofficial route with amazing speed. Under the title 'Bagman's Gazette', 'The Organiser' began his column for the *Darwin Northern Standard* in the Depression year of 1931 with a quotation from Lewis Carroll's famous nonsense poem 'The Walrus and the Carpenter'. The article was about wages and politics, suggesting that not much had changed since the strikes of forty years before:

> The time has come the Walrus said.
> To talk of many things;
> Of shoes, and ships and sealing wax,
> And cabbages and kings.

> Bagmen discussing politics at a recent session around the Camp fire touched on the so-called necessity for equal sacrifice, taking it for granted that all sections would be required by this to dub up in proportion so as to save the country from financial chaos. After disposing of the theory that lower wages would increase employment and quoting

their experiences in search of employment in the pastoral industry in Queensland, where wages are as low as 15/– a week, one bagman quoted the proposed British Budget as a sample of equal sacrifice. It is proposed to save Britain by reducing the unemployment dole by £66,500,000 and education grants, and teachers' salaries by £13,000,000. This makes a total of £79,500,000 out of £96,500,000 it is proposed to save. The workers even contribute a big part of the remaining £17,000,000.

Now if this equal, sacrifice were a real thing and if those who have no income can contribute £66,500,000 to the national income, how much can those who, do not work, never have worked, never will work, and have huge, incomes, contribute in this 'equal sacrifice' humbug? Then again in Australia if a worker on five quid a week can sacrifice 20 per cent of that for the national good, a judge or a politician or a bondholder should be able to sacrifice all the income he or she gets above five quid. They would then still be 20 per cent above the poor plugger that works for his bit and it is more questionable whether they are worth 20 per cent more.

The bagmen were unanimous that the only patriot expected (in war time or peace) to sacrifice everything for his Country is the toiler and they furthermore thought that it is time the Workers of Australia put up a fight against this 'equal sacrifice' humbug and wage a reduction campaign of the super patriots, but they are only bagmen.

A STUMP SPEECH

The 'stump speech' is a form of polished gibberish about nothing at all. Stump speeches featured in the United States during nineteenth century political campaigns and were also used as entertainment and as forms of 'spruiking' a product, often of the snake-oil variety. Australia has a similar tradition of these absurd but entertaining rants. This one is thought to

date from the early Federation period with its reference to
George Reid, leader of the first federal opposition, free trade
advocate and eventually prime minister from 1904–5.

Ladies and gentlemen—kindly turn your optics towards
me for a few weeks and I will endeavour to enlighten you
on the subject of duxology, theology, botanology, zoology
or any other ology you like. I wish to make an apology, yes
my sorefooted, black-eyed rascals, look here and answer
me a question I am about to put to your notice. I want
to be very lenient with you, but what shall it be, mark
you, what shall the subject of my divorce (excuse me),
discourse, this evening be? What shall I talk about? Shall
it be about the earth, sun, sea, stars, moon, Camp Grove
or jail? Now I wish to put before your notice the labour
question. It is simply deloructious—isn't that alright?
Yes, allow me to state the labour question is not what it
should be.

Now look here, when I was quite a young man I worked
very hard indeed, so hard, in fact, that I have seen the
drops of perspiration dropping from my manly brow onto
the pavement with a thud. Excuse me—yes, I say we shall
not work at all! Then again, my wooden, brainless youths,
answer me this: should men work between meals? No, no
certainly not; it is boisterous!

Other questions I would put before your notice tonight
are—why does Georgie Reid wear an eyeglass? Ha, ha my
friends we don't know where we are; therefore where we are
we do not know. Yes my noble-faced, flat-feeted, cockeyed,
rank-headed asses, I will put before your notice other questions but no longer will I linger on these tantalising subjects.
As time wags on and as I have to leave you; certainly I will
not take you with me, therefore I leave you. Now the best
of fools must part and as I see a policeman coming along
I will go. Goodnight!

THE PHANTOM BULLOCKY

The bullock driver, or 'bullocky', was an important member of the rural labour force in the era before the automobile and, in some places, for long after. The ability to control and work a team of sweating, bad tempered and reluctant beasts was highly prized and often handed down from father to son. A good bullocky could get work just about anywhere. It was a hard job, though, and the challenge of working bullock teams was a considerable one usually accomplished with a loud voice, special calls and extremely colourful language. The ability of a bullocky to swear—creatively and to good occupational purpose—was a measure of his status. Bush lore is full of songs, poems and stories about bullock drivers.

One particular tale, and its variants, has been well polished over the decades and, like quite a few other bush yarns, has also made it into literary form in Lance Skuthorpe's (1870–1958) 'The Champion Bullock Driver'. Bill Wannan included a version of the story—already of considerable age—in his *The Australian* (1954) and it has continued to be told and printed since then. Wannan's version includes a supernatural element that led him to call it 'The Phantom Bullocky':

> The boss is in need of a bullocky after his eight-yoke team of especially wild beasts had already sent fourteen bullockies to their graves. A bushman appears looking for a job, the boss asks him if he can swear well enough to handle a team and he replies that 'his conversation had set the stringybark trees on fire' in especially trying circumstances. The boss decides to give the bloke a trial and asks him to demonstrate his skills by imagining that eight panels of the wood and wire fence are a team of eight bullocks. The boss then gives the bloke the whip used by the fourteen deceased teamsters 'the handle was six feet, the lash eighteen feet of plaited greenhide, and there was two foot of silk cracker'.

The bloke runs the whip through his fingers then begins to work the fence, swearing, cheering and cracking the whip. Before long there is a blue flame running across the top fence wire. Suddenly the graves of the fourteen dead bullockies open and they jump out, each with a whip, and hail the bloke as King of the Bullockies, cheering and swearing and cracking their whips along the now fiery fence wire. Suddenly the fence posts began to move forward, just like a team of reluctant bullocks. The phantom bullockies and the bloke continued exhorting the fence onward in the traditional manner, plying their whips all the while until the fence strained so hard it ripped out the stringybark tree against which it had been strained and moved off at a flying pace over the hill with the bloke behind. The fourteen phantom bullockies gave another rousing cheer and disappeared back into their graves. The bloke returned with the fence and the amazed boss says he is the best bullocky he has ever seen and he can have the job. The bloke then laughs, gives another cheer and jumps into the air. 'He never came down again.'

Later versions of the tale are essentially the same, though drop the phantom bullockies and the bloke's disappearance into thin air, simply ending with him taking the job. Another variation has the outstanding bullocky doing much the same but letting the fence disappear into the backblocks. When he asks the boss if he can have the job, the boss replies, 'Any man who starts up a team an' fergits to stop 'em is no bloody good to me!'

A FINE TEAM OF BULLOCKS

They've been telling this yarn since Cooper's (or Cooper) Creek was first named, and probably long before:

A bullock driver had a crack team of beasts and on one particular trip was forced to get across a heavily flooded Cooper's Creek. Usually this is an impossible task, but on this occasion the floodwaters didn't look too deep, so the bullocky decided to give it a try.

He drew his team and wagon of wool up on the northern bank and spoke lovingly to them in the tender way that bullockies have, telling them that they now had a big challenge to get across the torrent. The bullocky then walked into the water and found that it was just up around his knees, showing his animals that it was not too dangerous.

He then went back and spoke lovingly to each and every one of the twenty-two beasts in the team. He told them what fine beasts they were and how he wanted them to pull together across the stream. Off they went, the lead bullock bravely forging ahead and the bullocky shouting encouragement to the team.

After a titanic effort, the bullocks, the wool wagon and the bullocky made it onto dry land at the other side. 'Whoa,' cried the bullocky, 'time for a rest.' As they settled down the bullocky looks back and sees with amazement that his champion team of bullocks have pulled the river 200 metres out of its course.

Without a word of a lie.

LANGUAGE!

Another bullock driver tale highlights the anti-authoritarianism and irreverence heard in much Australian folk humour. This one involves a bullocky in very trying circumstances, berating his beasts in the traditional colourful manner. The local parson happens by and sanctimoniously asks the bullocky if he knows where such language will take him. 'Yair,' the irate driver replies, 'to the bloody sawmill—or I'll cut every bastard bullock's bloody throat.'

The propensity of bullockies, or teamsters, to bad language was prodigious and legendary. It is the basis of a recitation known as Holy Dan in which an unusually righteous bullocky does not swear like the other bullockies when their beasts die of thirst in the Queensland drought. Instead, he counsels the other drivers and said it was:

> The Lord's all-wise decree,
> And if they'd only watch and wait,
> A change they'd quickly see.

But eventually even Holy Dan's twenty bullocks begin to die of thirst, and he entreats the Lord to send rain. No matter how hard he prays, the rain fails to fall and finally there is only one bullock left:

> Then Dan broke down—good Holy Dan—
> The man who never swore.
> He knelt beside the latest corpse,
> And here's the prayer he prore:

> 'That's nineteen Thou hast taken, Lord,
> And now you'll plainly see
> You'd better take the bloody lot,
> One's no damn good to me'.

> The other riders laughed so much,
> They shook the sky around,
> The lightning flashed, the thunder roared,
> And Holy Dan was drowned.

DROVING IN A BAR

The drover is a classic figure of bush lore and legend. Herding animals through heat, dust, mud and flies was tough and unpleasant work, but it seems to have inspired a great deal of humour, often based on enormous lies, like this one:

> They were boasting in the bar about the biggest mob of cattle they'd ever driven here, there and every bloody

where. One had drove a mob of 6000 from Perth to Wave Hill. At least, he had six thousand when he started but when he finished over two years later, he had 10 000. And so it went on.

An old bloke sat quietly in the corner, taking it all in. When there was a cool moment in the hot air, he piped up. 'You blokes talk about droving! Let me tell you about a real drive with a really BIG mob. Me and a mate broke the Australian droving record. We picked up a big mob at Barkly. Took us two days to ride right round 'em, it was that big. Anyway, we started with this mob and drove them clear down to Hobart.'

The bar fell into a stunned silence before one of the young blokes piped up. 'Ow'd ya get 'em across the Bass Strait?' he asked sarcastically.

The old drover looked closely at him and said, 'Don't be stupid, son, we went the other way.'

SLOW TRAINS

Modern Australia's founding and development coincided with the railway boom. The various colonial railways were eventually linked together by the Trans-Australian Railway, or 'the Trans', from 1917. Vital though the railways have been for the national economy, they do not necessarily run on time. Slow trains feature in railway yarns told throughout Australia. Versions of the following story have been collected in Tasmania, Queensland, South Australia, the Northern Territory and Western Australia.

The story often begins when a male passenger jumps off a train as it approaches the platform and rushes up to the stationmaster. The man asks for an ambulance to take his wife to hospital, as she is about to have a baby. The stationmaster rings the ambulance then turns to the man and says, 'She shouldn't have been travelling in that condition.' The man replies, 'She wasn't in that condition when she got on the train.'

Another slow train tale features the 'Spinifex Express' which used to run from Port Hedland to Marble Bar. It was always a pretty slow old trip and on one of these a passenger looked out the windows and saw the engine driver throwing seeds out on to the side of the track. All day the passenger watched as they crawled along. All the time the engine driver kept spreading what looked to the passenger to be tomato seeds. Eventually the passenger's curiosity got the better of him and he walked up to the engine and asked the driver, 'Why are you throwing tomato seeds onto the side of the line?'

The driver turned slowly round, fixed the passenger with a doleful eye and drawled: 'The guard's picking tomatoes.'

Some railway yarns revolve around the always-tense relationship between head office and the men working on the rail system itself. This story is told of named individuals, usually stationmasters, whose reports to head office were notoriously long and convoluted. Eventually head office formally instructed the stationmaster (in this Victorian version named Flanagan) to drastically shorten his reports in the future. The next time he had to report a derailment he wrote: 'off again, on again, gone again. Flanagan'.

SERVICE!

In this railway yarn, a passenger receives impeccable service:

A passenger boarded the train in Melbourne intending to get off at Albury. But when the conductor checked his ticket he had to tell him that the train didn't stop at Albury. The passenger went into a panic. 'I have to get off at Albury, it's a matter of life and death.' And pleaded with the conductor to stop the train for him.

The conductor said, 'Sorry, Sir, we can't stop the train at an unscheduled station but I do have a suggestion. I will ask the driver to slow down at Albury and I'll help you to alight from the train. It will be tricky and dangerous, but if I hold you outside the door by the collar and you start running we should be able to get you down without injury when your legs reach the right speed.'

The passenger was so desperate to get to Albury that he immediately agreed to this hazardous suggestion. 'Just one thing though,' said the conductor, 'after you're down be sure to stop running before you reach the end of the platform.' The plucky passenger nodded his agreement.

As the train approached Albury, the engine driver duly slowed down as much as he could. As soon as the platform came in sight, the conductor opened the door and held the passenger out over the platform. He began running in the air as he had been instructed and the train was about halfway along the station before the conductor gently lowered him down. He hit the platform and staggered but managed to stay upright, losing momentum gradually as he slowed his running legs. He managed to come to a teetering stop just before the end of the platform. Just then the last car rolled past and he was suddenly grabbed again by the collar and hauled back onto the train. Shocked, he twisted around to see the guard smiling happily at him—'Expect you thought you'd missed your train, Sir!'

MEEKATHARA ICE BLOCKS

Another favourite Western Australian railway story involves the Meekatharra gold escort:

On the old gold train, two security men were always locked into the van with the valuable cargo and it was always very hot. One day they had a bottle of whisky with them and asked the guard for some ice to cool down the drink.

The guard was friendly and soon produced a lump of ice. Of course, it melted away pretty quickly, so they asked for more ice. He brought it to them again. After a while their ice melted and they asked the guard for more. Once more he obligingly produced a nice fresh lump of ice from somewhere or other. This went on until the bottle was almost empty and they needed ice for one last drink each. Again they asked the guard for ice. But this time he said, 'Sorry boys, I don't think I'd better get you any more. The body's beginning to show.'

THE REDBACK SPIDER

A popular bush recitation tells the tale of a drunken shearer's undeserved good fortune with the help of a redback spider:

By the sluggish River Gwydir
Lived a wicked red-backed spider,
Who was just about as vicious as could be:
And the place that he was camped in
Was a rusty Jones's jam-tin
In a paddock by the show-grounds at Moree.

Near him lay a shearer snoozin':
He had been on beer and boozin'
All through the night and all the previous day;
And the rookin' of the rookers,
And the noise of showground spruikers,
Failed to wake him from the trance in which he lay.

Then a crafty-lookin' spieler
With a dainty little sheila
Came along collecting wood to make a fire.
Said the spieler, 'He's a boozer
And he's goin' to be a loser:
If he isn't, you can christen me a liar.'

'Hustle round and keep nit honey,
While I fan the mug for money,
And we'll have some little luxuries for tea.'
She answered, 'Don't be silly:

You go back and boil the billy.
You can safely leave the mug to little me!'

As she circled ever nearer,
'Till she reached the dopey shearer
With his pockets bulgin', fast asleep and snug:
But she did not see the spider
That was ringin' close beside her,
For her mind was on the money and the mug.

The spider sighted dinner,
He'd been daily growing thinner;
He'd been fasting and was hollow as an urn.
As she eyed the bulging pocket,
He just darted like a rocket
And he bit that rookin' sheila on the stern.

Then the sheila raced off squealin',
And her clothes she was un-peelin':
To hear her yells would make you feel forlorn.
One hand the bite was pressin',
While the other was undressin',
And she reached the camp the same as she was born!

Then the shearer, pale and haggard,
Woke up and back to town he staggered,
Where he caught the train and gave the grog a rest:
And he'll never know the spider,
That was camped beside the Gwydir,
Had saved him sixty smackers of the best!

THE GREAT AUSTRALIAN ADJECTIVE

First published in 1897, W.T. Goodge's brief poetic take on swearing manages to summarise the entire colourful field of Australian bad language:

The sunburnt —— stockman stood
And, in a dismal —— mood,
Apostrophized his —— cuddy;
'The —— nag's no —— good,
He couldn't earn his —— food —
A regular —— brumby,
——!'

He jumped across the —— horse
And cantered off, of —— course!
The roads were bad and —— muddy;
Said he, 'Well, spare me —— days
The —— Government's —— ways
Are screamin' —— funny,
——!'

He rode up hill, down —— dale,
The wind it blew a —— gale,
The crank was high and —— floody.
Said he: 'The —— horse must swim,
The same for —— me and him,
It's something —— sickenin',
——!'

He plunged me into the —— creek,
The —— horse was —— weak,
The stockman's face a —— study!
And though the —— horse was drowned
The —— rider reached the ground
Ejaculating : '——?
——!'

(*A 'cuddy' is a small horse.)

The great Australian adjective was also useful to describe conditions in Darwin during World War II:

This bloody town's a bloody cuss,
No bloody trams, no bloody bus,
And no one cares for bloody us,
In bloody, bloody Darwin.

The bloody roads are bloody bad,
The bloody folks are bloody mad,
They even say 'you bloody cad'
In bloody, bloody Darwin.

All bloody clouds and bloody rain,
All bloody stones, no bloody drains,
The council's got no bloody brains,
In bloody, bloody Darwin.

Everything's so bloody dear,
A bloody bob for bloody beer,
And is it good? no bloody fear,
In bloody, bloody Darwin.

The bloody 'flicks' are bloody old,
The bloody seats are bloody cold,
And can't get in for bloody gold,
Oh bloody, bloody Darwin.

The bloody dances make me smile,
The bloody band is bloody vile,
They only cramp your bloody style,
Oh bloody, bloody Darwin.

No bloody sports, no bloody games,
No bloody fun with bloody dames,
Won't even give their bloody names,
In bloody, bloody Darwin.

Best bloody place is bloody bed,
With bloody ice on bloody head,

And then they think you're bloody dead,
In bloody, bloody Darwin.

The bush has not only been implicated in the art of swearing. Many of the colourful expressions and idioms of Australian speech depend on a knowledge of the bush or at least some familiarity with its characteristics. If you are 'flat to the boards like a lizard drinking', you are far too busy to be bothered by anything else. 'Stone the crows', 'Fair crack of the whip' and 'In a pig's arse', or simply 'pigs', are venerable and well-known expressions.

The large stock of vernacular insults in Australian speech include many with a bush connection:

Mad as a cut snake
Kangaroos in the top paddock
White ants in the billy (crazy)
Useless as piles to a boundary rider
Ugly as a box of blowflies
More arse than a paddock-full of cows (cheeky; forward; overconfident)
Lower than a snake's belly

Or you could simply be described as a Drongo or a galah.

A few of the many other bush similes in the great Australian slanguage include:

Fit as a mallee bull
Pissed as a parrot
Stir the possum
It's Sydney or the bush
Bald as a bandicoot
As lean as a whip
As dry as a sunstruck bone

W.T. Goodge gave us yet another classic on the same subject:

'Tis the everyday Australian
Has a language of his own,
Has a language, or a slanguage,
Which can simply stand alone.
And a 'dickon pitch to kid us'
Is a synonym for 'lie',
And to 'nark it' means to stop it,
And to 'nit it' means to fly.

And a bosom friend's a 'cobber',
And a horse a 'prad' or 'moke',
While a casual acquaintance
Is a 'joker' or a 'bloke'.
And his lady-love's his 'donah'
or his 'clinah' or his 'tart'
Or his 'little bit o' muslin',
As it used to be his 'bart'.

And his naming of the coinage
Is a mystery to some,
With his 'quid' and 'half-a-caser'
And his 'deener' and his 'scrum'.
And a 'tin-back' is a party
Who's remarkable for luck,
And his food is called his 'tucker'
Or his 'panem' or his 'chuck'.

A policeman is a 'johnny'
Or a 'copman' or a 'trap',
And a thing obtained on credit
Is invariably 'strap'.
A conviction's known as 'trouble',
And a gaol is called a 'jug',
And a sharper is a 'spieler'
And a simpleton's a 'tug'.

If he hits a man in fighting
That is what he calls a 'plug',
If he borrows money from you
He will say he 'bit your lug'.
And to 'shake it' is to steal it,
And to 'strike it' is to beg;
And a jest is 'poking borac',
And a jester 'pulls your leg'.

Things are 'cronk' when they go wrongly
In the language of the 'push',
But when things go as he wants 'em
He declares it is 'all cush'.
When he's bright he's got a 'napper',
And he's 'ratty' when he's daft,
And when looking for employment
He is 'out o' blooming graft'.

And his clothes he calls his 'clobber'
Or his 'togs', but what of that
When a 'castor' or a 'kady'
Is the name he gives his hat!
And our undiluted English
Is a fad to which we cling,
But the great Australian slanguage
Is a truly awful thing!

LORE OF THE TRACK

An extensive body of folklore grew up around the swagman who 'humped his drum' along the 'tucker track'. One of the many classic yarns highlights the legendary reluctance of swagmen to indulge in more conversation than was necessary:

A couple of swaggies are tramping along together in the usual silence. Around mid-afternoon they come across the bloated carcass of a large animal on the side of the road. That night as they settle down in their camp, one says to the other, 'Did you notice that dead horse we saw this afternoon?'

It wasn't until lunchtime the following day that the other swaggie answered: 'It wasn't a horse, it was a bullock.'

The next morning he woke up but his mate was nowhere to be seen. But he'd left a note. It read: 'I'm off, there's too much bloody argument for me.'

The swaggie's dry sense of humour features in more than a few yarns:

One day out on the track out the back of Bourke, a swaggie runs out of food. Somewhere along the Darling River he comes across a ramshackle selection. He knocks on the door of the tumbledown shack and asks the farmer's wife for some food for his dog, thinking perhaps that this would encourage her sympathy. But the wife refuses, saying she can't be handing out food to lazy tramps and flea-bitten mongrels.

'Alright then missus,' says the swaggie, 'but can yer lend me a bucket?'

'What do you want that for?' she asks suspiciously.

'To cook me dog in.'

In this nugget from the 1930s the swaggie is called a 'tramp', but his sense of humour and irreverence towards the Arch–deacon and his four white ponies is pure bush:

Archdeacon Stretch, of Victoria, had been transferred to a big parish in New South Wales, where a kindly-disposed squatter, evidently somewhat partial to archdeacons, presented him with four handsome creamy ponies and a fine Abbott buggy. One day this Archdeacon was spinning along behind his creamies at a merry pace when he espied a tramp at the roadside whom he at once took aboard. Whether actuated by a purely generous impulse, or a wish to obtain the services of a gate-opener along the pastoral route, this article is little concerned. After a while, the tramp said: 'My word, that is a fine team of creamies, sir; when's the rest of the circus coming along?'

As well as having a sense of humour, the swaggie could, however, also display compassion to those less fortunate than himself:

Billy Seymour was another well-known swagman of the 'Outback' tracks, but he has since turned cane-farmer, and the bush roads know him no more. Travelling somewhere over Muttaburra way one time Billy called at a roadside humpy, and appealed to the woman who presented herself at the door, to fill his ration bags. The woman was sympathetic but said that she had very little food in the house. Her husband had been away droving for three months, and she had received no money from him during his absence. If he didn't write soon she couldn't imagine what she was going to do.

Billy pulled his old battered tobacco-box from his pocket and opening it, drew from its interior a crinkled and worn one-pound note. 'Here Missus,' he said, 'take this; I was saving it until I got to town, but spare me days I reckon you need it more than I do.'

SNIFFLING JIMMY

Another colourful swagman ended up in the first AIF, where the skills of living off the land and on one's wits stood him in good stead:

Nomads of the long and dusty track!! Yes, I've met them and studied their habits and characteristics, and many of them have been strange folk indeed. Most of them belonged to the past generation of 'matilda-waltzers' who have since disappeared from the roads, and their place has been taken by others who will never possess the rare humor or suffer the hardships of the men I am now going to tell about. Throw a log on the fire, draw closer to the cheering blaze and listen:

Just before I left North Queensland in 1914 to enlist in the A.I.F. I met a well-known track character who was better known as 'Sniffling Jimmy.' He was a short nuggety-built fellow with a freckled face and a mop of fiery red hair that would have turned a Papuan green with envy. I.e., if the natives of our vast Northern island have a liking for red hair. He was about 35 years of age and said that in his time he had walked through nearly every city and township between Melbourne and Townsville. He rarely did any work, and with a merry twinkle in his eye he said that when a boy his mother was much concerned about his constitution, so he promised her that he would never do a day's work if he could help it.

Jimmy was one of the very few teetotal swagmen I have met, and when he refused my offer to come in and have 'one' he said that he never touched anything stronger than water in his life. However, his specialty was soliciting free rations at some wayside squatter's homestead or farmer's home. Rarely has a swagman ever uttered such a pathetic oration. If his appeal to have his bag filled met with an abrupt refusal he would rattle off something like the following: 'Oh, have a heart lady; If it wasn't for me weak constitution I wouldn't be compelled to beg for food. You see. I was reared in poverty and besides me mother and an invalid father, there were 13 other children in our family. There wasn't enough money coming into the house to provide sufficient nourishment for all of us and as a result I did not get much to eat.'

'But you appear healthy enough,' said a Proserpine woman one day.

'Ah yes lady,' replied Jimmy, 'but you know that outside appearances are often deceptive; me constitution is injured in me interior.'

One day in 1915 I was carrying a bag of bombs from Monash Gully to Courtney's Post at Anzac, and about half way I came upon four men digging an eight-foot trench, through shaly ground, under snipers' fire. I instantly recognised one of the men as 'Sniffling Jimmy.'

'Hullo! You are working at last,' I said.

'Oh yes,' he replied, 'army rations agree with me constitution.'

Just then a sniper's bullet lifted the dirt a few inches away from where he was working and he began to dig the pick frantically into the ground. I passed on and did not meet him again, but I hope he returned to Australia without loss of health or limb.

THE POETIC SWAGGIE

Others less literary and unknown also caught the swaggie's lifestyle and ethos from another angle:

Kind friends, pray give attention
To this, my little song.
Some rum things I will mention,
And I'll not detain you long.
I'm a swagman on the wallaby,
Oh! don't you pity me.

At first I started shearing,
And I bought a pair of shears.
On my first sheep appearing,
Why, I cut off both its ears.
Then I nearly skinned the brute,
As clean as clean could he.
So I was kicked out of the shed,
Oh! don't you pity me, &c.

I started station loafing,
Short stages and took my ease;

So all day long till sundown
I'd camp beneath the trees.
Then I'd walk up to the station,
The manager to see.
'Boss, I'm hard up and I want a job,
Oh! don't you pity me,' &c.

Says the overseer: 'Go to the hut.
In the morning I'll tell you
If I've any work about
I can find for you to do.'
But at breakfast I cuts off enough
For dinner, don't you see.
And then my name is Walker.
Oh! don't you pity me.

And now, my friends, I'll say good-bye,
For I must go and camp.
For if the Sergeant sees me
He may take me for a tramp;
But if there's any covey here
What's got a cheque, d'ye see,
I'll stop and help him smash it.
Oh! don't you pity me.
I'm a swagman on the wallaby,
Oh! don't you pity me.

Shopkeepers would often provide passing swaggies with the means to take them through to the next stage of their journey. Henry Lawson noted this during his trek to Hungerford in 1892:

We saw one of the storekeepers give a dead-beat swagman five shillings worth of rations to take him on into Queensland. The storekeepers often do this, and put it down on the loss side of their books. I hope the recording angel listens, and puts it down on the right side of his book.

This was not because Hungerford was a prosperous place, only consisting of 'two houses and a humpy in New South Wales, and five houses in Queensland. Characteristically enough, both the pubs are in Queensland.' It was one of the unspoken obligations of bush life in which it was customary to provide assistance to travelers down on their luck.

Swagmen were not necessarily poorly educated, and in some cases were not even poor. There are many examples of swagmen who knew the classics, literature, art and philosophy as well as some professors. Sometimes these were men who had fallen on hard times, frequently due to the grog, perhaps gambling or other problems. Some had the means to live a settled life but chose to carry their drums along the tracks of Australia. A well-known case is that of Joseph Jenkins (1818–1898). After an early life as a successful farmer in Wales, Jenkins apparently suffered a breakdown of some sort aggravated by drinking and took passage to the colony of Victoria. Here he took to the road, taking whatever work he could get and writing award-winning poetry and campaigning in local newspapers to better the lot of bush workers. He kept a journal of his wanderings, later published as the *Diary of a Welsh Swagman* (1975), in which he wrote about politics, social conditions and Aboriginal people, among many other topics.

Many men spent parts of their lives as swaggies, sometimes as a necessity, sometimes as a way of seeking their fortunes as in the classic fairytales about ne'er-do-wells eventually doing well. Famous examples are the bush entrepreneur R.M. Williams and the novelist Donald Stuart. Even aristocrats were known to shoulder their swags from time to time.

WHERE THE ANGEL TARBOYS FLY

In 1908, a swaggie calling himself 'Vagrant' gave a blow-by-blow account of the great tallies of some legendary blade men. He managed to include a little verse, a yarn or two and a wonderful story made up of many stories about the competitive and boastful life of the shearer:

The shearing figures quoted in the 'Western Champion' of the 12th of September as to shearing tallies, are not quite correct. Andy Brown did not shear at Evesham in 1886. In 1887 Jimmy Fisher shore fifty lambs in one run before breakfast there. I do not know the time; but they used to ring the bell mighty early those days. I have seen spectral-like forms creeping across the silent space between the galley and the shed long before the kookaburra woke the bush with his laughing song, and he is a pretty early bird.

The same year Black Tom Johnson got bushed in the gloom of that space, and lost half a run before breakfast. Fisher shore 288 at Kynuna the following year: he was a wonderful man for his 8 st. of humanity. The same year Alf Bligh shore 254 at Isis Downs; he and Charlie Byers were the first two men to cut 200 sheep on the Barcoo. The same year Bill Hamilton, now M.L.A., shore 200 sheep at Manfred Downs, and to him belongs the credit of shearing the first 200 on the Flinders.

The next year Bill died at Cambridge Gulf; but as he is alive and all right now, the account was exaggerated. Bill says: 'That 200 at Manfred Downs was no "cake walk".' He used twelve gallons of water cooling down. Alick Miller shore 4163 sheep in three weeks and three days at Charlotte Plains, in 1885, and Sid ('Combo') Ross shore nine lambs in nine minutes at Belalie, on the Warrego, the year before.

In the early eighties there were a good number of 200-a-day men in New South Wales; but none of those celebrated personages ventured a pilgrimage northwards until 1887, when quite a number of fast men stormed the west, and their advent started a new era in the shearing world, improved tools and methods entirely superseding the old Ward and Payne, and Sorby school, and the old rum drinking ringers of the roaring days were gradually relegated to the 'snagger brigade.' Paddy M'Can, Jack Bird, Tom Green ('the Burdekin ringer'), Ned Hyles, Jack Ellis (Bendigo), Mick Hoffman (the Peak Downs ringer), Billy Cardham, Jim Sloane, Jack Collins, and George Taylor ('the Native') had to give way to the younger brigade with improved Burgon and Ball tools, and new ideas, and, with the advent of Jack Howe, Christy Gratz, 'Chinee' Sullivan, Billy Mantim, George Butler, Jimmy Power, Alick Miller, Jack Reid, Allan M'Callum, and others, 180 and 200 were common enough.

Later, when machinery was introduced, tallies took a further jump. Jimmy Power shore 323 at Barenya in 1892 by machines. The same year Jack Howe shore 321 by hand at Alice Downs, his tallies for the week previous being 249, 257, 259, 263, 267, 144, a total of 1439 for the week. I doubt if this record has ever been beaten. I will say right here that Jack Howe was the best shearer I have ever seen at work. The only one approaching him was Lynch, of the Darling River, New South Wales.

No doubt figures get enlarged in circulation, and tall tallies in the bar-room mount up with the fumes of bottled beer—there is a lot of sheep shorn there. Shearers do not lie, as a rule: they boast and make mistakes casually. Jack Howe once told me the biggest mistake he ever made was in trying to shake hands with himself in a panel mirror in an hotel in Maoriland. He had just landed, and made for the first hotel. You see, he had grown a beard on the trip over, and looked like a chap he used to know on the Barcoo. The mistake was considerably intensified by the barmaid's smile, as she watched Jack's good-natured recognition of an old shearing mate from Queensland.

At Kensington Downs in 1885, a big Chinaman named Ah Fat rang the shed. He could shear all right, too. The men used to take day about to run him [take turns to beat him]; but the Chow had too much pace. A shearer named George Mason made great preparations to 'wipe him out' one day, and, after nearly bursting himself up to dinner-time, discovered that Ah Fat was not on the board: he was doing a lounge in the hut that day. I think that Chinaman must have died; everyone loved him, and, like Moore's 'Young Gazelle,' with its gladsome eye, he was sure to go—

To that shed beyond the sky,
Where the angel tarboys fly,
And the 'cut' will last for ever, and
The sheep are always dry.

These records may be of interest to the survivors of the old school, and may, perhaps, stir up the dormant memories of the younger ones. They have been culled from past records, written on the backs of stolen telegram forms from almost every post office between Burketown and Barringun, and are given for what they merit.

BOWYANG BILL AND THE COCKY FARMER

'Bowyang Bill' recalled an experience of his younger days, just around the turn of the twentieth century. If Bill is to be believed, on this occasion at least, he worked very hard for one of the notoriously tight-fisted and hard-handed cocky farmers. (A 'bowyang' was a length of string tied around trousers just below the knee to keep them up. They were commonly worn by working men in the nineteenth century and many illustrations of swaggies feature them.)

Bowyang Bill begins his story with a short verse that could be a memorial for the swaggies' way of life and death:

For they tramp and go as the world rolls back,
They drink and gamble, and die;
But their spirits shall live on the outback track.
As long as the years go by.

Remember those cockies who used to wake a fellow at 2 a.m. in the morning to start the day's work? They are not so plentiful as they were 30 odd years back, but there's still a few of them milking cows or growing spuds in this State.

All this takes me back to the time when I tied my first knot in the swag and started out along the dusty tracks to make my fortune. After many weeks I came to Dawson's place. He was a long, lean hungry sort of codger, and his bleary eyes sparkled when I agreed to work for five bob a week and tucker. I didn't know Dawson or I would have wasted no time in re-hoisting Matilda and proceeding on my way. I worked 16 hours a day on that place, and lived mostly on damper and flybog. I used to get up so early in the morning that I was ashamed to look at the sleeping fowls when I passed their camping place. I never saw those fowls moving about their yard. They were sleeping on their roosts when I went to work, and they were snoozing on the same roosts when I returned to the house at night.

Things went on like this until another young cove came along with a swag. It was also his first experience 'carrying the bundle,' and no doubt that was why he also agreed to work for Dawson. He said his name was Mullery. We had tea at 11 p.m. the day he arrived, and it was midnight when we turned into our bunks in the harness-room. Before I went to sleep I told Mullery what sort of a place it was, but he said he would stick it—until he earned a few bob to carry him along the track. In the next breath he told me he was greatly interested in astronomy. I didn't know what that was until he explained he was interested in the stars. 'Well, by cripes,' I said, 'you'll get plenty of opportunities to examine them here.'

That cove was over the odds. I'm just dozing off when he leans over and says, 'Do you know how far it is from here to Mars?' Pulling the old potato bag wagga from my face I told him I hadn't the faintest idea, as I had never travelled along the road to the blanky place. He mentioned the millions of miles it was from here to there. 'Did you measure the distance with a foot-rule?' I asked as I again drew the wagga over my face.

When old Dawson pushed his head through the door at 2 a.m. I was awake but the new chap was dead to the world. Dawson went across and yanked the blanket off him. 'Here, hurry up', he growled, 'and get those cows milked before they get sun-stroke.' 'What's going to give them sunstroke?' asked Muller, as innocent as you like. 'Why, the blanky sun, of course,' roared Dawson. The new chap made himself more comfortable in his bunk, then he drawled, 'There's no danger of that, sir, and allow me to inform you that at this time of the year the sun is 93 million miles from the earth.'

'You're a liar,' yelled Dawson, shaking the hurricane lamp in Mullery's face, 'and if you come outside I'll prove it to you. Why, the darned sun is just peeping over the tops of the gum trees half-a-mile from here, and by the time it's well above them you'll be on the track again. Yes, you're sacked, so get out of here quick and lively.'

A GOOD FEED

This one is an old favourite:

The horse breaker had been living on mutton, tea and damper for months and was well ready for a break on the coast. As he rode through the country one night, he came to a farm run by an old cocky and his attractive young wife. He asked the cocky if he could have a bed for the night and something to eat. The uncharacteristically generous cocky said that he could share the evening meal and stay for the night. But there was only one bed, so they'd all have to sleep together. This was fine with the horse breaker and he sat down at the table as the farmer's wife served dinner, making eyes at him as she did so. The food was wonderful and an awful lot better than the diet he'd been living on and the young wife was much easier on the eyes than the horses he'd been breaking. Unfortunately, the cocky and his wife were not heavy eaters and he hadn't eaten his fill when the meal was cleared away and the leftovers placed in the meat safe.

As the meal was over and there was not a lot else to do, they all agreed to turn in for the night. The cocky slept in the middle of the bed, with his wife on one side and the horse breaker on the other. It wasn't long before the old bloke was fast asleep and snoring and not long after that before the horse breaker and the young woman were fondling each other's hands across her husband's sleeping body. This went on for some time when there was a dreadful squawking from the chook yard. The cocky sat bolt upright in bed: 'There's that bloody fox again,' he cried as he jumped, grabbed his rifle and headed out into the night. 'Now's our chance,' said the young wife to the horse breaker. 'Too right,' he answered enthusiastically as he rolled across the bed towards her waiting arms. But to her surprise, he jumped right over her, ran to the meat safe and ate up the rest of the food.

THE SWAGMAN'S UNION

Folklore has it that there was such a thing as a 'Swagman's Union'. According to this account, an organisation of this type was formed in the 1870s and had some interesting rules by which its members were allegedly regulated:

The old-time swagman is fast disappearing, but to-day my thoughts go back to some of the real old-time 'whalers' of the Murrumbidgee and other Southern watercourses (writes 'Bill Bowyang'). The genuine 'whaler' in the halcyon days of yore was a feature of the Murrumbidgee tracks and along the routes fringing some of the Western Queensland rivers.

Those who carried the swag on the Lachlan were known as the 'Lachlan Cruisers' but there were also the 'Darling Whisperers,' the 'Murray Sundowners,' and the 'Bogan Bummers.' Each member cherished an unbounding pride in his clan, and there were at times fierce fights under the big river gums when some favored fishing hole was usurped by an interloper from an alien band.

Scanning an old scrap book recently I came across an interesting record of an occurrence that at the time created a great stir in swag men circles throughout the West. It tells of a meeting that was held to bring about a combination of the scattered units of swaggiedom in a society known as the 'Amalgamated Swagmen of Australia.' This first union was formed in a bend of the Lachlan, near Forbes, in 1877, and a conference of delegates from far and wide gathered for the occasion. They were a motley crew, frowsy dead beats, loony-hatters, and aggressive cadgers.

By the fitful flames of yarran and myall fires, officers were elected, branches formed, and rules drawn up. Sir William Wallaby was the first President, and Sir John Bluey, secretary; T. Billy Esq. is named as treasurer, and Dr. Johnny Cake medical adviser. The well-known firm of Walker and Tucker were solicitors. The rules were as follows:

1. No member to be over 100 years old.
2. Each member to pay one pannikin of flour entrance fee. Members who don't care about paying will be admitted free.
3. No member to carry swags weighing over ten pounds.
4. Each member to possess three complete sets of tucker bags, each set to consist of nine bags.
5. No member to pass any station, farm, boundary rider's hut, camp, or private house without 'tap-ping' and obtaining rations or hand outs.
6. Each member to allow himself to be bitten by a sheep. If a sheep bites a member he must immediately turn it into mutton.
7. Members who defame a 'good' cook, or pay a fine when run in, shall not be allowed to enter the Kingdom of Heaven. Amen.

8. No members allowed to hum baking powder, tea, flour, sugar, or tobacco from a fellow unionist.

9. Non-smoking members must 'whisper' for tobacco on every possible occasion, the same as smokers.

10. At general or branch meetings non-smoking hums must give up their whispered tobacco to be distributed amongst the officers of the society.

11. Any member found without at least two sets of bags filled with tucker will be fined.

12. No member to own more than one creek, river, or billabong bend. To sell bends for old boots or sinkers is prohibited.

13. No member to look for or accept work of any description. Members found willing will be at once expelled.

14. No member to walk more than five miles per day if rations can be hummed.

15. No member to tramp on Sundays at any price.

This union is many years defunct and its original members as widely scattered as the ashes of their long-dimmed camp-fires, yet the spirit and the rules are adhered to sacredly, even in these days, by those who hump the swag. Par chance these rules extend to Paradise, and the sturdy beggars still tramp through eternity with Matilda up.

Amongst the old time 'whalers', Scotty the Wrinkler was perhaps the most famous. A garrulous Scotch man of scholarly attainments, he had, perhaps, less need to cadge than any other. Scotty I always recognised as somewhat of a poseur. His habits were so settled that he dwelt most of the year in a huge hollow log on the banks of the Murrumbidgee, near Narrandera, and he even acquired his name from the original holder, who was a Darling River Whisperer.

A GLORIOUS SPREE

Australia's long love affair with the grog begins with the 'Rum Corps' in colonial New South Wales and extends to the present.

Along the way have been told many beery tales of mammoth sprees and monumental hangovers. The balladry of the bush overflows with references to alcohol, much of it 'sly' or illegal. The 'hocussed' or adulterated shanty grog took down many a shearer's cheque. A famous example occurs in 'On the Road to Gundagai', where a bloke named Bill and his mate make the mistake of camping at Lazy Harry's sly grog tent on their way to Sydney with the season's shearing wages:

> In a week the spree was over and our cheque was all
> knocked down
> So we shouldered our Matildas and we turned our backs
> on town.
> And the girls stood us nobblers as we sadly said goodbye,
> And we tramped from Lazy Harry's on the road to Gundagai.

In vain did the forces of law and order try to police and control the sly-grog trade. Colonists mostly insisted on their right to a drink and the grog quickly became an element of the 'fair go' ethos, as events at Pakenham demonstrated in 1879:

> An interesting raid was made by the revenue officers of the Shire of Berwick, on Wednesday last, on a number of unlicensed shanty-keepers, who for some time past have been carrying on an illicit traffic in liquor in the neighbourhood of a large quarry near the Gippsland railway, about seven miles from Berwick, from which metal has been obtained for the Oakleigh end of the line. At this place a large camp of quarry men and stonebreakers has been formed consisting of about 100 tents and shanties of all kinds and descriptions, and as there are no public houses in the locality sly grog-selling is carried on to a great extent.
>
> It came to the knowledge of the Revenue officers a few days ago that a large quantity of spirituous liquor had been sent up to the camp and having determined to take some action to put a stop to this illicit traffic, the revenue

inspector, Mr. Robinson, visited the place on Wednesday last, accompanied by the inspector of licensed premises, Mr A. Cartledge, and three mounted constables, and made a sudden descent on the camp before the casks and cases; containing the liquor, could be removed or secreted by their owners. At the first place which was visited, that of Mr. R. Stout's, about a dray load of stock was seized and placed in a dray which had been provided for the occasion.

In the meantime a large number of the navvies had assembled, and seeing the state of affairs commenced looting the shanties and grogshops in spite of the efforts of the police, who endeavoured to roll back the casks into the tents as the mob took them out, but of course were outnumbered, and the result was that casks of bottled beer and cases of brandy, whisky, &c. were smashed open and rifled. By this time the mob had increased to about 100 persons, and an assault was made on the police by a party armed with pickhandles, sticks and other weapons, and the police were rather severely handled—so much so that they had to produce their revolvers, and the revenue officer's party took advantage of the tranquilising effect which this manoeuvre produced to retire from the camp.

The scene that ensued baffles description; yelling and screaming the mob either stoved in the ends of the casks and opened the cases and removed their contents for immediate consumption, or took them away into the bush for a future occasion. It is estimated that about £30 of spirituous liquor was taken or destroyed by the mob, including the dray load, which the inspector had seized.

Not surprisingly the police were planning to summon the known rioters to court.

THE DIMBOOLA CAT FARM

Modern electronic narratives include tales circulated on paper, usually produced with some form of reprographic machine, such as the typewriter, spirit duplicator, Gestetner or, from the late 1940s, the electronic photocopier. Since the 1980s the facsimile machine, followed by email and the internet, have also provided opportunities for business send-up stories to be created and re-created. As with urban legends and some other story forms, these are often international in scope and circulation, but they are also characterised by adaptation to local circumstances.

One of the earliest known examples of these stories in Australia is a satirical item usually titled 'The Dimboola Cat Farm':

WILD CAT SYNDICATE, DIMBOOLA

Dear Sir,

Knowing that you are always interested and open for an investment in a good live proposition. I take the liberty of presenting to you what appears to be a most wonderful business, in which no doubt you will take a lovely interest and subscribe towards the formation of the Company. The objects of the Company are to operate a large cat ranch near Dimboola, where land can be purchased cheap for the purpose.

To start with we want 1,000,000 cats. Each cat will average about 12 kittens per year; the skins from 1/6 for the white one to 2/6 for the pure black ones. This will give us 12,000,000 skins a year to sell at an average of 2/- each, making our revenue about £2500 per day.

A man can skin about 100 cats a day, at 15/- per day wages, and it will take 100 men to operate the ranch; therefore the net profit per day will be £2425. We feed the cats on rats and will start a rat ranch; the rats multiply four times as fast as the cats.

We start with 1,000,000 rats and will have four rats per cat from which the skins have been taken, giving each rat one quarter of a cat. It will thus be seen that the whole business will be self-acting and automatic throughout. The cats will eat the rats and for the rats' tails we will get the government grant of four pence per tail. Other by-products are guts for tennis racquets, whiskers for wireless sets, and cat's pyjamas for Glenelg flappers. Eventually we will cross the cats with snakes, and they will skin themselves twice a year, thus saving the men's wages for skinning and also getting two skins per cat per year.

Awaiting your prompt reply, and trusting that you will appreciate this most wonderful opportunity to get rich quick.

Yours faithfully
Babbling Brook, Promoter

A half-century or so later, the story was still going the rounds. It appeared in the form of a photocopied A4 sheet and with a few modern additions such as conversion to decimal currency and a more modern enticement to invest: 'The offer to participate in this investment opportunity of a lifetime has only been made to a limited number of individuals—so send your cheque now!' Otherwise, it was the same bizarre tale.

A FARMER'S LAMENT

Life on the land is full of troubles, many originating in Canberra:

It all started back in 1966, when they changed to dollars and overnight my overdraft doubled.

I was just getting used to this when they brought in kilograms and my wool cheque dropped by half.

Then they started playing around with the weather and brought in Celsius and millimetres, and we haven't had a decent fall of rain since.

As if this wasn't enough, they had to change over to hectares and I end up with less than half the farm I had.

So one day I sat down and had a good think. I reckon with daylight saving I was working eight days a week, so I decided to sell out.

Then, to cop it all, I had only got the place in the agent's hand when they changed to kilometres and I find I'm too flaming far out of town!

WHAT'S ON, COOKIE?

Bush cooks were the butt of many humorous anecdotes and yarns, especially the shearer's cook, also known as a 'babbling brook', or just a 'babbler', in rhyming slang. For her work on Western Australian shearing sheds, author June Lacy collected many occupational anecdotes, including this one recorded from shearing legend Reg Dunbar at Kingsley in 1995:

It was the first shed and first meal after getting off the plane. The bell rings for tea. 'What's on cookie?' was the usual question. 'Good soup mate, I can recommend it,' is the standard answer. 'Good soup, right on,' I replied and lifted the pot lid. A sheep's head was staring at us. A bit of wool still on it—teeth, ears, and the tongue protruding, with a couple of carrots and onions trying to knock out the eyes. Hell, straight from the killing-pen. Turned me off soup forever. The Union Rep took one look and bellowed in no uncertain terms, 'You won't cook for us any more. You're sacked, you bastard. You never wiped his nose!'

This story well illustrates the terse mode of yarn-spinning, telling the personal experience with a humorous sting in the tale that is at once amusing, suggestive of the toughness of the shearing life and falling squarely within a tradition that would be familiar to anyone involved in this line of work.

THE MAIDEN COOK

This epic from the early twentieth century tells how a drover's cook learned the trade. (Tooraweenah is in New South Wales, near Gilgandra, and Gummin is probably Gummin Gummin station in the Warrumbungles, near Coonabarabran.)

He was working on a road job,
Out Tooraweenah way,
But he didn't like the work at all,
And he didn't like the pay.

He was getting six and sixpence,
And he didn't think it right,
For he had to work so hard all day
That he couldn't sleep at night.

He camped on an early riser,
On some leaves beneath a fly,
And he was always up before
The stars were off the sky.

He had only half a blanket,
And the nap was worn off that;
So for convenience sake he slept in
His trousers, boots, and hat.

He longed for something better,
And he longed for change of life,
So he took a job of cooking,
Off a drover chap, named Fyfe.

And he drove along to Gummin,
With a free and easy mind,
And never once regretted
The job he'd left behind.

They were shearing at the station
And the drovers and the cook
Stopped the night and had their supper
With the shearers' 'Babbling Brook.'

They were taking sheep from Gummin,
Three thousand head or more,
And the drover's cook was happy,
Though he'd never cooked before.

And they rose up in the morning
Before the break of day;
And when the sun had risen,
They were a mile upon their way.

When the evening meal was over,
And his mates were all asleep,
The maiden cook then set to work
To kill his maiden sheep.

He tied its legs together
Put an edge upon his knife,
And by the camp fire murdered
The first sheep in his life.

It took him hours to skin it,
'Twas a picture then to see,
As on a rope it dangled
Beneath a leaning tree.

But he soon got used to killing,
And to fixing up the breaks,
And he soon got used to cooking
Stews and chops, and bread and cakes.

But he never had such trouble,
In the present or the past,
As the night he baked the damper,
When the rain was falling fast.

Beneath a leaning gum tree
He built a roaring fire,
Put the dough into an oven,
Which hung upon a wire.

The rain then fell in torrents,
And the cook was in a state,
As he stood above the oven,
Like a jockey losing weight.

With his overcoat he sheltered
That damper from the rain,
And he swore by all that's holy
That he'd never cook again.

And he cursed and swore like blazes;
But it didn't matters mend,
So he cooked on to the finish,
Till they reached their journey's end.

And he left his mates in Gulgong,
For a different way they took.
But the boss before he said adieu
Gave a reference to the cook.

THE FARMER'S WILL

Life on the land has always been tough, but dying on it can be even harder, as the maker of this will suggests:

I've left my soul to me banker—he's got the mortgage on it anyway.

I've left my conversion calculator to the Metrification Board. Maybe they'll be able to make sense of it.

I have a couple of last requests. The first one is to the weatherman: I want rain, hail and sleet for the funeral. No sense in finally giving me good weather just because I'm dead.

And last, but not least, don't bother to bury me—the hole I'm in now is big enough. Just cremate me and send me ashes to the Taxation Office with this note: 'Here you are, you bastards, now you've got the lot'.

A Farmer

*Mr V.J. White, Assistant Chief Protector of Aborigines
in the Northern Territory, with 'Paddy' the camel, near
Ayers Rock (Uluru), 1935.*

7

THE LAWS OF LIFE

*They like to make it tough—but they can't make it tough
enough!*

Anon

RULES FOR BEING HUMAN

1. You will receive a body. You may like it or hate it, but it
   will be yours for the entire period this time around.
2. You will learn lessons. You are enrolled in a full-time
   informal school called life. Each day in this school you
   will have the opportunity to learn lessons. You may like
   the lessons or think them irrelevant and stupid.
3. There are no mistakes, only lessons. Growth is a process
   of trial and error, experimentation. The 'failed' experi-
   ments are as much a part of the process as the experiment
   that ultimately 'works'.
4. A lesson is repeated until learned. A lesson will be
   presented to you in various forms until you have learned
   it. When you have learned it, you can go on to the next
   lesson.

5. Learning lessons does not end. There is no part of life that does not contain its lessons. If you are alive, there are lessons to be learned.

6. 'There' is no better than 'here'. When your 'there' has become a 'here' you will simply obtain another 'there' that will, again, look better than 'here'.

7. Others are merely mirrors of you. You cannot love or hate something about another person unless it reflects to you something you love or hate about yourself.

8. What you make of your life is up to you. You have all the tools and resources you need. What you do with them is up to you. The choice is yours.

9. Your answers lie inside you. The answers to life's questions lie inside you. All you need to do is look, listen, and trust.

10. You will forget all this . . .

APPLICATION FOR AUSTRALIAN CITIZENSHIP

A popular send-up of the citizenship test for migrants wishing to become Australian citizens:

Australian Government Department of Immigration and Multicultural and Indigenous Affairs

You must answer 75% (28 or more out of 37) of these questions correctly in order to qualify for Australian Citizenship.

1. How many slabs can you fit in the back of a Falcon Ute while also allowing room for your cattle dog?

2. When packing an Esky do you put the ice, or the beer, in first?

3. Is the traditional Aussie Christmas dinner:
   a) At least two roasted meats with roast vegetables, followed by a pudding you could use as a cannonball. Also ham. In 40°C heat.

    b) A seafood buffet followed by a barbie, with rather a lot of booze. And ham. In 40°C heat.

    c) Both of the above, one at lunchtime and one at dinnertime. Weather continues fine.

4. How many beers in a slab?

5. You call that a knife, this is a knife.

True or False?

6. Does 'yeah-nah' mean?

    a) 'Yes and no'

    b) 'Maybe'

    c) 'Yes I understand but No I don't agree'

7. The phrases 'strewth' and 'flamin' dingo' can be attributed to which TV character?

    a) Toadie from *Neighbours*

    b) Alf from *Home & Away*

    c) Agro from *Agro's Cartoon Connection*

    d) Sgt Tom Croydon from *Blue Heelers*

8. When cooking a barbecue do you turn the sausages:

    a) Once or twice

    b) As often as necessary to cook

    c) After each stubby

    d) Until charcoal

9. Name three of the Daddo brothers.

10. Who was the original lead singer of AC/DC?

11. Which option describes your ideal summer afternoon:

    a) Drinking beer at a mate's place

    b) Drinking beer at the beach

    c) Drinking beer watching the cricket/footy

    d) Drinking beer at a mate's place while watching the cricket before going to the beach

12. Would you eat pineapple on a pizza? Would you eat egg on a pizza?

13. How many cans of beer did David Boon consume on a plane trip from Australia to England?

14. How many stubbies is it from Brissy to the Gold Coast in a Torana travelling at 120 km/h?

15. Who are Scott and Charlene?
16. How do you apply your tomato sauce to a pie?
    a) Squirt and spread with finger
    b) Sauce injection straight into the middle
17. If the police raided your home, would you:
    a) Allow them to rummage through your personal items
    b) Phone up the nearest talkback radio shock jock and complain
    c) Put a written complaint in to John Howard and hope that he answers it personally
18. Which Australian Prime Minister held the world record for drinking a yardie full of beer the fastest?
19. Have you ever had/do you have a mullet?
20. Thongs are:
    a) Skimpy underwear
    b) Casual footwear
    c) They're called jandals, bro
21. On which Ashes tour did Warney's hair look the best?
    a) 1993
    b) 1997
    c) 2001
    d) 2005
22. What is someone more likely to die of:
    a) Redback spider
    b) Great white shark
    c) Victorian police officer
    d) King brown snake
    e) Your missus after a big night
    f) Drop bear
23. How many times must a steak be turned on a conventional four-burner barbie?
24. Can you sing along to Cold Chisel's 'Khe Sanh'?
25. Explain both the 'follow-on' and 'LBW' rules in cricket and discuss the pros and cons for the third umpire decisions in the latter . . .
26. Name at least 5 items that must be taken to a BBQ.

27. Who is the current Australian test cricket captain:
    a) Ricky Ponting
    b) Don Bradman
    c) John Howard
    d) Makybe Diva
28. Is it best to take a sick day:
    a) When the cricket's on
    b) When the cricket's on
    c) When the cricket's on
29. What animal is on the Bundaberg Rum bottle?
30. What is the difference between a pot and a middy of beer?
31. What are budgie smugglers?
32. What brand and size of Esky will you be purchasing?
33. Did you cry when Molly died on a *Country Practice*?
34. A 'Hoppoate' is:
    a) A breed of kangaroo
    b) A kind of Australian 'wedgie'
    c) A disgraced Rugby League player
35. What does having a 'chunder' mean?
36. When you were young, did you prefer the Hills Hoist over any swing set?
37. What does the terminology 'True Blue' mean?

Your Score _____

For Office Use Only.
In
Out
Can have another crack at it

CHILDREN'S PROVERBS

'From the mouths of babes', as the old saying goes. This is a variation of the 'what they said' form of humour and it's been around as long as we've had children.

Here's a modern take from a primary school teacher who collected well-known proverbs. She gave each child in her class the first half of a proverb and asked them to come up with the remainder of the proverb. It's hard to believe these were actually done by eight-year-olds, because the last one is classic!

Strike while the . . . *insect is close.*
Never underestimate the power of . . . *ants.*
Don't bite the hand that . . . *looks dirty.*
Better to be safe than . . . *punch an older boy.*
If you lie down with dogs, you'll . . . *stink in the morning.*
It's always darkest before . . . *Daylight-Saving Time.*
You can lead a horse to water but . . . *how?*
No news is . . . *impossible.*
A miss is as good as a . . . *Mr.*
You can't teach an old dog new . . . *math.*
Love all, trust . . . *me.*
The pen is mightier than the . . . *pigs.*
An idle mind is . . . *the best way to relax.*
Where there's smoke, there's . . . *pollution.*
Happy is the bride who . . . *gets all the presents.*
A penny saved is . . . *not much.*
Two's company, three's . . . *the Musketeers.*
Don't put off 'til tomorrow what . . . *you put on to go to bed.*
Laugh and the whole world laughs with you, cry and . . . *you have to blow your nose.*
There are none so blind as . . . *Stevie Wonder.*
Children should be seen and not . . . *smacked or grounded.*
If at first you don't succeed . . . *get new batteries.*
You get out of something only what you . . . *see in the picture on the box.*
When the blind leadeth the blind . . . *get out of the way.*
Better late than . . . *pregnant*!

TO THE CITIZENS OF THE USA

This spoof letter was written while George W. Bush was POTUS—President of the United States of America (2001–09). It purports to be the work of the famous English comedian John Cleese. Unlikely though that is, the sentiments expressed were commonly heard in Australia as well as the rest of the world. It has an uncanny relevance to the situation from 2017 onwards and, like all humour, says as much about the joker as the target, possibly more:

To the citizens of the United States of America:

In the light of your failure to elect a competent President of the USA and thus to govern yourselves, we hereby give notice of the revocation of your Independence, effective today. Her Sovereign Majesty Queen Elizabeth II will resume monarchical duties over all states, commonwealths and other territories. Except Utah, which she does not fancy.

Your new Prime Minister (The Right Honourable Tony Blair, MP for the 97.85% of you who have until now been unaware that there is a world outside your borders) will appoint a Minister for America without the need for further elections.

Congress and the Senate will be disbanded. A questionnaire will be circulated next year to determine whether any of you noticed. To aid in the transition to a British Crown Dependency, the following rules are introduced with immediate effect:

1. You should look up 'revocation' in the Oxford English Dictionary. Then look up 'aluminium'. Check the pronunciation guide. You will be amazed at just how wrongly you have been pronouncing it. The letter 'U' will be reinstated in words such as 'favour' and 'neighbour', skipping the letter 'U' is nothing more than laziness on your part. Likewise, you will learn to spell 'doughnut'

without skipping half the letters. You will end your love affair with the letter 'Z' (pronounced 'zed' not 'zee') and the suffix 'ize' will be replaced by the suffix 'ise'.

You will learn that the suffix 'burgh' is pronounced 'burra' e.g. Edinburgh. You are welcome to respell Pittsburgh as 'Pittsberg' if you can't cope with correct pronunciation. Generally, you should raise your vocabulary to acceptable levels. Look up 'vocabulary'. Using the same twenty seven words interspersed with filler noises such as 'like' and 'you know' is an unacceptable and inefficient form of communication. Look up 'interspersed'.

There will be no more 'bleeps' in the Jerry Springer show. If you're not old enough to cope with bad language then you shouldn't have chat shows. When you learn to develop your vocabulary then you won't have to use bad language as often.

2. There is no such thing as 'US English'. We will let Microsoft know on your behalf. The Microsoft spell-checker will be adjusted to take account of the reinstated letter 'u' and the elimination of '-ize'.

3. You should learn to distinguish the English and Australian accents. It really isn't that hard. English accents are not limited to cockney, upper-class twit or Mancunian (Daphne in Frasier). You will also have to learn how to understand regional accents—Scottish dramas such as 'Taggart' will no longer be broadcast with subtitles. While we're talking about regions, you must learn that there is no such place as Devonshire in England. The name of the county is 'Devon'. If you persist in calling it Devonshire, all American States will become 'shires' e.g. Texasshire, Floridashire, Louisianashire.

4. Hollywood will be required occasionally to cast English actors as the good guys. Hollywood will be required to cast English actors to play English characters. British sit-coms such as 'Men Behaving Badly' or 'Red Dwarf'

will not be re-cast and watered down for a wishy-washy American audience who can't cope with the humour of occasional political incorrectness.

5. You should relearn your original national anthem, 'God Save The Queen', but only after fully carrying out task 1. We would not want you to get confused and give up half way through.

6. You should stop playing American 'football'. There is only one kind of football. What you refer to as American 'football' is not a very good game. The 2.15% of you who are aware that there is a world outside your Borders may have noticed that no one else plays 'American' football. You will no longer be allowed to play it, and should instead play proper football. Initially, it would be best if you played with the girls. It is a difficult game.

   Those of you brave enough will, in time, be allowed to play rugby (which is similar to American 'football', but does not involve stopping for a rest every twenty seconds or wearing full kevlar body armour like nancies). We are hoping to get together at least a US Rugby sevens side by 2005.

   You should stop playing baseball. It is not reasonable to host an event called the 'World Series' for a game which is not played outside of America. Since only 2.15% of you are aware that there is a world beyond your borders, your error is understandable. Instead of baseball, you will be allowed to play a girls' game called 'rounders' which is baseball without fancy team stripes, oversized gloves, collector cards or hotdogs.

7. You will no longer be allowed to own or carry guns. You will no longer be allowed to own or carry anything more dangerous in public than a vegetable peeler. Because we don't believe you are sensible enough to handle potentially dangerous items, you will require a permit if you wish to carry a vegetable peeler in public.

8. July 4th is no longer a public holiday. November 2nd will be a new national holiday, but only in England. It will be called 'Indecisive Day'.

9. All American cars are hereby banned. They are crap and it is for your own good. When we show you German cars, you will understand what we mean. All road intersections will be replaced with roundabouts. You will start driving on the left with immediate effect.

   At the same time, you will go metric with immediate effect and without the benefit of conversion tables. Roundabouts and metrication will help you understand the British sense of humour.

10. You will learn to make real chips. Those things you call French fries are not real chips. Fries aren't even French, they are Belgian, though 97.85% of you (including the guy who discovered fries while in Europe) are not aware of a country called Belgium. Those things you insist on calling potato chips are properly called 'crisps'. Real chips are thick cut and fried in animal fat. The traditional accompaniment to chips is beer which should be served warm and flat. Waitresses will be trained to be more aggressive with customers.

11. As a sign of penance, 5 grams of sea salt per cup will be added to all tea made within the Commonwealth of Massachusetts, this quantity to be doubled for tea made within the city of Boston itself.

12. The cold tasteless stuff you insist on calling beer is not actually beer at all, it is lager. From November 1st only proper British Bitter will be referred to as 'beer', and European brews of known and accepted provenance will be referred to as 'Lager'. The substances formerly known as 'American Beer' will henceforth be referred to as 'Near-Frozen Gnat's Urine', with the exception of the product of the American Budweiser company whose product will be referred to as 'Weak Near-Frozen Gnat's Urine'. This will allow true Budweiser (as manufactured

for the last 1000 years in Pilsen, Czech Republic) to be sold without risk of confusion.

13. From November 10th the UK will harmonise petrol (or 'Gasoline' as you will be permitted to keep calling it until April 1st 2005) prices with the former USA. The UK will harmonise its prices to those of the former USA and the former USA will, in return, adopt UK petrol prices (roughly $6/US Gallon—get used to it).

14. You will learn to resolve personal issues without using guns, lawyers or therapists. The fact that you need so many lawyers and therapists shows that you're not adult enough to be independent. Guns should only be handled by adults. If you're not adult enough to sort things out without suing someone or speaking to a therapist then you're not grown up enough to handle a gun.

15. Please tell us who killed JFK. It's been driving us crazy.

16. Tax collectors from Her Majesty's Government will be with you shortly to ensure the acquisition of all revenues due (backdated to 1776).

17. Last, but not the least, and for heaven's sake . . . it's Nuclear as in 'clear' NOT Nucular.

Thank you for your co-operation and have a great day.
John Cleese

SIGNS OF YOUR TIMES

As we stagger over the hill, certain signs become apparent—to ourselves and to others. Police men and women look very young and music in pubs and restaurants is always too loud (and you can't understand the words, anyway). But there are even more challenges, as 'A Curmudgeon's Guide to Ageing Gracelessly' notes:

You spend longer and longer in the bathroom in the mornings.
There's never anything worth watching on TV.

People may give up their seat to you on public transport or offer to help you get up or down the stairs.

You become invisible.

Food doesn't taste like it used to and they put lids on jars too tightly for you to unscrew.

You are effortlessly overtaken by almost everyone when walking at your top speed.

Young people's faces all begin to look the same.

You can't remember the word for . . . ?

You learn never to trust a fart.

You begin to wonder how much funerals cost—and should you be saving up?

You avoid bending down, becoming amazingly adept at lifting small objects with your feet.

When travelling you need a ridiculous amount of space to pack your pills.

What's the matter with everyone!?

You've never noticed how bright that flower is.

People don't laugh at your jokes. Even if they didn't laugh very much before, now you start to notice it.

Every now and then, you put your underwear on inside-out—and don't notice until you undress for bed.

Dogs and cats seem to want to go to sleep on your lap a lot.

All electronic devices are designed for aliens—by aliens!

No one else on the road knows how to drive properly.

You break the habit of a lifetime and begin to read instructions—but you can't understand them.

Guided tours and cruises seem like an adventurous way to travel.

You need to express your opinions much more forcefully.

You recall what happened in the good old days much more accurately than anyone else.

You actually did everything in *The Dangerous Book for Boys/Girls*.

You don't know who incredibly famous celebrities are—and you don't want to. But you know who Enid Blyton was.

There are lots more signs of your times, but now you're depressed enough. In the end, you become so tired, weak and slow that the only remaining defence is to be unremittingly nice to everyone—especially those old bastards!

FACEBOOK FOR THE CHRONOLOGICALLY CHALLENGED

Another sign of the times for the digitally challenged generation:

For those of my generation who do not, and cannot, comprehend why Facebook exists:

I am trying to make friends outside of Facebook while applying the same principles. Therefore, every day I walk down the street and tell passers-by what I have eaten, how I feel at the moment, what I have done the night before, what I will do later and with whom.

I give them pictures of my family, my dog, and of me gardening, taking things apart in the garage, watering the lawn, standing in front of landmarks, driving around town, having lunch, and doing what anybody and everybody does every day.

I also listen to their conversations, give them the 'thumbs up' and tell them I like them.

It works just like Facebook.

I already have four people following me: two police officers, a private investigator and a psychiatrist.

MAKING A DIFFERENCE

This one emphasises the importance of staying occupied after retirement:

As we get older we sometimes begin to doubt our ability to 'make a difference' in the world. It is at these times that our hopes are boosted by the remarkable achievements of other 'seniors' who have found the courage to take on challenges that would make many of us wither.

Harold Schlumberg is such a person. THIS IS QUOTED FROM HAROLD:

'I've often been asked, "What do you do now that you're retired?"'

'Well . . . I'm fortunate to have a chemical engineering background and one of the things I enjoy most is converting beer, wine and whiskey into urine. It's rewarding, uplifting, satisfying and fulfilling. I do it every day and I really enjoy it.'

Harold is an inspiration to us all.

GO AUSSIE, GO!

A perennial source of humour is national character. This irreverent round-up of Australian prejudices and paranoias manages to hit pretty well every non-politically correct subject of the present, the past and, probably, the future.

WE, the people of the broad brown land of Oz, wish to be recognised as a free nation of blokes, sheilas and the occasional wanker. We come from many lands (although a few too many of us come from New Zealand) and although we live in the best country in the world, we reserve the right to bitch and moan about it whenever we bloody like. We are one nation but we're divided into many States.

First, there's Victoria, named after a queen who didn't believe in lesbians. Victoria is the realm of Mossimo turtlenecks, cafe latte, grand final day and big horse races. Its capital is Melbourne, whose chief marketing pitch is that 'it's liveable'. At least that's what they think. The rest of us think it is too bloody cold and wet.

Next, there's NSW, the realm of pastel shorts, macchiato with sugar, thin books read quickly and millions of dancing queens. Its capital Sydney has more queens than any other city in the world and is proud of it. Its mascots are Bondi lifesavers who pull their Speedos up their cracks to keep the left and right sides of their brains separate.

Down south we have Tasmania, a State based on the notion that the family that bonks together stays together. In Tassie, everyone gets an extra chromosome at conception. Maps of the State bring smiles to the sternest faces. It holds the world record for a single mass shooting, which the Yanks can't seem to beat no matter how often they try.

South Australia is the province of half-decent reds, a festival of foreigners and bizarre axe murders. SA is the state of innovation, where else can you so effectively reuse country bank vaults and barrels as in Snowtown, just out of Adelaide (also named after a queen). They had the Grand Prix, but lost it when the views of Adelaide sent the Formula One drivers to sleep at the wheel.

Western Australia is too far from anywhere to be relevant in this document. It's main claim to fame is that it doesn't have daylight saving because if it did all the men would get erections on the bus on the way to work. WA was the last state to stop importing convicts and many of them still work there in the government and business.

The Northern Territory is the red heart of our land. Outback plains, sheep stations the size of Europe, kangaroos, jackaroos, emus, Uluru and dusty kids with big smiles. It also has the highest beer consumption of anywhere on the planet and its creek beds have the highest aluminium content of anywhere too. Although the Territory is the centre piece of our national culture, few of us live there and the rest prefer to fly over it on our way to Bali.

And there's Queensland. While any mention of God seems silly in a document defining a nation of half-arsed agnostics, it is worth noting that God probably made Queensland. Why he filled it with dickheads remains a mystery.

Oh yes and there's Canberra. The least said the better.

We, the citizens of Oz, are united by the Pacific Highway, whose treacherous twists and turns kill more of us each year than die by murder. We are united in our lust for international recognition, so desperate for praise we leap in joy when a rag tag gaggle of corrupt IOC officials tells us Sydney is better than Beijing. We are united by a democracy so flawed that a political party, albeit a redneck gun-toting one, can get a million votes and still not win one seat in Federal Parliament while bloody Brian Harradine can get 24,000 votes and run the whole country. Not that we're whingeing, we leave that to our Pommy immigrants. We want to make 'no worries mate' our national phrase, 'she'll be right mate' our national attitude and 'Waltzing Matilda' our national anthem (So what if it's about a sheep-stealing crim who commits suicide).

We love sport so much our news readers can read the death toll from a sailing race and still tell us who's winning. And we're the best in the world at all the sports that count, like cricket, netball, rugby, AFL, roo-shooting, two-up and horse racing. We also have the biggest rock, the tastiest pies and the worst-dressed Olympians in the known universe. We shoot, we root, we vote. We are girt by sea and pissed by lunchtime. And even though we might seem a racist, closed-minded, sports-obsessed little people, at least we're better than the Kiwis.

25 LESSONS IN LIFE

Many of life's lessons are learned in childhood, then passed down through the generations:

1. My mother taught me TO APPRECIATE A JOB WELL DONE.
   'If you're going to kill each other, do it outside. I just finished cleaning.'
2. My mother taught me RELIGION.
   'You better pray that will come out of the carpet.'

3. My mother taught me about TIME TRAVEL.
   'If you don't straighten up, I'm going to knock you into the middle of next week!'

4. My mother taught me LOGIC.
   'Because I said so, that's why.'

5. My mother taught me MORE LOGIC.
   'If you fall out of that swing and break your neck, you're not going to the store with me.'

6. My mother taught me FORESIGHT.
   'Make sure you wear clean underwear, in case you're in an accident.'

7. My mother taught me IRONY.
   'Keep crying, and I'll give you something to cry about.'

8. My mother taught me about the science of OSMOSIS.
   'Shut your mouth and eat your supper.'

9. My mother taught me about CONTORTIONISM.
   'Will you look at that dirt on the back of your neck!'

10. My mother taught me about STAMINA.
    'You'll sit there until all that spinach is gone.'

11. My mother taught me about WEATHER.
    'This room of yours looks as if a tornado went through it.'

12. My mother taught me about HYPOCRISY.
    'If I told you once, I've told you a million times. Don't exaggerate!'

13. My mother taught me the CIRCLE OF LIFE.
    'I brought you into this world, and I can take you out.'

14. My mother taught me about BEHAVIOUR MODIFICATION.
    'Stop acting like your father!'

15. My mother taught me about ENVY.
    'There are millions of less fortunate children in this world who don't have wonderful parents like you do.'

16. My mother taught me about ANTICIPATION.
    'Just wait until we get home.'

17. My mother taught me about RECEIVING.
    'You are going to get it when you get home!'

18. My mother taught me MEDICAL SCIENCE.
    'If you don't stop crossing your eyes, they are going to get stuck that way.'
19. My mother taught me ESP.
    'Put your sweater on; don't you think I know when you are cold?'
20. My mother taught me HUMOUR.
    'When that lawn mower cuts off your toes, don't come running to me.'
21. My mother taught me HOW TO BECOME AN ADULT.
    'If you don't eat your vegetables, you'll never grow up.'
22. My mother taught me GENETICS.
    'You're just like your father.'
23. My mother taught me about my ROOTS.
    'Shut that door behind you. Do you think you were born in a barn?'
24. My mother taught me WISDOM.
    'When you get to be my age, you'll understand.'
25. And my favourite: My mother taught me about JUSTICE.
    'One day you'll have kids, and I hope they turn out just like you.'

WHY CUCUMBERS ARE BETTER THAN MEN

A popular item from the gender wars:

Cucumbers are better than men because . . .
The average cucumber stays hard for a week.
The average cucumber is at least 6 inches long.
A cucumber never suffers from performance anxiety.
Cucumbers are easy to pick up.
You can fondle cucumbers in a supermarket . . .
. . . and you know how firm it is before you take it home.

Cucumbers can get away any weekend.
A cucumber will always respect you in the morning.

A cucumber doesn't ask, 'Am I the first?'
Cucumbers don't care if you are a virgin.
Cucumbers won't tell other cucumbers you're not a virgin
  anymore.
With cucumbers you don't have to be a virgin more than
  once.

Cucumbers don't have sex hang-ups.
You can have as many cucumbers as you can handle.
You only eat cucumbers when you feel like it.
Cucumbers never need a round of applause.
Cucumbers won't ask:—
    Am I the best?
    How was it?
    Did you come? How many times?

A cucumber won't mind hiding in the fridge when your
  mother comes over.
A cucumber will never make a scene because there are
  other cucumbers in the fridge.
No matter how old you are, you can always get another
  cucumber.
A cucumber will never give you a hickey.
Cucumbers can stay up all night . . . and you won't have
  to sleep on the wet spot.
Cucumbers won't leave you wondering for a month.

Cucumbers won't tell you a vasectomy will ruin it for
  them.
A cucumber never forgets to flush the toilet.
A cucumber doesn't flush the toilet when you are in the
  shower.
Cucumbers don't compare you to a centrefold.
Cucumbers don't tell you they like you better with long
  hair.
A cucumber will never leave you for:—

Another woman.
Another man.
Another cucumber.

You always know where your cucumber has been.
Cucumbers don't have mid-life crisis.
Cucumbers don't play the guitar and try to find themselves.
A cucumber doesn't tell you he's outgrown you
    intellectually.
Cucumbers never expect you to have little cucumbers.
It's easy to drop a cucumber.

WHY BEER IS BETTER THAN WOMEN

Of course, there is a male riposte:

Beer is better than women because . . .

You don't have to wine and dine beer.
Your beer will always wait patiently in the car while you
    play football.
Beer is never late.
A beer doesn't get jealous when you grab another beer.
Beer never has a headache.
A beer won't get upset if you come home with another beer.
You can have more than one beer in a night, and not feel
    guilty.
Beer doesn't demand equality.
You can have a beer in public.
A beer won't tell you it's pregnant for fun.
A beer doesn't have in-laws.
No matter what the package, a beer still looks good.
Beer doesn't complain about farting.
The only thing a beer tells you is when it's time to go to the
    bathroom.
You don't need a licence to live with a beer.

Beer doesn't care how much you earn.

Beer won't complain about your choice of vacation.

You never have to promise to respect a beer in the morning.

You can put all your old beers in one room, and they won't fight.

PERSONAL GROWTH AND DEVELOPMENT COURSES

The self-help and therapy industries have long been favourite targets of folk humour, as in this spoof list of possibilities:

1100	Creative Suffering
EC-6	100 Other Uses for Vacuum Cleaners
1100	Overcoming Peace of Mind
EC-7	How to Convert a Wheelchair into a Dune Buggy
1102	You and Your Birthmark
H202	Creative Tooth Decay
1103	Guilt Without Sex
H204	Exorcism and Acne
1104	The Primal Shrug
H205	The Joys of Hypochondria
1105	Ego Gratification Through Violence
H210	High Fibre Sex
1106	Moulding Your Child's Behaviour Through Guilt and Fear
H210	Suicide and Health
H220	Biofeedback and How to Stop It
1107	Dealing with Post-Realisation Depression
H302	Skate Yourself to Regularity
H406	Understanding Nudity
1108	Whine Your Way to Alienation
H408	Tapdance Your Way to Social Ridicule
1109	How to Overcome Self-Doubt Through Pretence and Ostentation
H409	Optional Body Functions

1130	'I made $100 in Real Estate'
C800	How to Draw Genitalia
1131	Career Opportunities in El Salvador
C102	Needlecraft for Junkies
C105	Cuticle Crafts
1231	Packaging and Selling Your Child
C110	Gifts for the Senile
1300	How to Profit From Your Body
C606	Christianity and RV Maintenance
1310	Money Can Make You Rich
E406	Repair and Maintenance of Your Virginity
1434	Bonsai Your Pet
G105	Sinus Drainage at Home
1342	How You Can Convert Your Room into a Garage

Name_____Phone_____

LIFETIME HOROSCOPE

It's all written in the stars:

Aquarius: Jan 20–Feb 18. You have an inventive mind and are inclined to be progressive. You lie a lot. On the other hand, you are inclined to be careless and impractical, causing you to make the same mistakes repeatedly. Everyone thinks you are stupid.

Pisces: Feb 19–Mar 20. You have a vivid imagination and often think you are being followed by the CIA, KGB and FBI. You have a minor influence over associates and people resent you for flaunting your power. You lack confidence and are generally afraid to do anything. Pisces people often have sex with small animals.

Aries: Mar 21–Apr 19. You are the planner type and hold most people in contempt. You are quick tempered, impatient and scornful of advice. You are a prick.

Taurus: Apr 20–May 20. You're practical and persistent. You have a dogged determination and work like hell. Most people think you are stubborn and bullheaded. Actually, you are nothing but a damn communist.

Gemini: May 21–June 20. You are a quick and intelligent thinker. People like you because you are bisexual. However, you are inclined to expect too much for too little. This means you are cheap. Geminis are notorious for thriving on incest.

Cancer: June 21–July 22. You are sympathetic and understanding to other people's problems. They think you are a sucker. You are always putting things off, and that is why you will always be on welfare and never worth a cent.

Leo: July 23–Aug 22. You consider yourself a born leader, while others think you are pushy. Most Leos are bullies. You are vain and cannot take criticism. Your arrogance is disgusting. Leo people are thieving bastards.

Virgo: Aug 23–Sept 22. You are the logical type and hate disorder. This nitpicking is excessive and sickening to your friends. You are cold and unemotional and often fall asleep while making love. Virgos make excellent bus drivers and pimps.

Libra: Sept 23–Oct 22. You are the artistic type and have a difficult time with reality. If you are a man, you are more than likely gay. Changes of employment and monetary gains are excellent. Most Libra women make excellent whores. All Libras will eventually die of venereal disease.

Scorpio: Oct 23–Nov 21. You are shrewd in business and cannot be trusted. You shall achieve the pinnacle of success because of your lack of ethics. You are a perfect son-of-a bitch. Most Scorpios are mentally retarded.

Sagittarius: Nov 22–Dec 21. You are optimistic and enthusiastic. You have a reckless tendency to rely on luck since you lack talent. The majority of Sagittarians are drunks and dope fiends. People laugh at you a great deal because you are always getting fucked.

Capricorn: Dec 22–Jan 19. You are conservative and afraid of taking risks. You don't do much of anything and are lazy. There has never been a Capricorn of any importance. Capricorns should avoid standing still for very long periods of time, as they tend to attract pigeons.

A ROTTEN DAY

Who hasn't had a few of these?

You can tell it's going to be a rotten day when . . .

You wake up face down on the pavement.

You put your bra on backwards and it fits better.

You call suicide prevention and they put you on hold.

You see a *60 Minutes* news team waiting in your office.

You want to put on the clothes you wore home from the party and they aren't there.

You turn on the news and they're showing emergency routes out of the city.

You wake up to discover your waterbed has broken, then remember you don't have a waterbed.

Your car horn goes off accidentally and remains stuck as you follow a group of Hell's Angels down the motorway.

Your wife wakes up feeling amorous and you have a headache.

Your boss tells you not to bother taking off your coat.

You call your answering service and they tell you it's none of your business.

Your blind date turns out to be your ex-wife.

Your income tax cheque bounces.

You put both contact lenses in the same eye.

Your pet rock snaps at you.

Your wife says, 'Good morning, Bill,' and your name is George.

Author unknown . . . but troubled.

WHAT THEY WANTED

Another venerable item of office humour, still relevant today:

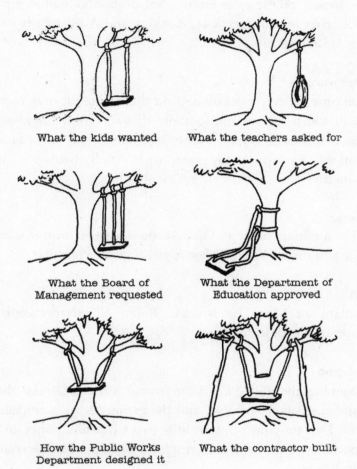

What the kids wanted

What the teachers asked for

What the Board of
Management requested

What the Department of
Education approved

How the Public Works
Department designed it

What the contractor built

THE IMPOSSIBLE EXAMINATION

This is an old favourite in schools and universities as well as offices and anywhere else where they want people to sit a test:

Instructions: Read each question thoroughly. Answer all questions. Time limit—four hours. Begin immediately.

History

Describe the history of the Papacy from its origins to the present day, concentrate specifically but not exclusively, on the social, political, economic, religious and philosophical impact on Europe, Asia, America and Africa. Be brief, concise and specific.

Literature

Compose an epic poem based on the events of your own life in which you see and footnote allusions from T.S. Eliot, Keats, Chaucer, Dante, Norse mythology and the Marx brothers. Critique your poem with a full discussion of its metrics.

Music

Write a piano concerto. Orchestrate it and perform it with flute and drum. You will find a piano under your seat.

Art

Explain the Mona Lisa's smile. Relate all interpretations associated with it.

Religion

Assuming the Judeo-Christian moral structure, take the stand for Adam and Eve, and the eating of the forbidden fruit. Explain your position fully to a Chassidic Rabbi and answer his arguments. An Anglican bishop will moderate this debate.

Logic

Using accepted methodology, prove all four of the following: the universe is infinite; truth is beauty; there is not a little person who turns off the light in the refrigerator when you close the door; and that you are the person taking this exam. Now disprove all of the above. Be specific; show all work.

Philosophy
Sketch the development of human thought; estimate its significance. Compare with the development of any other kind of thought.

Epistemology
Take a position for or against truth. Prove the validity of your position.

Medicine
You have been provided with a razor blade, a piece of gauze, and a bottle of Scotch. Remove your own appendix. Do not suture until your work has been inspected. You have fifteen minutes.

Biology
Create life. Estimate the differences in subsequent human culture if this form of life had developed five hundred years earlier, with special attention to the probable effects on the English Parliamentary system. Prove your thesis.

Psychology
Employing principles from the major schools of psychoanalytic thought, successfully subject yourself to analysis. Make appropriate personality changes, bill yourself and fill out all medical insurance forms. Now do the same to the person seated to your immediate left. Also, based on your degree of knowledge of their works, evaluate the emotional stability, degree of adjustment, and repressed frustrations of each of the following: Alexander of Aphrodisias, Ramesses II, Gregory of Nicea, Hammurabi. Support your evaluations with quotations from each man's work, making appropriate references. It is not necessary to translate.

Sociology
Estimate the sociological problems that might accompany the end of the world. Construct an experiment to test your theory.

Economics
Develop a realistic plan for refinancing the national debt. Trace the possible effects of your plan in the following areas: Cubism, the Donatist controversy, the wave theory of light. Outline a method from all points of view. Point out deficiencies in your argument as demonstrated in your answer to the last question.

Computer Science
Define computer. Define Science. How do they relate? Why? Create a generalised algorithm to optimise all computer decisions. Assuming an 1130 CPU supporting 50 terminals, each terminal to activate your algorithm, design the communications to interface and all the necessary control programs.

Management Science
Define Management. Define Science. How do they relate? Why? Create a generalised algorithm to optimise all managerial decisions.

Public Speaking
2,500 riot-crazed students are storming the classroom. Calm them. You may use any ancient language except Latin or Greek.

Physics
Explain the nature of matter. Include in your answer an evaluation of the impact of the development of mathematics on science.

Modern Physics

Disprove Einstein's Theory of Relativity. Construct an experiment to prove your position.

Engineering

The disassembled parts of a high-powered rifle have been placed in a box on your desk. You will also find an instruction manual, printed in Swahili. In ten minutes a hungry Bengal tiger will be admitted to the room. Take whatever action you feel is appropriate. Prove your assertions, and be prepared to cost- and motion-justify your decision.

Agricultural Science

Outline the steps involved in breeding your own super high yield, all weather hybrid strain of wheat. Describe its chemical and physical properties and estimate its impact on world food supplies. Construct a model for dealing with world-wide surpluses. Write your Nobel Prize acceptance speech.

Comprehension

Three-minute time test. Read everything before doing anything. Put your name in the upper right-hand corner of this page. Circle the word name in sentence three. Sign your name under the title of this paper, after the title write yes, yes, yes. Put an X in the lower left-hand corner of this paper. Draw a triangle around the X you just put down. On the back of this paper multiply 703 x 668. Loudly call out your name when you get to this point. If you think you have followed directions carefully to this point, call out 'I have.' Punch three small holes in the top of this paper. If you are the first person to get this far, call out 'I am the first person to this point, I am leading in following directions.' On the reverse side of this paper add 8950 and 9850. Put a circle around your answer and put a square around the circle. Now that you have finished reading carefully, do only sentence two.

Political Science
There is a red telephone on the desk behind you. Start World War III. Report at length on its socio-political effects, if any.

Jurisprudence
In Part 2 of Shakespeare's *Henry VI*, Jack Cade, the leader of the Populist revolt, proposes that the first order of business following a successful coup d'e'tat could be to 'kill all the lawyers'. In light of the present populist mood in the world, assess the utility and any potential impact of such a policy today.

Mathematics
Give today's date, in metric.

Chemistry
Transform lead into gold. You will find a tripod and three logs under your seat. Show all work including Feynman diagrams and quantum functions for all steps. You have fifteen minutes.

General Knowledge
Describe in detail. Be objective and specific.
For Extra Credit
Define the Universe. Give two examples.

DO NOT BREAK THE CHAIN

The chain letter has long been a widespread form of global folklore. The usual form of the letter is a story that claims good luck and riches will be showered on the recipient who mails the letter to a number of others. If the recipient of the chain letter fails to do this, something dreadful is usually threatened. In recent years these older chain letters, while still circulating by mail and even through emails, have been joined by some playful parodies. This 'Chain Letter for Women', as it is usually called, is itself a parody of a much earlier spoof chain letter involving husbands sending their wives on, known since at least the 1950s:

Dear Friend,

This letter was started by a woman like yourself, in the hope of bringing relief to the tired and discontented. Unlike most chain letters, this one does not cost anything. Just send a copy to five of your friends who are tired and discontent. Then bundle up your husband or boyfriend and send him to the woman whose name appears at the top of the list.

When your name comes to the top you will receive 16,374 men, and some of them are bound to be a hell of a lot better than the one you already have.

Do not break the chain. Have faith. One woman broke the chain and got her own husband back.

At the time of writing, a friend of mine had already received 184 men. They buried her yesterday, but it took three undertakers 36 hours to get the smile off her face!!!

AN INVITATION

Not the sort of letter you would like to receive, even in the 1980s.

> The Very Rev. Thomas Jones-White
> Minister, M,S,. B,D,.St. M
> Crown Street,
> SURRY HILLS, SYDNEY, N.S.W.

CHURCH OF EVANGELISM, SYDNEY

Dear Horace,

Perhaps you have heard of me and my nationwide campaign in the cause of temperance. Each year for the past fourteen

I have made a tour of Australia, delivering a series of lectures on the evils of drinking.

On these tours I have been accompanied by my young friend and assistant, Clyde Linson. Clyde, a young man of good family and excellent background, is a pathetic example of a life ruined by excessive indulgence in whisky and women. Clyde would appear with me at lectures and sit on the platform—drunk, wheezing, staring at the audience through bleary and blood-shot eyes, sweating profusely, picking his nose, belching and breaking wind, and making obscene gestures at the ladies, while I would point him out as an example of what over-indulgence can do to a person.

This winter, unfortunately, Clyde died. A mutual friend has given me your name, and I wonder if you would be available to take Clyde's place on my 1984 tour.

Yours in Evangelism
MINISTER

THE ARMY RECRUIT'S LETTER

This golden oldie is known in English, Canadian, American, Swiss and German versions. Here's an Australian rendition that leads a lively life on the internet:

Dear Mum & Dad,

I am well. Hope youse are too. Tell me big brothers Doug and Phil that the Army is better than workin' on the farm— tell them to get in quick smart before the jobs are all gone! I wuz a bit slow in settling down at first, because ya don't hafta get outta bed until 6am. But I like sleeping in now, cuz all ya gotta do before brekky is make ya bed and shine ya boots and clean ya uniform. No cows to milk, no calves to feed, no feed to stack—nothin'!! Ya haz gotta shower though, but it's not so bad, coz there's lotsa hot water and even a light to see what ya doing!

At brekky ya get cereal, fruit and eggs but there's no kangaroo steaks or possum stew like wot Mum makes. You don't get fed again until noon and by that time all the city boys are dead because we've been on a 'route march'—geez it's only just like walking to the windmill in the back paddock!!

This one will kill me brothers Doug and Phil with laughter. I keep getting medals for shootin'—dunno why. The bullseye is as big as a possum's bum and it don't move and it's not firing back at ya like the Johnsons did when our big scrubber bull got into their prize cows before the Ekka last year! All ya gotta do is make yourself comfortable and hit the target! You don't even load your own cartridges, they comes in little boxes, and ya don't have to steady yourself against the rollbar of the roo shooting truck when you reload!

Sometimes ya gotta wrestle with the city boys and I gotta be real careful coz they break easy—it's not like fighting with Doug and Phil and Jack and Boori and Steve and Muzza all at once like we do at home after the muster.

Turns out I'm not a bad boxer either and it looks like I'm the best the platoon's got, and I've only been beaten by this one bloke from the Engineers—he's 6 foot 5 and 15 stone and three pick handles across the shoulders and, as ya know, I'm only 5 foot 7 and eight stone wringin' wet, but I fought him till the other blokes carried me off to the boozer.

I can't complain about the Army—tell the boys to get in quick before word gets around how good it is.

Your loving daughter, Sheila.

APPLICATION FOR AN AUSTRALIAN PASSPORT

A very angry citizen vents on the bureaucracy. But the writer of the letter does have a point, despite the invective:

Dear Mr Minister,

I'm in the process of renewing my passport, and still cannot believe this. How is it that K-Mart has my address and telephone number, and knows that I bought a television set and golf clubs from them back in 1997, and yet the Federal Government is still asking me where I was born and on what date? For Christ sakes, do you guys do this by hand?

My birth date you have in my Medicare information, and it is on all the income tax forms I've filed for the past 40 years.

It is also on my driver's licence, on the last eight passports I've ever had, on all those stupid customs declaration forms I've had to fill out before being allowed off planes over the past 30 years.

It's also on all those insufferable census forms that I've filled out every 5 years since 1966.

Also . . . would somebody please take note, once and for all, that my mother's name is Audrey, my father's name is Jack, and I'd be absolutely bloody astounded if that ever changed between now and when I drop dead!

****! What do you people do with all this information we keep having to provide?

I apologize, Mr Minister. But I'm really pissed off this morning. Between you and me, I've had enough of all this bullshit!

You send the application to my house, then you ask me for my bloody address! What the hell is going on with your mob? Have you got a gang of mindless Neanderthals working there!

And another thing, look at my damn picture. Do I look like Bin Laden? I can't even grow a beard for God's sakes. I just want to go to New Zealand and see my new granddaughter. (Yes, my son interbred with a Kiwi girl). And would someone please tell me, why would you give a shit whether or not I plan on visiting a farm in the next 15 days? In the unlikely event I ever got the urge to do something weird to a sheep or a horse, believe you me, I'd sure as hell not want to tell anyone!

Well, I have to go now, 'cause I have to go to the other side of Sydney and get another bloody copy of my birth certificate—and to part with another $80 for the privilege of accessing MY OWN INFORMATION!

Would it be so complicated to have all the services in the same spot, to assist in the issuance of a new passport on the same day?

Nooooo, that'd be too bloody easy and makes far too much sense!

You would much prefer to have us running all over the bloody place like chickens with our heads cut off, and then having to find some 'high-society' idiot to confirm that it's really me in the goddamn photo! You know the photo . . . the one where we're not allowed to smile? You bloody morons.

Signed—An Irate Australian Citizen.

According to the source of this item: 'The above is an actual letter sent to the DFAT (Department of Foreign Affairs and Trade) Immigration Minister. The Government tried desperately to censure the author, but got nowhere because every legal person who read it couldn't stop laughing!'

TAKE A RUNNING JUMP AT YOURSELF!

The range, colour and variety of Australian slang is truly a wondrous thing. There are words and phrases for every conceivable, and some inconceivable, situations—good, bad and dire. This is just as well, because life serves up more troubles than you can poke a stick at, and we need a full armoury of the slanguage just to get by. Here are a few useful examples for dealing verbally with life's irritations and the morons who cause them, selected from an infinite array of possibilities.

Traditionally, the Australian art of invective was practised at its sharpest in the art of 'barracking', or boisterously supporting one's own football side by abusing the opposing team, its supporters and the referee. The exact content of barracking varies from game to game and supporter to supporter, but a few selected football examples recorded in 1917 give the flavour:

Yer couldn't pass the sugar before the tea gets cold.

Little man to big man: 'Garn, you're overgrown; you forgot to get yurself pruned this year.'
Big man replies: 'Get away, yer little sawed off. Pity yer mother didn't put some superphosphates in yer grub when you was young, mighter made yer grow a bit.'

Since the 1980s, barracking has been joined by the practice of 'sledging' in which individual players—especially in cricket—seek to undermine their opponents' morale by witty barbs like that Dennis Lillee allegedly deployed against more than one opposing batsman over his lengthy career: 'I can tell you why you're batting so badly, you've got some shit on the end of your bat.' The batsman would usually flip his bat over to check the end, and then Lillee would say: 'Wrong end mate.'

Being 'all over the place like a mad woman's knitting' is just one of many ways to describe someone who lacks organisation or purpose. You could also be 'running 'round like a chook with its head cut off', have 'more rattles than a millionaire's baby' or simply not 'know if you're Arthur or Martha'.

Our linguistic inventiveness is even more marked when it comes to scorning the closely related lack of effectiveness or value. One might be 'useless as screen doors on a submarine', 'as much use as an ashtray on a motorbike', or—no offence to the godly—'as useless as tits on a nun'.

Australians must be particularly prone to bad luck, judging by the many ways to describe the affliction. 'Couldn't take a trick', 'couldn't win a pie at a Big Ben picnic', or 'couldn't win a Catholic raffle, even if I was the Pope' are a few possibilities, and there are many more: 'If I fell into a rose garden I'd land in dog shit', 'If it rained gravy everyone would have a frying pan and I'd have the gridiron' or 'Couldn't get a root in a brothel'.

As a result of these misfortunes, you might be 'up a gum tree' or 'up shit creek', usually 'without a paddle'. Misery may be the consequence, leaving one 'as happy as a bastard on Father's Day', 'about as happy as a cat shitting razor blades' or bearing 'a face like a dropped pie'.

Stinginess is a characteristic widely deplored, particularly when it comes time to 'shout' drinks, like the bloke who 'wouldn't shout if a shark bit him'. The same miser could also be described as having 'short arms and long pockets', as someone who 'wouldn't give you a shock if he owned the power-house', or is 'meaner than Hungry Tyson', the noted bush tight-fist.

Straight-out insults are many, usually in the form of physical descriptions such as 'ugly as a plateful of mortal sins' or having 'a head like a half-sucked mango'. An especially elaborate insult is, 'If I was as two-faced as you and had a face like that, I'd wear the other one.' Imputed stupidity also falls into this category: 'If brains were made of dynamite, he/she wouldn't have enough to blow his/her head off' and 'If brains were made of elastic you wouldn't have enough to make a garter for a canary's leg'.

Additionally, someone might be 'a sandwich short of a picnic', as 'silly as a two-bob watch', 'silly as a hatful of arse-holes' or with 'not enough sense to come in out of the rain'.

Books have been written on the slanguage and it is both celebrated and deplored in roughly equal measure. One thing is certain though, there is no chance of it going away any time soon. As older idioms fade away, they are replaced by shiny bright new ones like 'budgie smugglers', the favoured swimwear of a former prime minister. A 'milkshake duck' refers to something that is at first positive but is subsequently revealed to be much less so, a common experience in the era of fake news. 'Milkshake duck' was coined by Australian cartoonist Ben Ward in 2016 and 'went viral' on Twitter and the internet. It was selected as the word of the year by the learned folks at *Macquarie Dictionary* in 2017 and shows signs of staying on as one more linguistic reminder of the ironclad laws of life.

A cart of memories: young lads gallivanting for the day, South Australia, circa 1909.

MOMENTS LIKE THESE . . .

If you didn't laugh, you'd cry.

Traditional saying

UP, UP AND AWAY!

A very short but intrepid journey was taken over Sydney by an early 'aeronaut', Mr C.H. Brown. On the night of 17 January 1859, assisted by his partner Mr Dean, the aeronaut boarded his gas-powered balloon in the Domain and cast off 'with about twenty-eight pounds weight of fireworks attached to my car'. The fireworks—perhaps ill-advised for a contrivance powered by combustible hydrogen—were for a publicity stunt promoting the delights of ballooning. Mr Brown's troubles began almost immediately, when he found the balloon had 'but little ascension power': it would not rise. He quickly threw the anchor overboard, and then a bag of ballast. Still dangerously low, he threw a second bag of ballast overboard while above Hyde Park, 'by which means [he] ascended gently to a height of about a mile as [he] judged from the expansion of the balloon'.

Hopefully there was nobody taking the evening air in Hyde Park at that moment.

Despite these early troubles, Brown flew on and discharged the fireworks, at which 'deafening shouts reached [his] ears from the thousands of people assembled in the Domain and Hyde Park':

> I hailed the crowd in Hyde Park, some of whom inform me that my shouts were heard by them. I heard distinctly the sounds of a band of music at the Rotunda, Woolloomooloo, over which I passed. From the time of my leaving the Domain, until my descent, the shouts of the people and the barking of dogs did not become inaudible.

But now Mother Nature added to his own fireworks show: he flew high into the centre of an electrical storm, writing that 'at times the lightning appeared to form a complete and immense circle around me'. Despite this he reported feeling 'quite secure' and enjoyed the view of the city of Sydney at night, 'with its thousands of lights present[ing] a beautiful sight'.

Once the fireworks, which had been smouldering on the ground for ten minutes, seemed to be extinguished, Brown began his descent. But now the daring young man in his flying machine really got into trouble. A sudden gust of wind sent him off-course towards Randwick but he didn't notice in time. Instead he descended more quickly, and then 'passing over the Orphan Asylum, at Randwick, came down with great violence in a garden, a few hundred yards further'. He writes, 'My first impression was, that my neck was broken, but a second or two afterwards, finding myself unhurt, I prepared for another shock, which I expected would be more violent than the first.' The balloon, after violently colliding with the ground, had lifted again and he now prepared for a second crash landing:

> I twisted one leg around a rope, held one of the car-ropes with my left hand, and the string of the valve with my right.

Down I came again with a frightful shock, and the balloon dragged me at a terrific rate through the scrub, the car cutting through the bushes like a knife. I expected every moment would be my last, but endeavoured to keep cool, and determined to endeavour to save myself by dropping over the side of the car, and setting the balloon free.

After having been dragged along in this manner for at least a mile, expecting every moment to plunge into the bay, I put my legs over the side of the car and waited for a favourable opportunity to get completely out. At last I sprang from the car, and was thrown violently on my hands and face into a bush. I soon got on my feet, and followed the balloon at least three quarters of a mile, when I lost sight of it.

Poor Mr Brown's wandering balloon was found near Botany Bay, four or five kilometres from where he had 'first struck the earth', as he put it. He had been in the air for just twenty minutes. Brown and Dean soon left for Melbourne for further ballooning antics. As the reporter of this aerial farce wrote, tongue in cheek: 'Monday's ascent concluding, for the present, aeronautic expeditions in New South Wales.'

ALL'S WELL THAT ENDS WELL

Early in 1876 the ex-mayor of Geelong took a trip to Tasmania, referred to as 'the Tight Little Island'. While there, he took the train from Launceston to Hobart and back again, describing his eventful journey in a letter to his constituents. They would have been very amused at his entertaining yarn and may have quietly decided not to travel by train if they ever visited Tassie:

We went to Hobart Town on Thursday week by the train, and certainly found the mode of management original. The carriages and engine having to turn sharp curves are made, the first to travel on two sets of wheels called the Bogie principle, whilst the latter have the doors at each end, not fastened. They are connected together with a pin, which allows them to move to the right or left easily. Without mentioning the particulars of our down journey other than to say that the rails being very light and placed on small sleepers without the necessary weight to keep them down, floated on the water when the flood came, and were in many places clear of the permanent way, in others the soil had been washed from under the sleepers. About seventeen miles had been damaged, so we had to do this by coach.

After waiting some time four horses were brought-knocked up, having just come a journey of 27 miles. We started with a very heavy load, and it was not long before the pace was reduced to a walk. The coachman asked me if I could drive, I answered in the affirmative, at once arranged the reins in the most scientific manner possible, and there I sat in my glory whilst the coachman got down and ran or walked alongside the horses, which, by means of a tickle now and again with the whip, he succeeded in making go at the rate of fully four miles an hour. Anyone meeting us must have thought we were a comical turn-out—myself driving, a priest on the box next to me holding an umbrella over my head, the coachman running by the side cracking his whip, and some of the passengers also stretching their legs alongside of him. However, we got safely to Hobart Town, and now for the return journey.

The line, I may mention, is on the narrow gauge, 3ft. 6in. wide. The carriages have no springs similar to those used on the Victorian lines, but rest on spiral wire springs, and these, when travelling fast, nearly shake the inside from you. During the latter part of the journey I was glad to stand, as when we were travelling at the rate of forty miles an hour to make up for lost time the motion was almost unbearable. The hour at which it was announced the train would start was 8.30 sharp, but at that hour everything apparently had to be got ready. The water was carried in three four-hundred gallon tanks lashed on a truck, coals on a truck behind. However we got off at last at about 9 o'clock, and progressed steadily for about an hour and a half when the train came to a full stop. We all jumped out to see what was up, and found the draft of the boiler was so strong that the small pieces of coal had been drawn through the tubes so as to choke the three or four bottom rows; the back pan had to be opened and cleaned out, then steam was again raised, and away we went.

After some time we stopped at a station to drop some freight, which occupied some time, as it consisted of two bags of sugar. Away we went again, and were suddenly brought to a dead stop. On looking out I saw some of the passengers collecting wood to assist in livening the fire, so I ran back, and shouted 'All hands forward to collect wood,' and amid general laughter we all lent a hand.

Once more we started on our journey round curves so sharp that the train with the engine at one end and a guard's van at the other nearly described a half-circle. Suddenly another stop was made at Jerusalem. Having got to this remarkable locality we all jumped out to amuse our selves while the freight for the thriving place was deposited on the sand. Some of the passengers played at duck stone; others threw up one stone and tried to hit it with another; a priest amused him self playing with his dog. I saw the goods unloaded; they consisted of two or three bags of sugar, some packages of canvas and a case, the whole being saturated with boiled oil. It appeared they had placed a kerosene tin of boiled oil on the top of the goods, and had succeeded in piercing the tin by carelessly placing some scythes against it.

After a great deal of time had been lost in discussing this accident, and who was to remove a box covered with boiled oil from the van, the hands generally objecting to touch it, we made another start, and in about an hour pulled up over a creek, at which we were to take in water by bucketing it up. After some discussion about a rope, during which some of the passengers suggested that we should tie our pocket handkerchiefs together, they set to work. The chief engineer, with the rope, dropped a bucket into the stream, hauled it up, handed it to the man who took the tickets, and who transferred it to the second engineer, and the latter emptied it into the 400-gallon tank. Meanwhile, a garden being near, a number of passengers, accompanied by the third engineer, rushed and helped themselves to fruit. After some time the ticket collector, finding the bucketing rather hard work, sang out for the third engineer to assist, the latter thereupon was seen rushing up with both hands filled with fruit, and took the place of the first engineer, being cautioned not to break the bucket, as that was the only one they had.

The watering was completed in about half an hour; we made another start, and an hour afterwards pulled up at the large tank, at which I supposed a sufficient supply of water would be taken in in about ten minutes. Not so, however; when they tried the hose, which was new, they found it impossible to get either end on, so had to use a V-shaped piece of wood to support it near the aperture in the tank, and the poor fellow who held this got well soused with water.

The mayor and his well-shaken travelling companions arrived back at Launceston at 8.30 pm—'All's well that ends well,' he wrote, 'and I thoroughly enjoyed my trip to Hobart Town.'

THE OOZLUM BIRD

The Oozlum bird is an Australian version of a mythical creature also found in British and American traditions. 'Ouzel' is a name given to a variety of bird species in the British Isles, most commonly it seems the blackbird. In Ireland the water ouzel is associated with the danger of malignant disease, while the blackbird is the carrier of numerous superstitions, as in English folklore. The ouzel also appears in Welsh mythology and in that of the Ainu, the Aboriginal inhabitants of what is now Japan. Intriguingly, in the Japanese belief system, the ouzel is associated with improved sight, perhaps echoed in the Australian version's capabilities, or lack of them.

Our Oozlum bird flies backwards, either because it wishes to gaze admiringly at its own tail feathers or to keep the dust out of its eyes. Or it could be because it likes to know where it has been because it does not know where it is going. It can be large enough for a human to ride upon. If startled, the Oozlum bird may fly in smaller and smaller circles until it eventually disappears into its own fundamental orifice—sometimes in a puff of blue smoke.

The journalist, humourist and poet W.T. Goodge penned a few verses featuring the Oozlum bird and also helpfully explained how the town of Birdsville got its name. The poem begins by introducing 'Ginger Joe' of the Diamantina:

> He was old and he was ugly,
> He was dirty, he was low . . .

Joe was also a noted teller of tall tales and the best anyone ever heard him tell was about Jock McPherson's trip to Sydney on the famously speedy Oozlum bird. According to Joe, this is just how it happened:

> 'You can talk about yer racehorse
> And the pace as he can go,
> But it just amounts to crawlin',
> Nothink else!' said Ginger Joe.
> 'And these cycle blokes with pacers,
> You can take my bloomin' word,
> They're a funeral procession
> To the blinded Oozlum Bird!
>
> 'Do yez know Marengo station?
> It's away beyond the Peak,
> Over sixty miles from Birdsville
> As you go to Cooper's Creek,

Which the blacks call Kallokoopah,
And they tell you that Lake Eyre
Was one time an inland ocean.
Well, the Oozlum Bird is there!

'Bet yer boots it ain't no chicken,
It's as big and wide across
As the bird what beats the steamships,
What's it called? The albatross!
That's the bird! And old King Mulga
Used to tell the boys and me
They were there when Central 'Stralia
Was a roarin' inland sea!

'I was cook at old Marengo
When McTavish had the run,
And his missus died and left him
With a boy—the only one.
Jock McPherson was his nephew,
Lately came from Scotland, too,
Been sent out to get "experience"
As a kind of Jackeroo!

'Well, this kid of old McTavish
Was a daisy. Strike me blue!
There was nothing, that was mischief,
That the kiddy wouldn't do!
But he was a kindly kinchen
And a reg'lar little brick,
And we all felt mighty sorry
When we heard that he was sick!

'But, McTavish! Well, I reckon
I am something on the swear,
But I never heard sich language
As McTavish uttered there;

For he cursed the blessed country,
And the cattle and the sheep,
And the station-hands and shearers
Till yer blinded flesh would creep.

'It was something like a fever
That the little bloke had got,
And McTavish he remembered
(When he'd cursed and swore a lot),
That a chemist down in Sydney
Had a special kind of stuff
Which would cure the kiddy's fever
In a jiffy, right enough!

'So he sends me into Birdsville
On the fastest horse we had,
And I has to wire to Sydney
For the medsin for the lad.
They would send it by the railway,
And by special pack from Bourke;
It would take a week to do it
And be mighty slippery work.

'Well, I gallops into Birdsville
And I sends the wire all right;
And I looks around the township,
Meanin' stopping for the night.
I was waitin' in the bar-room—
This same bar-room—for a drink
When a wire comes from McPherson,
And from Sydney! Strike me pink!

'I had left him at Marengo
On the morning of that day!
He was talking to McTavish
At the time I came away!

And yet here's a wire from Sydney!
And it says: "Got here all right.
Got the medsin. Am just leaving.
Will be home again to-night!"

'Well, I thought I had the jim-jams,
Yes, I did; for, spare me days!
How in thunder had McPherson
Got to Sydney, anyways?
But he'd got there, that was certain,
For the wire was plain and clear.
I could never guess conundrums,
So I had another beer.

'In the morning, bright and early,
I was out and saddled up,
And away to break the record
Of old Carbine for the Cup.
And I made that cuddy gallop
As he'd never done before;
And, so-help-me-bob, McPherson
Was there waiting at the door!

'And the kid was right as ninepence,
Sleepin' peaceful in his bunk,
And McTavish that delighted
He'd made everybody drunk!
And McPherson says: "Well, Ginger,
You did pretty well, I heard;
But you must admit you're beaten,
Joe—I rode the Oozlum Bird!"

'Said he'd often studied science
Long before he'd came out here,
And he'd struck a sort of notion,
Which you'll think is mighty queer—

That the earth rolls round to eastward
And that birds, by rising high,
Might just stop and travel westward,
While the earth was rolling by!

'So he saddled up the Oozlum,
Rose some miles above the plain,
Let the Earth turn underneath him
Till he spotted the Domain!
Then came down, and walked up George-street,
Got the stuff and wired to me;
Rose again and reached Marengo
Just as easy as could be!

'"But," says I, "if you went westward
Just as simple as you say,
How did you get back?" He answered:
"Oh, I came the other way!"
So in six-and-twenty hours,
Take the yarn for what it's worth,
Jock McPherson and the Oozlum
Had been all around the earth!

'It's a curious bird, the Oozlum,
And a bird that's mighty wise,
For it always flies tail-first to
Keep the dust out of its eyes!
And I heard that since McPherson
Did that famous record ride,
They won't let a man get near 'em,
Couldn't catch one if you tried!

'If you don't believe the story,
And some people don't, yer know;
Why the blinded map'll prove it,
Strike me fat!' said Ginger Joe.

'Look along the Queensland border,
On the South Australian side,
There's this township! christened Birdsville,
'Cause' of Jock McPherson's ride!'

Another variation exists in the United States military, where an 'Oozlefinch' has been the official mascot of the Air Defense Artillery since the early twentieth century. As befits an air force mascot, the featherless Oozlefinch flies at the incredibly fast pace that sped Jock McPherson to Sydney and back, but has the additional military advantage of tearing enemy aircraft from the skies. Like our own species, the Oozlefinch flies backwards, but is not thought to perform the same unique vanishing act when alarmed.

THE BLACK STUMP

Where is it? How did it originate? What does it mean?

That iconic Australian expression 'beyond the black stump' or 'not this side of the black stump' refers to any location considered to be far away from the speaker. Usually this means well beyond the rural urban fringe, in the bush and in all likelihood the outback. No one is quite sure where the outback begins and ends, but we all know that it's a long way away and very big. So important is the black stump that it has evolved its own considerable body of lore and legend to explain its existence.

Some stories rely on what the dictionary makers call etymology, the history of a word from its origins—at least as far as these can be determined—and its appearance in books, newspapers and other documentary sources. It seems that there are various tantalising allusions to the black stump in nineteenth-century sources of this kind, but nothing very conclusive. We have to wait until the twentieth century to find references of this sort. Before that, so the story goes, the term originated among rural carriers who used fire-blackened tree stumps as way finders. 'Turn left at the third black stump after the river,' and so on. Needless to say, there is no evidence for this belief whatsoever. Which, of course, does not mean it is wrong, just unsubstantiated.

A number of bush towns claim the honour of being the location of the original black stump. As in all good folklore, each has an elaborate tale to justify its claim. In Coolah, New South Wales, it is said that one of the early 'limits of location' involved the boundary of a property known as the 'Black Stump Run'. Later, in the 1860s, an inn was built in the area and named 'The Black Stump Inn'. This establishment was an important stop for travellers and so 'beyond the black stump' came into use as a reference to going beyond the boundaries of settlement. Variations on this theme include the suggestion that fire-blackened stumps functioned as unofficial markers for property boundaries.

A colourful legend underlies the claim of the Riverina village of Merriwagga to be the location of the original blackened stump. In 1886 the wife of a passing carrier, Barbara Blain, was burned to death when her dress caught alight in the flames of the campfire. It is said that in describing the body, her husband said it resembled a black stump. A local waterhole is named Black Stump Tank.

Not to be outdone by New South Wales, the Queensland town of Blackall has a scientific legend to bolster its claim. A surveying party visited the area in the late 1880s and established a site for observing longitude and latitude. Theodolites mounted on tree stumps were used for this work, a number of which were fire-blackened. The remote country beyond this site was considered to be 'beyond the black stump'.

Just how remote and isolated the black stump and beyond could be is highlighted in at least one yarn:

Some time in the 1930s a boundary rider is well out beyond the black stump. He comes across an old prospector who asks him how the war is going. Taken aback, the boundary rider tells him that the 1914–18 war has been over for years.

'Really!' exclaims the prospector. 'Can you tell me who won it?'

'Our mob won, of course.'

The prospector cackled. 'I expect Queen Vic is happy then, she never liked the bloody Boers.'

It has also been said that the term originated in an Indigenous story. A giant Aboriginal man once threw an enormous spear high into the sky. When it eventually returned to earth most of the wooden spear had been burned away, leaving only the blackened stump in the ground where it fell. Apparently, the legend does not say exactly where the spear fell, which is the whole point (ouch!) of the tale.

There are also outrageous assertions that New Zealand actually originated the phrase. The Kiwis might use it but, of course, they got it from us!

Whatever we might think of these passionately held claims to the first black stump, they do not explain those other essentials of bush geography like Oodnagallabie, Woop Woop, Bullamakanka or simply 'out to buggery'. Where are these places?

YEARNING FOR YOWIES

What are we going to do about all these yowies? They're turning up everywhere around the nation in almost plague proportions. At least that is the impression given by the various websites dedicated to hunting the wild yowie. The big, hairy creatures that have been reported since the early colonial period are being regularly sighted in the bush, in the suburbs and even in a bloke's garage. In 2010 a Canberra man met a hairy, apelike creature in his garage. Apparently, it wanted to communicate—but who knows what?

Canberra, Queanbeyan and surrounding areas have long been yowie hotspots. They became such a nuisance in the 1970s that a $200,000 reward was offered by the Queanbeyan Festival Board to anyone who could capture one of the elusive creatures. The money has never been claimed but that has had no effect on yowie sightings, which go back a long time.

In 1903, Graham Webb of Uriarra recalled an encounter with 'some strange animal' that took place many years earlier:

> We were out in Pearce's Creek (a small stream between the Tidbinbilla Mountains and the Cotter River) in search of cattle. In the early part of the day we came upon the remains of a cow of ours. We recognised this beast by the head, as the blacks would only take the tongues out. That the blacks had speared and roasted was evidenced by their stone oven which was close by. We searched the creek during the day, and having seen no indications of cattle being there, we decided to return to where the cow had been killed, and camp there for the night, as it was a good place for the safe keeping of our horses. The weather was very hot and dry; it was in the month of March, there was no moon, none of us had a match. We had supper as usual, and lay down.
>
> Some time during the night, I think it must have been late, I awoke (the others were asleep) and I heard a noise similar to what an entire horse makes. I heard it again and awoke the others. We heard it some four or five times, and the noise ceased, but we could hear it walking along on the opposite side of the range, and when in a line with our camp, we could hear it coming down in our direction. As it came along we could hear its heavy breathing. About this time the dogs became terrified and crouched against us for protection. On account of a fallen tree being on the side the thing was coming, it had to come on one side or the other to get to where we were. My brother Joseph was on the lower side of this tree, I was on the upper side and my brother William in the centre. Not many seconds passed before Joseph sang out, 'here the thing is,' and fired a small pistol he carried at it. Neither William nor myself, coming to the scrub got a sight of it. Joe says it was like a black-fellow with a blanket on him.

We did not hear it going away. We then tried to set our dogs after it, thinking they might find out where the thing went, but we could not get them to move. Had this thing been a little later in coming we could have seen what it was, as the day began to dawn in less than a quarter of an hour after Joe fired at it.

Webb also mentioned another incident in which Aboriginal people had killed a creature like the one that terrified him and his brothers:

The locality where the blacks killed it was below the junction of the Yass River with the Murrumbidgee. The animal got into some cliffs of rocks, and the blacks got torches to find out where it was hidden and then killed it with their nullah nullahs. There was a great many blacks at the killing, and he saw two dragging it down the hill by its legs. It was like a black man, but covered with grey hair.

The yowie is considered by many to be related to the yeti or 'abominable snowman' of the Himalayas. A few years ago, an Oxford University geneticist claimed to have matched DNA from alleged yeti hair samples to those of a polar bear. This claim raised enormous interest around the world, though has been challenged on the basis that polar bears are not likely to have ever existed in Nepal. Probably not in Australia, either.

Other speculations about the yowie include the possibility that the creature is a remnant of an earlier species. Aboriginal legends are often put forward as evidence for this.

Meanwhile, the hunt for our very own long-armed and hairy monster goes on. Sightings are regularly reported in many places. In the Queensland farming town of Kilcoy, they are so enthusiastic about their venerable yowie legends that they have erected a yowie statue in the local park, now called Yowie Park. In another sighting hotspot, the town of Mulgowie, the locals speak enthusiastically of sightings and speculations on the nature of their mysterious monster, the poetic Mulgowie Yowie. They have yowies in Woodenbong, New South Wales. They're in the Blue Mountains, near Taree, throughout Queensland and there are infestations in the ACT. We love a good yowie yarn almost as much as newspapers, radio and television, where even the sniff of a yowie is elevated to a major event. It seems that we really don't want to let our yowie go. If only someone could actually produce one. Perhaps we could grasp it by the leg?

MY BOYFRIEND GAVE ME AN APPLE

Children have their own repertoire of humour in the form of games, rhymes and parodies. 'My Boyfriend Gave Me an Apple' is an old and still widely practised clapping game. Here's one of many versions sung in school playgrounds:

> My boyfriend gave me an apple,
> My boyfriend gave me a pear,
> My boyfriend gave me a kiss on the lips,
> Then threw me down the stairs.

> I gave him back the apple,
> I gave him back the pear,
> I gave him back the kiss on the lips,
> Then pushed him down the stairs.

> I kicked him over London,
> I kicked him over France,
> I kicked him over the USA
> In just his underpants.

And then there are the parodies of advertising jingles and pop culture in general. This well-known ditty sending up 'On Top of Old Smokey' has been around since at least the 1951 hit song:

On top of spaghetti, all covered in cheese,
I lost my poor meatball when somebody sneezed.

It rolled off the table and onto the floor,
And then my poor meatball rolled out of the door.

It rolled down the garden and under a bush,
And then my poor meatball was nothing but mush.

Also in the 1950s and early 1960s, the Flick brand of insecticide used this jingle:

If there are white ants in the floor,
Borers in the door,
Silverfish galore
Get a Flick man, that's your answer
Remember, one Flick and they're gone.

In the Cold War fears of the era, this became:

If there are Russians in the floor
Soviets at the door
Communists galore—
Get an A Bomb, that's your answer
Remember: one flash—and they're ash!

The pop culture of the 1970s produced this popular playground rhyme on the now-defunct Trans-Australia Airways:

Jingle bells, Batman smells,
Robin flew away,
Wonder Woman lost her bosom
Flying TAA.

The famous 'Happy Little Vegemites' song was parodied when the HIV-AIDS epidemic first appeared in the 1980s and the previously suppressed topic of prophylactics came to the attention of younger children through public health campaigns. The original Vegemite jingle goes like this:

> We're happy little Vegemites, as bright as bright can be,
> We all enjoy our Vegemite for breakfast, lunch and tea.
> Mummy says we're growing stronger every single day
> Because we love our Vegemite,
> We all enjoy our Vegemite,
> It puts a rose in every cheek.

The kids turned it into this:

> We're happy little condoms,
> We come in packs of six
> You buy us at the chemist and you stick us on your ——

Sorbent toilet paper—or 'tissue', to be proper—has been a staple of Australian shopping lists since the 1950s. Around that time, the company featured an advertising jingle that went:

> What's the gentlest tissue in the bathroom you can issue?
> New, new, new, new Sorbent
> What's the biggest-selling brand of toilet tissue in the land?
> New, new, new, new Sorbent.

This was quickly subverted:

> What's the gentlest fibre you can use to wipe your Khyber?
> New, new, new newspaper.
> If it's aggravating you can read it while you're waiting,
> New, new, new newspaper.
> If you've got the runnies,
> You can always read the funnies
> New, new, new newspaper.

A SEASONAL GUIDE TO WIVES

In the nineteenth and early twentieth centuries, a lot of information about the weather, planting times and the seasons in general was handed down through the generations in almanacs and farmers' guides. They also carried other items that could turn out to be useful for the man on the land. If he needed to determine the nature of a potential wife, he could turn to folklore for an indication of what married life might be like. All he needed to know was the birth month of his potential wife, then he could consult this handy guide:

A January bride will be a prudent housewife and sweet of temper.

A February bride will be an affectionate wife and a loving mother.

A March bride will be a frivolous chattermag, given to quarrelling.

An April bride is inconsistent, not over wise, and only fairly good looking.

A May bride is fair of face, sweet tempered and contented.

A June bride is impetuous and open handed.

A July bride is handsome but quick of temper.

An August bride is sweet-tempered and active.

A September bride is discreet and forthcoming, beloved of all.

An October bride is fair of face, affectionate but jealous.

A November bride is open-handed, kind-hearted, but inclined to be lawless.

A December bride is graceful in person, fond of novelty, fascinating, but a spendthrift.

HENRY SPRUIKS HEENZO

Under the title of 'The Tragedy—A Dirge', Henry Lawson penned this advertisement for cough medicine during World War I. He must have been hard up, as usual:

Oh, I never felt so wretched, and things never looked so
    blue,
Since the days I gulped the physic that my Granny used to
    brew;
For a friend in whom I trusted, entering my room last night,
Stole a bottleful of Heenzo from the desk whereon I write.

I am certain sure he did it (though he never would let on),
For he had a cold all last week, and to-day his cough is
    gone:
Now I'm sick and sore and sorry, and I'm sad for
    friendship's sake
(It was better than the cough-cure that our Granny used
    to make).

Oh, he might have pinched my whisky, and he might have
    pinched my beer;
Or all the fame or money that I make while writing here—
Oh, he might have shook the blankets and I'd not have
    made a row,
If he'd only left my Heenzo till the morning, anyhow.

So I've lost my faith in Mateship, which was all I had to
    lose
Since I lost my faith in Russia and myself and got the
    blues;
And so trust turns to suspicion, and so friendship turns
    to hate,
Even Kaiser Bill would never pinch his Heenzo from a
    mate.

SPIFLER- —— -CATE HIM!

C.J. Dennis, later to write the classic *Songs of a Sentimental
Bloke* and other once much-loved verse, knocked out this ditty
in 1908. It was not originally meant for publication and was

to be sung to the tune of 'Onward Christian Soldiers' (try it). But the verses exhorting men to step up for their country found their way into the *Bulletin* magazine and became an instant hit. Dennis was influenced by W.T. Goodge's 'The Great Australian Adjective' to create yet another poetic riff on what was then Australia's most popular swear word. It works a bloody treat.

Fellers of Australier,
Blokes an' coves an' coots,
Shift yer —— carcases,
Move yer —— boots.
Gird yer —— loins up,
Get yer —— gun,
Set the —— enermy
An' watch the —— run.

Chorus:
Get a —— move on,
Have some —— sense.
Learn the —— art of
Self de- —— -fence.

Have some —— brains be-
Neath yer —— lids.
An' swing a —— sabre
Fer the missus an' the kids.
Chuck supportin' —— posts,
An' strikin' —— lights,
Support a —— fam'ly an'
Strike fer yer —— rights.

Chorus:
Get a —— move, etc.

Joy is —— fleetin',
Life is —— short.

Wot's the use uv wastin' it
All on —— sport?
Hitch yer —— tip-dray
To a —— star.
Let yer —— watchword be
'Australi- —— -ar!'
Chorus:
Get a —— move, etc.

'Ow's the —— nation
Goin' to ixpand
'Lest us —— blokes an' coves
Lend a —— 'and?
'Eave yer —— apathy
Down a —— chasm;
'Ump yer —— burden with
Enthusi- —— -asm.

Chorus:
Get a —— move, etc.

W'en the —— trouble
Hits yer native land
Take a —— rifle
In yer —— 'and.
Keep yer —— upper lip
Stiff as stiff kin be,
An' speed a —— bullet for
Pos- —— -terity.

Chorus:
Get a —— move, etc.

W'en the —— bugle
Sounds 'Ad- —— -vance'
Don't be like a flock uv sheep

In a —— trance.
Biff the —— foeman
Where it don't agree.
Spifler- —— -cate him
To eternity.

Chorus:
Get a —— move, etc.

Fellers of Australier,
Cobbers, chaps an' mates,
Hear the —— enermy
Kickin' at the gates!
Blow the —— bugle,
Beat the —— drum,
Upper-cut and out the cow
To kingdom- —— -come!

Chorus:
Get a —— move on,
Have some —— sense.
Learn the —— art of
Self de- —— -fence!

Dennis updated the poem in 1915 to take account of World War I, which was then raging, including this amended verse:

W'en the —— bugle
Sounds 'Ad- —— -vance'
Don't be like a flock er sheep
In a —— trance
Biff the —— Kaiser
Where it don't agree
Spifler- —— -cate him
To Eternity.

TOUGH TIMES

Australians are proud of their ability to withstand tough times, and no more so than in marriage, as shown by this classic example:

> An old Aussie battler lays dying. He calls his faithful wife of 60 years to his bedside and says: 'Shirl, when we started out in the Depression and the business went bust, you stuck by me.'
>
> 'Yes I did, Darl,' she says.
>
> 'And when I was sent to the front line during the war and lost me leg, you stayed with me.'
>
> 'Of course I did, Darl,' she replies.
>
> 'Then the farm flooded, the drought came and the bushfires finally wiped out the farm, but you were still there.'
>
> 'I know I was, Darl.'
>
> 'Now I'm here, dying in pain and useless, but you're still at my side.'
>
> 'I am, Darl.'
>
> 'Shirl . . .'
>
> 'Yes Darl.'
>
> 'You're bloody bad luck.'

AUSTRALIAN TOURISM

The questions and answers in this item of internet humour are said to have been asked by intending visitors to Australia. They display the abiding prejudices about 'Pommies' and 'Yanks', together with the characteristic element of self-deprecation:

> Q: Does it ever get windy in Australia? I have never seen it rain on TV, how do the plants grow? (UK).
>
> A: We import all plants fully grown and then just sit around watching them die.

Q: Will I be able to see kangaroos in the street? (USA)
A: Depends how much you've been drinking.

Q: I want to walk from Perth to Sydney—can I follow the railroad tracks? (Sweden)
A: Sure, it's only three thousand miles, take lots of water.

Q: Is it safe to run around in the bushes in Australia? (Sweden)
A: So it's true what they say about Swedes.

Q: Are there any ATMs (cash machines) in Australia? Can you send me a list of them in Brisbane, Cairns, Townsville and Hervey Bay? (UK)
A: What did your last slave die of?

Q: Can you give me some information about hippo racing in Australia? (USA)
A: A-fri-ca is the big triangle shaped continent south of Europe. Aus-tra-lia is that big island in the middle of the Pacific which does not . . . oh forget it. Sure, the hippo racing is every Tuesday night in Kings Cross. Come naked.

Q: Which direction is North in Australia? (USA)
A: Face south and then turn 180 degrees. Contact us when you get here and we'll send the rest of the directions.

Q: Can I bring cutlery into Australia? (UK)
A: Why? Just use your fingers like we do.

Q: Can you send me the Vienna Boys' Choir schedule? (USA)
A: Aus-tri-a is that quaint little country bordering Germany, which is . . . oh forget it. Sure, the Vienna Boys Choir plays every Tuesday night in Kings Cross, straight after the hippo races. Come naked.

Q: Can I wear high heels in Australia? (UK)
A: You are a British politician, right?

Q: Are there supermarkets in Sydney and is milk available all year round? (Germany)
A: No, we are a peaceful civilisation of vegan hunter/gatherers. Milk is illegal.

Q: Please send a list of all doctors in Australia who can dispense rattlesnake serum. (USA)
A: Rattlesnakes live in A-meri-ca which is where YOU come from. All Australian snakes are perfectly harmless, can be safely handled and make good pets.

Q: I have a question about a famous animal in Australia, but I forget its name. It's a kind of bear and lives in trees. (USA)
A: It's called a Drop Bear. They are so called because they drop out of gum trees and eat the brains of anyone walking underneath them. You can scare them off by spraying yourself with human urine before you go out walking.

Q: Do you have perfume in Australia? (France)
A: No, WE don't stink.

Q: I have developed a new product that is the fountain of youth. Can you tell me where I can sell it in Australia? (USA)
A: Anywhere significant numbers of Americans gather.

Q: Can you tell me the regions in Tasmania where the female population is smaller than the male population? (Italy)
A: Yes, gay nightclubs.

Q: Do you celebrate Christmas in Australia? (France)
A: Only at Christmas.

Q: I was in Australia in 1969 on R+R*, and I want to contact the girl I dated while I was staying in Kings Cross. Can you help? (USA)
A: Yes, and you will still have to pay her by the hour.

Q: Will I be able to speak English most places I go? (USA)
A: Yes, but you'll have to learn it first.

* Many American servicemen came to Australia for 'rest and recuperation' leave from the war in Vietnam.

THE NAKED CARAVANNER

Fear of being caught in the nude or otherwise embarrassing situations in a public place are the themes of a number of contemporary fables, such as 'The Fart in the Dark' and 'The Surprise Party'. In this legend, the 'someday you're gonna get caught' syndrome is well and truly played out—with unhappy consequences:

A man and his wife take a caravanning holiday in the outback. It is very hot and the wife decides she would like a rest. She decides to climb into the caravan while the husband drives on to the next town, some hundreds of kilometres away.

Inside the van it is very hot, so the wife strips down to her briefs and goes to sleep. After a while she is wakened by a loud bang. The car has had a blowout on the driver's-side front wheel. While the husband swears and drags the jack and spare out to fix the flat, the wife decides she needs a pee. There is no one and nothing to be seen as far as the eye can see in any direction, so she gets out of the van and squats in the scrub beside the highway.

The husband finishes changing the wheel and, not realising that his wife has left the van, climbs in the car and roars off into the distance, leaving her near-naked by the road.

Fortunately, after a few minutes a bikie roars up. The wife, embarrassed but desperate, flags him down and asks for the bikie to chase after her husband with the caravan. The obliging bikie agrees, so she hops on behind him and they roar off in chase of the caravan.

They catch up with the caravan but cannot attract the husband's attention. So the bikie decides to overtake and wave the husband down. As he roars past, the husband, seeing his wife in only her briefs on the back of the motor-cycle, is so shocked that he runs the car off the road and is killed in the smash.

This is pretty much how the most commonly encountered version of this tale goes in Australia. American versions usually have the male and female roles reversed. I first heard this one told in Australia around 1986 and it was certainly around for a good while before then. It was collected in New South Wales as early as 1978 by Bill Scott and was known in Perth in the mid-1980s. An Adrienne Eccles of Unley, SA, sent a good version to Jan Brunvand that he published in his 1993 book *The Baby Train*. In the South Aussie version, the action takes place on the conveniently located Nullarbor Plain and it happened to 'a friend's uncle and aunt'. Fair dinkum.

ROAMING GNOMES

Fantastic journeys undertaken by garden gnomes have long featured in modern legend. As the stories go, garden gnomes have been going missing for decades, if not longer. It seems that these prized ornaments have a habit of disappearing in the middle of the night. Some time later, maybe days, weeks or months, their disconsolate owners receive a letter or email from a distant holiday location informing them that their gnome or gnomes are having a great time. Usually there is a photograph of the gnome reclining by the pool or beside the sea. Then, sometimes years later, the vanished gnomes may mysteriously reappear in the gardens from which they disappeared.

The disappearing gnome story might have originated in the practice of stealing gnomes from gardens and placing them in unexpected locations, such as a freeway verge. This is reported in a post to the Museum of Hoaxes blog as happening in Sydney in 1978. This prank seems to have evolved into stealing gnomes then demanding a ransom for their return. Some time around the middle of the 1980s, reports of gnomes simply disappearing on holidays began to circulate.

Gnome roaming has now moved on the World Wide Web, where there are innumerable reports of their antics to be found. The gnomes have even made it into the movies in the French film *Amelie*.

And it's not just the gnomes who have taken to travel. All manner of garden ornaments have taken off, including flamingos, rabbit and frogs.

Is it all an elaborate international prank, another urban legend or something much more sinister?

In case your gnome has taken an unscheduled trip to Bali or wherever and has not returned, help may be at hand. The enterprising residents of the Dardanup area in the Ferguson Valley of south-western Australia have created Gnomesville, 'the magical home to over 3000 gnomes who have migrated here from all over Australia and around the world'. Here, a whole roundabout is full of miscellaneous wandering dwarves who, for whatever reasons, have not returned to their homes.

So, if you're wondering what happened to your gnome, take a trip of your own to Dardanup and see what you can find. Even if your gnome is not on the roundabout, there is a shop, so you could always give another lump of coloured concrete a good home.

HER MAJESTY RESPONDS

When the Whitlam government was dismissed in 1975 and replaced with the Fraser government, it precipitated a constitutional crisis. In the early hours of the following morning, someone in the Prime Minister's Department decided that Her Majesty Queen Elizabeth should be informed. After all, she was, and is, the Queen of Australia and our ultimate head of state.

The call was placed to Buckingham Palace and Her Majesty eventually came on the line. The official from the Prime Minister's Department nervously said: 'I need to report to Your Majesty that Whitlam is out, and Fraser is in.'

There was a slight pause at the British end of the line then, in her well-rounded vowels, the Queen said: 'Why ring me at this hour to tell me the cricket score?'

TIGGA'S TRAVELS

The tale of a globetrotting ginger cat entertained the world's media and social media for some months in 2015. Tigga was his name, though he was rechristened 'Ozzie' near the end of his adventurous life.

Tigga's rise to global stardom began in mid-2015 when he was found in a garden in County Armagh. A cat protection volunteer took him to the vet for a check-up. To everyone's surprise, Tigga's microchip revealed that he was from Australia.

But not by direct flight, it seems. The microchip also indicated that Tigga had been residing in London during 2004. He turned up as a stray at a veterinary clinic there, though how he travelled from the English capital to Australia and then to Ireland was a total mystery.

Even more curiously, according to the electronic data on Tigga's microchip, he was born in 1989, making him an incredible twenty-five years old. Cats are mostly long gone by then, so this one was probably the oldest living feline ever.

How did Tigga get from London to Australia and then to County Armagh? And how could he be so old?

The puzzle persisted while Irish cat protectors looked after Tigga and began a search for more information. Carers and Tigga reportedly crossed their paws while they waited for news of the tomcat's background. Eventually social media provided the answer to the riddle.

Tigga belonged to a well-travelled couple moving between Ireland and Australia. They left their pet with friends in Armagh, but he ran away and lived rough on the streets and in the gardens of the locals until he was picked up in June.

It also turned out that he was not as old as he seemed. A misprint in the original records meant that he was born in 1999, not 1989.

Sadly, this tale has an unhappy ending. Despite gaining an extra ten years of youth, Tigga became ill while in care. An untreatable liver condition took him away before his owners could be reunited with their paw-loose pet. He died without fear or pain 'and surrounded by love', members of the Armagh cat protection group wrote on Facebook.

Tigga's ashes made the long journey back to Australia, ending his unusual life of travel, adventure and global stardom. Vale Tigga.

RUNNING NAKED WITH THE BULLS

Australians like to celebrate and enjoy themselves. No surprise there. But we seem to have a particular affinity for activities that are a bit off the wall and seem to take a perverse delight in parodying pretty well everything.

The Darwin Beer Can Regatta is a light-hearted make-do event involving vessels made of empty beer cans. The Henley-on-Todd Regatta in Alice Springs features homemade craft racing along the dry bed of the Todd River. Cockroach races were established as a regular event at Kangaroo Point, Brisbane, on Australia Day 1982. The Tolmie Sports of north-eastern Victoria were established in 1886 and feature events associated with rural life, including riding events. The main event is the woodchopping in the form of the Tolmie 3-man Challenge. This is a team event involving running and riding mountain bikes as well as chopping wood. But as well as these more or less orthodox forms of competition, the Tolmie event features novelty footraces, baking competitions, nail driving and spud peeling bouts.

Over in the west, the Broome Cup, often though not necessarily held in July, has developed a beer-fuelled crab racing session that follows the horse races, as well as a two-up school. In Marble Bar, Western Australia, the annual races have been run mid-year since 1893. Even then, it's hot in the Pilbara and so in recent years the races have been followed by the 'mixed breed undie run'. Those so inclined strip down to their underwear and enjoy a 100-metre sprint along the racetrack.

But in the Queensland mining town of Weipa, they took these amusements to a new level. Beginning in 1993 and intended to mark the first rain of the wet season, the locals invented a new tradition for themselves. They called it 'Running Naked with the Bulls'. Why? Because that's exactly what they did. The first event involved 150 local miners streaking nude along a 2-kilometre course at 2 am. Other than their joggers, the miners carried only a plastic shopping bag for donations to the Royal Flying Doctor Service.

After that, things settled down, more or less, though the running has had what they call 'a chequered history'. The event rapidly established itself on the local calendar and became an international event as well. In 1998 it was believed to have set a record for the highest number of naked people ever to be interviewed. The ABC conducted the interviews from a telephone box along the course as the runners joggled past. Not wanting to appear sexist, the organisers decided that women were also allowed to run naked with the bulls in 1999.

Sadly, the event was closed down in 2001 due to complaints about indecency. There has been recent pressure to revive it, though, as Weipa is in need of the tourist income the event attracted. Local police are said to oppose its reintroduction. The future of running naked with the bulls remains uncertain at the time of writing.

But even when a local custom like this does spring up spontaneously, the commercial world is quick off the mark. A local resident and participant was heard on ABC Radio National back in November 1998 telling of the difficulties the event had encountered with sponsorship. It was not that the locals were against sponsorship for their start of the wet season celebration, just that some sponsors were inappropriate. A large brothel chain wished to sponsor the event but the participants had to decline. There was no moral problem; it was just that the brothel wanted the runners to wear a t-shirt advertising their business. Reluctantly, the runners could not oblige.

YOU NEED MINTIES

'Minties moments' became part of Australian lingo almost from the time they first went on sale in the 1920s. Wrapping the lollies in a cartoon and caption beginning 'It's moments like these . . .' was an advertising gimmick that 'went viral' long before anyone even thought of the internet. As early as 1927 the slogan was recognised as one of the most popular modern catchcries:

> At the present time, one hears the phrase wherever one goes. The makers of 'Minties', Messrs. James Stedman-Henderson's, of 'Sweetacres', receive dozens of suggestions by every post from people instancing 'Moments like these', when 'Minties' would have been most acceptable. 'It's moments like these' has proved itself to be one of the most catchy catchphrases that has ever caught on, and it shows no signs yet of fading out of public recognition.

The sweet, sticky and dentally dangerous treats were well established in everyday life by the 1940s, when up to three new cartoons a week appeared on advertising hoardings and print commercials. Many commercial artists, some now well-known, were employed to turn out the miniature mishaps and pratfalls that were the basis of the slogan. These moments required a consoling Mintie, possibly several.

So well established was the Minties slogan that it had even entered underworld parlance by 1930. Thomas Herbert Skinner, a criminal known as the 'Grey Shadow', was in court facing a ten-year sentence for armed robbery when he exclaimed loudly, 'It's moments like these you certainly do need Minties.'

In 1943, the demands of a wartime economy forced the manufacturers to stop making Minties. They ran large advertisements in the press, apologising to their customers. The advertisement also explained that the company was doing its bit for the war effort by using its factory facilities for 'giving the troops a "round the clock" service of Dehydrated Vegetables processed in our own plant at Sweetacres'. Not a lot of consolation. This was definitely a 'Minties moment'.

Minties situations were many, ranging from the banal to the absurd.

One showed a bride and groom about to cut their wedding cake when the groom is elbowed out of the way by his mother-in-law, who takes over the cake slicing, her look strongly implying that the husband will have little say in matters from now on.

Another cartoon depicted schoolboys pranking their teacher with a bucket of water balanced over the door. The teacher walks through and the bucket overbalances the wrong way, threatening to wet the chief prankster.

In another, a string of frankfurters cooking at a hot dog stand is shown snapping at two frightened dogs. An elephant is standing on a girl's doll as a boy tries to extricate it, watched by the distressed owner.

A brick structure on top of a very tall building is being demolished by two workmen. One is standing on top of the bricks, while the other below smashes away at the bricks, leaving his mate above in imminent danger of almost certain death.

Mildly amusing, these moments were produced in their hundreds, perhaps thousands, and the lollies themselves were consumed by generations of Australians and New Zealanders.

Minties are now manufactured in South-east Asia and the formula has been reworked to make them softer, presumably to safeguard against the loss of fillings that the old ones were known to sometimes cause. Wimps!

ACKNOWLEDGEMENTS

As always, many people have contributed to the making of this book, unknowingly and knowingly. Of the latter, my thanks to Maureen Seal, Rob Willis, Olya Willis, Warren Fahey, Mark Gregory, and staff at Allen & Unwin. Many of the items in this collection come from earlier books in the 'Great Australian Stories' series, now mostly out of print.

NOTES

INTRODUCTION: AN EDGE LIKE A CHAINSAW

Lea Winerman, 'A Laughing Matter', *American Psychological Association*, vol. 37, no. 7 at www.apa.org/monitor/jun06/laughing, accessed February 2019, reporting on the research of Robert R. Provine and associates.

A good example of this is F. Hardy & A. Mulley, *The Needy and the Greedy: Humorous Stories of the Racetrack*, Canberra, Libra Books, 1975.

Wilbur Howcroft, *Dungarees and Dust: A diverse collection of rural reminiscences, both true and legendary, spiced with an assortment of bush ballads and nonsense doggerel*, Melbourne, The Hawthorn Press, 1978, p. 81, titled 'Easy Explanation' and featuring a grazier and handyman. Another in Bill Wannan, *Come in Spinner: A Treasury of Popular Australian Humour*, Adelaide, Rigby, 1976 [1964], p. 173, featuring a stationmaster and railway inspector.

CHAPTER 1: BULL

WHAT A HIDE

Traditional but this version from Bill Wannan, *Come in Spinner: A Treasury of Popular Australian Humour*, p. 47.

THE SPLIT DOG

A version (from SA) in Bill Wannan, *Come in Spinner*, p. 25, citing English and North Carolina variants, and giving other bush dog tales.

Ron Edwards, *Fred's Crab and Other Bush Yarns*, Kuranda, Rams Skull Press, 1989, pp. 185–6.

DROP BEARS

There is a fascinating entry on drop bears at the Australian Museum website, www.australianmuseum.net.au/learn/animals/mammals/drop-bear/, accessed February 2019.

HOOP SNAKES

See Bill Scott, *Complete Book of Australian Folklore*, Sydney, PR Books, 1988, pp. 220–1, quoting Martin Brennan, *Reminiscences of the Goldfields and Elsewhere in New South Wales*, Sydney, William Brooks, 1907.

Maurie Fields, *Dinkum Aussie Yarns*, Southdown Press, 1988, p. 25.

GIANT MOZZIES

Bill Wannan, *The Australian: Yarns, ballads, legends and traditions of the Australian people*, Adelaide, Rigby, 1954, pp. 87–8. See also Bill Wannan, *Come in Spinner*, pp. 31–2, and Wilbur Howcroft, *Dungarees and Dust*, p. 55.

Collected from 'Bob' at the Cessnock Show sometime in the late twentieth century and retrieved from the internet in February 2008.

CROOKED MICK AND THE SPEEWAH

Quoted in Bill Wannan, *Crooked Mick of the Speewah and Other Tall Tales*, Melbourne, Lansdowne Press, 1965, pp. 76–7.

Bill Wannan, *Come in Spinner*, pp. 66–70.

June Lacy, *Off-Shears: The Story of Shearing Sheds in Western Australia*, Perth, Black Swan Press, 2002.

DINKUM!

F.J. Mills ('The Twinkler'), *Square Dinkum: A volume of original Australian wit and humour*, Melbourne, Melville & Mullen, 1917.

THE EXPLODING DUNNY

Versions in the *Sydney Morning Herald*, 31 August 1988, and *Northern Territory News*, 18 September 1997.

THE WELL-DRESSED 'ROO

Graham Seal, *Great Australian Urban Myths (rev. edn)*, Sydney, HarperCollins, 2001, p. 120.

LOADED ANIMALS

Graham Seal, *Great Australian Urban Myths*, 2001, p. 76.

Henry Lawson, 'The Loaded Dog', *Joe Wilson and His Mates*, London, Blackwood, 1901.

THE BLACKOUT BABIES

Graham Seal, *Great Australian Urban Myths*, 2001, p. 17.

THE MOST BEAUTIFUL LIES

Mark Twain, *Following the Equator*, Hartford, American Publishing Company, 1897.

THE POMMIES AND THE YANKS

Anon, *Lest We Forget: Digger Tales 1914–19, 1939–1941*, Melbourne, nd (1941?), np.

Australasian Post, 26 April 1956.

Anon, *Marching On: Tales of the Diggers*, Petersham, Geo Nye, nd (c. 1942).

League Post, 1 October 1932, np.

'Semaphore', *Digger Yarns (and some others) to Laugh At*, Melbourne, E.H. Gibbs & Sons, 1936.

Anon, *Digger Aussiosities*, Sydney, New Century Press, 1927.

AUSSIE EFFICIENCY

Another version at 'Is this an Aussie joke', *Yahoo Answers*, https://au.answers.yahoo.com/question/index?qid=20070827030349AADR4k2#, accessed September 2018.

CHAPTER 2: CHARACTERS

THE DRONGO

Bill Wannan, *Come in Spinner*, pp. 131–4, gives nine Drongo yarns. See also Bill Wannan, *The Australian*, Adelaide, Rigby, 1954, p. 137, which reprints the story about the origins of 'Drongo' from *Salt*, 8 April 1946.

Bill Wannan, *Come in Spinner*, pp. 131–4. See also Bill Wannan, *The Australian*, p. 137.

COUSIN JACKS

Wilbur Howcroft, *Dungarees and Dust*, p. 55; Bill Wannan, *Come in Spinner*, p. 130, also includes three other Cousin Jack stories.

TOM DOYLE

Ron Edwards, *The Australian Yarn*, Adelaide, Rigby, 1978 (1977), pp. 30–1; Bill Wannan, *Come in Spinner*, p. 141. Tom Doyle-isms published in *Australasian Post*, 30 October 1958.

THE WIDOW REILLY'S PIG

Bill Wannan, *The Folklore of the Irish in Australia,* Melbourne, Currey O'Neill, 1980, pp. 157–8. An earlier edition was published as *The Wearing of the Green*, Melbourne, Lansdowne Press, 1965.

THE CONVICT'S TOUR TO HELL

See www.frankthepoet.blogspot.com.au/2011/01/articles.html, with thanks to Mark Gregory, www.frankthepoet.blogspot.com/2011/01/songs.html, both accessed March 2019.

MAKE IT HOURS INSTEAD OF DAYS

Socius, 'Paying a Debt', *The Sydney Stock and Station Journal*, 18 April 1902, p. 12; 'Paying a Debt', *The Sydney Stock and Station Journal*, 27 May 1902, p. 3.

WHO WAS BILLY BARLOW?

See Joy Hildebrand, *Hey Ho Raggedy-o: A Study of the Billy Barlow Phenomenon* at www.warrenfahey.com/fc_barlow_book.html; also containing a large number of Billy Barlow ballads, www.warrenfahey.com.au/hey-ho-raggedy-o/, both accessed February 2019.

JACKY BINDI-I

Also the title of a widely sung Aboriginal folksong that satirises white attitudes and activities in general and dispossession of Indigenous land and culture in particular. See Graham Seal & Rob Willis (eds), *Verandah Music: Roots of Australian Tradition*, Curtin University Books, 2003.

This yarn has some similarities with the American tale of the 'Arkansas Traveller' in which a city slicker asks the yokel where the road goes and the yokel superciliously replies that he has been living in the area all his life and he has never seen the road go anywhere. The irritated city slicker calls the yokel a fool, whereon the local drawls, 'But I ain't lost.' In Australia, it is also told of a swagman (bagman) in Howcroft, *Dungarees and Dust*, p. 18.

Bill Wannan, *Come in Spinner*, pp. 142–6, includes ten Jacky Bindieye yarns.

John Meredith, 'Study in Black and White', *Quadrant* 13, Summer 1959–60, pp. 59–62.

Albert F. Calvert, *The Aborigines of Western Australia*, London, Simpkin, Marshall, Hamilton, Kent, 1894.

JIMMY AH FOO

Bill Wannan, *Come in Spinner*, p. 148.

SNUFFLER OLDFIELD

Ron Edwards, *The Australian Yarn*, pp. 32, 94.

CORNY KENNA

Bill Wannan, *Come in Spinner*, pp. 149–150. A Cornelius 'Corny' Kenna was buried at Ellerslie, Victoria in 1921 at the age of 77.

THE HODJA

C.E.W. Bean (ed.), *The Anzac Book*, London, Cassell, 1916, p. 24.
Steele Rudd, *On Our Selection*, Sydney, Angus & Robertson, 1899.

DAD MAKES A BLUE

Steele Rudd, *Our New Selection*, Sydney, Bulletin Newspaper Co., 1903, pp. 101–5.

DAD, DAVE AND MABEL

Bill Wannan, *The Australian*, pp. 91–2. See also Wannan, *Come in Spinner*, p. 118.
Maurie Fields, *Dinkum Aussie Yarns*, p. 66.

Bill Wannan, *Come in Spinner*, p. 117.

A.H. Fisher from Camden Park, SA, undated letter (c. 1960s), Wannan papers, National Library of Australia.

Maurie Fields, *Dinkum Aussie Yarns*, p. 5. For another Dad and Dave yarn involving Mabel, see Bill Wannan, *Come in Spinner*, pp. 117–8, and see Phillip Adams and Patrice Newell, *Official Aussie Joke Book*, Melbourne, Wilkinson Publishing, 2017, pp. 30–40, for a very large selection of Dad, Dave and Mabel yarns.

ANZAC CHARACTERS

See Graham Seal, *Inventing Anzac: The Digger and National Mythology*, St Lucia, University of Queensland Press, 2004.

HOW HE WORKED HIS NUT

Aussie, 15 December 1920, pp. 64–5, reprinted from the *Third Battalion Magazine*, nd.

TOM 'N' OPLAS

Collected from Chris Gray, Sydney, 1984, by Graham Seal.

THREE BLOKES AT A PUB

Fields, *Dinkum Aussie Yarns*, p. 14, and see also Phillip Adams and Patrice Newell, *Official Aussie Joke Book*, for more examples.

CHAPTER 3: HARD CASES

THE COCKY

Wannan, *Come in Spinner*, pp. 28–30, 118, 119. Other mean cocky yarns in Maurie Fields, *Dinkum Aussie Yarns*, Southdown Press, 1988, pp. 46, 56, 64; and Ron Edwards, *Fred's Crab and Other Bush Yarns*, p. 16.

'HUNGRY' TYSON

W.N. Willis, *The Life of W.P. Crick*, Sydney, 1909, quoted in Bill Wannan, *My Kind of Country: More Australian yarns, ballads, and legends*, Ringwood, Viking O'Neil, p. 171.

NINETY THE GLUTTON

Bill Wannan, *Come in Spinner*, pp. 150–1.

GALLOPING JONES

Ron Edwards, *The Australian Yarn*, pp. 27–9. See also *Fred's Crab*, p. 24.

CHRISTY PALMERSTON

Ron Edwards, *The Australian Yarn*, pp. 26–7 (collected 1969), 117 (collected 1972).

MOONDYNE JOE

Ian Elliot, *Moondyne Joe: The Man and the Myth*, Nedlands, University of Western Australia Press, 1978.

THE EULO QUEEN

Bill Beatty, *A Treasury of Australian Folk Tales and Traditions*, Sydney, Ure Smith, 1960, pp. 173–4.

WHEELBARROW JACK

Peter J. Bridge, *Russian Jack*, Perth, Hesperian Press, 2002.
Westralian Worker, 6 May 1904, p. 7, also the *Day Dawn Chronicle* and the *Murchison Advocate* over the relevant years.

LONG JACK

Aussie, 15 December 1920, p. 66, reprinted from *The Third Battalion Magazine*, c. 1917.

DIABOLICAL DICK

Collected from Archer Whitworth, Geraldton, by Wendy Lowenstein, and published in her newsletter, *Australian Tradition*, December 1969.
Scott, *Complete Book of Australian Folklore*, p. 241.

PUPPY PIE AND DOG'S DINNER

Bill Wannan, *Come in Spinner*, pp. 126–9. See also *The Australian*, p. 68. For another execrable station cook yarn, see also Alan Marshall in *Australasian Post*, 18 February 1954; also Wilbur Howcroft, *Dungarees and Dust*, p. 58.
J. Brunton Stephens, 'My Other Chinee Cook' in *The Australasian*, 8 March 1873, p. 7.
Western Australian Folklore Archive, Curtin University, Perth.

THE WORLD'S GREATEST WHINGER

There are various versions of this tale, including Fields, *Dinkum Aussie Yarns*, pp. 60–1, and in the 'Papers of Ian Turner', National Library of Australia, Canberra.

THE CAPTAIN OF THE PUSH

Henry Lawson, *Verses, Popular and Humorous*, Sydney, Angus & Robertson, 1900.

THE SOUVENIR KING

Australian War Memorial, 'Fifty Australians–Barney Hines', *Australian War Memorial*, Campbell, ACT, www.awm.gov.au/visit/exhibitions/fiftyaustralians/24, accessed March 2019.

MRS DELANEY

Patsy Adam-Smith, *Folklore of the Australian Railwaymen*, Adelaide, Seal Books, 1976 (first published 1969), p. 196.

DOPES
Versions in Sam Weller, *Old Bastards I Have Met*, Charters Towers, Sampal Investments, 1976, p. 106, and F. Hardy & A.G. Mulley, *The Needy and the Greedy: Humorous Stories of the Racetrack*, Canberra, Libra Books, 1975, p. 69.

TAKEN FOR A RIDE
Versions in Sam Weller, *Old Bastards I Have Met*, p. 106, and Hardy & Mulley, *The Needy and the Greedy*, p. 61.

BEA MILES
The Cumberland Argus, 14 September 1955, p. 1.
Sunday Times (Perth), 23 January 1955, pp. 1, 3.

DOING BUSINESS WITH REG
Graham Seal, *Great Australian Urban Myths*, Sydney, HarperCollins, 2001, p. 97.

AN UNWELCOME MIRACLE
The Spoof, 'An Australian, An Irishman and an Englishman . . .', The Spoof, www.thespoof.com/jokes/12275/an-australian-an-irishman-and-an-englishman, accessed September 2018 (published 2012).

CHAPTER 4: DIGGEROSITIES

A MILLION CAT-CALLS
Lyn MacDonald, *They Called it Passchendaele: The story of the Battle of Ypres and of the men who fought in it*, London, Penguin, 1993.

RELIGION
Australasian Post, 26 April 1956.

MONOCLES
Graham Seal, *Great Anzac Stories*, Sydney, Allen & Unwin, 2015, pp. 161–2.

FOOD AND DRINK
Anon., *Digger Aussiosities*, Sydney, New Century Press, 1927

ARMY BISCUITS
O.E. Burton in C.E.W. Bean (ed.), *The Anzac Book*, London, Cassell, 1916, p. 61.

BABBLING BROOKS
Smith's Weekly, 6 June 1925, with 'bastard' blanked out.
Albert Horace Cooper, *Character Glimpses: Australians on the Somme*, nd (1919?).
Smith's Weekly, Christmas edition 1942.
C.S. Hicks, *Who Called the Cook a Bastard?* Sydney, Keyline Publishing, 1972, p. 29.

C.E.W. Bean, *Official History of Australia in the War of 1914–1918, Vol VI: The Australian Imperial Force in France during the Allied Offensive, 1918,* Canberra, Australian War Memorial, vol. 6, 1946, p. 10.

THE CASUAL DIGGER
Australian Corps News Sheet, 6 November 1918.

OFFICERS
Anon, *Lest We Forget: Digger Tales 1914–1918, 1939–1941,* Melbourne, nd (1941?).

Anon, *Marching On: Tales of the Diggers,* Petersham, Geo Nye, nd (c. 1942).

League Post, 1 October 1932.

Fred Mills ('The Twinkler'), *Square Dinkum: A volume of original Australian wit and humour,* Melbourne, Melville & Mullen, 1917.

'Semaphore', *Digger Yarns (and some others) to Laugh At,* Melbourne, 1936.

Anon, *Digger Aussiosities,* np.

R. Fair (comp.), *A Treasury of Anzac Humour,* Brisbane, Jacaranda Press, 1965, pp. 11–12.

BIRDIE
R. Fair, *A Treasury of Anzac Humour,* p. 12.

The Listening Post, 17 August 1923, p. 21.

THE PIECE OF PAPER
'Methodical Madness', *Anzac Records Gazette,* 12 November 1915, p. 5.

Anon, *Digger Doings,* Petersham, Geo Nye, nd (c. 1943).

PARABLES OF ANZAC
C.E.W. Bean, *The Anzac Book,* p. 23.

BALDY BECOMES MOBILE
Author's collection.

THE ROO DE KANGA
Manchester Guardian, 27 September 1918, in H. Frank Molony diary, 8 August–17 December 1918, Mitchell Library, State Library of New South Wales, MLMSS 2883/Item 7.

BLIGHTY
Graham Seal, *Echoes of Anzac: The Voice of Australians at War,* Melbourne, Lothian, 2005, p. 102.

VERY IRRITATED
Author's collection.

THINKING AHEAD
Anon, There is a Cecil Hartt cartoon on this possibly apocryphal event in his bestselling *Humourosities*, London, Australian Trading and Agencies, 1917.

FINDING THE 'AWSTRALIANS'
Traditional.

PLEASE LET US TAKE TOBRUK!
Mud and Blood: 2/23 Australian Infantry Battalion newsletter, 25 June 1941.

COUNT YOUR CHILDREN
Sent to author from 'a bloke on the cab rank in Albany', 1980.

PARABLE OF THE KIT INSPECTION
From the *Vietnam Veterans' Federation Newsletter*, Queensland, Queensland Sub-Branch Inc, date unknown.

THE AIR FORCE WIFE
Author's collection.

CHAPTER 5: WORKING FOR A LAUGH

THE GARBOS' CHRISTMAS
Vane Lindesay, *Aussie-osities*, Richmond, Greenhouse, 1988; Bill Scott, *Complete Book of Australian Folklore*, Sydney, Summit Books, 1978 (1976), pp. 412–14.

A CHRISTMAS MESSAGE
Townsville Daily Bulletin, 4 June 1924, p. 9.

RECHTUB KLAT
Garry Maddox, 'Behind that tray of snags, there's a rechtub talking', *Sydney Morning Herald,* 27 May 2002.

THE WHARFIE'S REPLY
A version in Bill Wannan, *Come in Spinner,* p. 205.

THE UNION DOG
An internet version at The Politically Incorrect Collection, 'The Union Dog', www.pcuf.fi/~pjt/pink/union-dog.html, accessed January 2019.

WORKING ON THE RAILWAY
Graham Seal, *Larrikins, Bush Tales and Other Great Australian Stories*, Sydney, Allen & Unwin, 2014, p. 264.

HIGH-OCTANE TRAVEL
Graham Seal, *Larrikins, Bush Tales and Other Great Australian Stories*, p. 266.

RAILWAY BIRDS
Graham Seal, *Larrikins, Bush Tales and Other Great Australian Stories*, p. 267, from *The Railroad* magazine.

TOTAL ECLIPSE OF COMMUNICATION
Author's collection.

THE LAWS OF WORKING LIFE
Author's collection.

SOMEBODY ELSE'S JOB
Author's collection.

THE BASIC WORK SURVIVAL GUIDE
Author's collection.

TWELVE THINGS YOU'LL NEVER HEAR AN EMPLOYEE TELL THE BOSS
Author's collection.

EXCESSIVE ABSENCE
Author's collection.

THE END OF A PERFECT DAY
Author's collection.

TOTAL QUALITY MANAGEMENT [TQM]
Author's collection.

POLICY DEVELOPMENT
Author's collection.

THE BOAT RACE
Author's collection.

PROSPECTIVE EMPLOYEE ASSESSMENT
Author's collection.

SPECIALISED HIGH-INTENSITY TRAINING [S.H.I.T.]
Author's collection.

EARLY RETIREMENT
Author's collection.

DIFFERENCES BETWEEN YOU AND YOUR BOSS
Author's collection.

WHAT DO THEY REALLY MEAN?
Author's collection.

THE LITTLE RED HEN
Author's collection.
B. & E. Hader, *The Little Red Hen*, New York, MacMillan, 1928. See also J. Domanska (illustrator), *Little Red Hen*, Macmillan, 1973.

THE AIRLINE STEWARD'S REVENGE
Graham Seal, *Great Australian Urban Myths*, p. 114.

THE BOSS
Graham Seal, *The Bare Fax*, p. 27, and numerous variants in the Seal collection.

AFTER WORK . . .
Email to author, 1 February 2015.

MEETINGS
Author's collection and many variations on the internet.

PRAYER FOR THE STRESSED
A version at 'Prayer for the Stressed', *PM Humor*, www.pmhumor. com/, accessed October 2010.

THE JOB APPLICATION
Author's collection and another version at 'McDonalds Job Application', ThoughtCo., www.thoughtco.com/mcdonalds-job-application-3299516, accessed January 2019.

THE BOSS'S REPLY
Author's collection.

ODE TO PUBLIC SERVANTS
Author's collection.

JARGONING
Author's collection.

THE JARGON GENERATOR
Author's collection.

GOVERNMENTIUM
Author's collection.

THE SURPRISE PARTY
Graham Seal, *Great Australian Urban Myths*, p. 28.

THE SEX LIFE OF AN ELECTRON
Author's collection.

DEATH OF EMPLOYEES
Author's collection and in many, many variations.

WORKPLACE AGREEMENTS
Author's collection.

POPULATION OF AUSTRALIA
Author's collection.

CHAPTER 6: A SWAG OF LAUGHS

THE GREAT AUSTRALIAN YARN

Other versions in Bill Wannan, *The Australian*, Adelaide, Rigby, 1954,
p. 3, and Maurie Fields, *Dinkum Aussie Yarns*, *Australasian Post*,
nd (early 1990s), p. 6.

THE BAGMAN'S GAZETTE

'The Organiser', 'The Bagman's Gazette', *Northern Standard* (Darwin),
29 September 1931, p. 2.

A STUMP SPEECH

Imperial Songster 97, Sydney, J. Slater, 1907.

THE PHANTOM BULLOCKY

Another example in Ron Edwards, *The Australian Yarn*, Adelaide,
Rigby, 1978, pp. 216–18, in which the bullocks are so strong they
pull Cooper's Creek ten chains out of its course.
Lance Skuthorpe, *The Bulletin,* vol. 42, no. 2164, 4 August 1921,
p. 48.
Bill Wannan, *The Australian*, pp. 55–7.
Maurie Fields, *Dinkum Aussie Yarns*, pp. 29, 52.

A FINE TEAM OF BULLOCKS

Traditional.

LANGUAGE!

Maurie Fields, *Dinkum Aussie Yarns*, p. 17. For another bullock tale
from an early *Bulletin* magazine see Bill Scott, *Complete Book of
Australian Folklore*, Dee Why West, Summit Books, 1976, p. 226.

DROVING IN A BAR

Edwards, *The Australian Yarn*, pp. 235–6.

SLOW TRAINS

Patsy Adam-Smith, *Folklore of the Australian Railwaymen*, Adelaide,
Rigby, 1976, pp. 193–4.
Another version, featuring the Mullewa–Wiluna train, appears in Bill
Wannan, *Come in Spinner*, p. 168.
Patsy Adam-Smith, pp. 199–200, for another slow train tale in South
Australia. Also Bill Wannan, *Come in Spinner*, p. 173 for yet
another.
See also Patsy Adam-Smith, pp. 194–5.

SERVICE!

Graham Seal, *Larrikins, Bush Tales and Other Great Australian
Stories*, Allen & Unwin, Sydney, 2014, p. 265.

MEEKATHARA ICE BLOCKS

Bill Wannan, *Come in Spinner*, p. 170.

Also a version collected by the author from Western Australian
    railwaymen, Pinjarra, November 2002. The written
    communications or reports from railwaymen to their superiors,
    usually explaining some real or alleged infraction of the rules, is
    a popular sub-genre of railway yarning. A number of examples
    are included in M. Tronson (ed.), *Ripping Good Railway Yarns*,
    Wallacia, IFH Publishing Co., 1991, pp. 38–9, 149.

THE REDBACK SPIDER
Traditional.

THE GREAT AUSTRALIAN ADJECTIVE
W.T. Goodge, 'The Great Australian Adjective', *The Clipper*, 5 August
    1899, p. 8.
'Bloody Darwin', author's collection.
W.T. Goodge, 'The Australian Slanguage', *The Bulletin*, 4 June 1898,
    Red Page.

LORE OF THE TRACK
Bill Wannan, *Come in Spinner*, Adelaide, Rigby, 1976, p. 196.
Bill Bowyang, 'On the Track', *Townsville Daily Bulletin*, 4 June 1924,
    p. 9.
Will Carter, 'Australianities', *Nepean Times*, 1 April 1933, p. 6.

SNIFFLING JIMMY
Bill Bowyang, 'On the Track', *Townsville Daily Bulletin*, 4 June 1924,
    p. 9.

THE POETIC SWAGGIE
A.B. 'Banjo' Paterson (ed.), *Old Bush Songs*, Sydney, Angus
    & Robertson, 1906.
Henry Lawson, 'Hungerford', published in the Christmas edition
    of *The Bulletin*, 1893.

WHERE THE ANGEL TARBOYS FLY
Vagrant, 'Shearing Records', *North Queensland Register*, quoted in
    The Capricornian, 14 November 1908, p. 47.

BOWYANG BILL AND THE COCKY FARMER
Bill Bowyang, 'Tales of the Bush and Life Outback', *Narromine News
    and Trangie Advocate*, 16 February 1934, p. 6.

A GOOD FEED
Traditional; a version told by the folklorist A.L. Lloyd at 'Bush Humor
    – Yarn Telling', *Warren Fahey's Folklore Unit*, www.warrenfahey.
    com.au/bush-humour-yarn-telling/, accessed 15 March 2019.

THE SWAGMAN'S UNION
Burra Record, 11 February 1931.

A GLORIOUS SPREE
'Raid on sly grog-sellers at Pakenham', *South Bourke and Mornington Journal*, 19 March 1879, p. 3.

THE DIMBOOLA CAT FARM
Author's collection.

A FARMER'S LAMENT
Author's collection.

WHAT'S ON, COOKIE?
Bill Wannan, *The Australian*, p. 67, quoting Julian Stuart, *Australian Worker*, 31 October 1928.
Reg Dunbar, a noted Western Australian raconteur, also features alongside many other shearing industry yarn-spinners in Valerie Hobson, *Across the Board: Stories of Western Australian shearing as told by the people who worked in the sheds*, Gidgegannup, BackTrack Books, 2002.
June Lacy, *Off-Shears: The Story of Shearing Sheds in Western Australia*, p. 214.

THE MAIDEN COOK
Wellington Times, 24 March 1907, p. 6, from 'The Singer', Cooma, NSW.

THE FARMER'S WILL
Author's collection.

CHAPTER 7: THE LAWS OF LIFE

RULES FOR BEING HUMAN
Author's collection.

APPLICATION FOR AUSTRALIAN CITIZENSHIP
Circulated on the internet from 2006.

CHILDREN'S PROVERBS
Email to author, 29 June 2005.

TO THE CITIZENS OF THE USA
Author's collection.

SIGNS OF YOUR TIMES
Anon.

FACEBOOK FOR THE CHRONOLOGICALLY CHALLENGED
Email to author, April 2018.

MAKING A DIFFERENCE
Email to author, January 2014.

GO AUSSIE, GO!
Email to author, 16 January 2003.

25 LESSONS IN LIFE
Anon.

WHY CUCUMBERS ARE BETTER THAN MEN
Author's collection.

WHY BEER IS BETTER THAN WOMEN
Author's collection.

PERSONAL GROWTH AND DEVELOPMENT COURSES
Author's collection.

LIFETIME HOROSCOPE
Author's collection.

A ROTTEN DAY
Author's collection.

WHAT THEY WANTED
Author's collection.

THE IMPOSSIBLE EXAMINATION
Author's collection.

DO NOT BREAK THE CHAIN
Author's collection.

AN INVITATION
Author's collection.

THE ARMY RECRUIT'S LETTER
Many internet versions, see https://www.reddit.com/r/Jokes/comments/
    99l12s/an_australian_army_recruit_sends_home_a_letter/, accessed
    August 2019.

APPLICATION FOR AN AUSTRALIAN PASSPORT
Author's collection.

TAKE A RUNNING JUMP AT YOURSELF!
Fred J. Mills ('The Twinkler'), *Square Dinkum: A volume of original
    Australian wit and humour*, Melbourne, Melville & Muller, 1917.

CHAPTER 8: MOMENTS LIKE THESE . . .

UP, UP AND AWAY!
'Perilous Balloon Excursion', *The Maitland Mercury and Hunter River
    General Advertiser*, 22 January 1859, Maitland, p. 3.

ALL'S WELL THAT ENDS WELL
'Railway Travelling in Tasmania', *Launceston Examiner*, 10 February
    1876, p. 4.

THE OOZLUM BIRD
The first mention of Goodge's poem is in the *Sunday Times* (Sydney) on 19 December 1897, p. 18.

THE BLACK STUMP
Graham Seal, *Larrikins, Bush Tales and Other Great Australian Stories*, Sydney, Allen & Unwin, 2014, p. 104.

YEARNING FOR YOWIES
Queanbeyan Age, 7 August 1903, p. 2.

MY BOYFRIEND GAVE ME AN APPLE
Kate Darian-Smith & Nikki Henningham, *Childhood, Tradition and Change: Final Report of the Childhood, Tradition and Change Project*, June 2011, http://ctac.esrc.unimelb.edu.au/objects/project-pubs/FinalReport.pdf, accessed January 2019.
Author's collection.

A SEASONAL GUIDE TO WIVES
Anon, *Pageant of Humour*, Sydney, Gayle Publishing (?), 1920, said to be from an 1842 source.

HENRY SPRUIKS HEENZO
Henry Lawson, 'The Tragedy—A Dirge', *The Argus*, 23 July 1918, p. 6.

SPIFLER- —— -CATE HIM!
C.J. Dennis, '*The Australaise*', *The Bulletin*, Red Page, 12 November 1908.

TOUGH TIMES
Anon.

AUSTRALIAN TOURISM
Email to author, 2013.

THE NAKED CARAVANNER
Graham Seal, *Great Australian Urban Myths*, Sydney, HarperCollins, 2001, p. 35.

ROAMING GNOMES
'A few cases at Garden Gnome Sale', www.gardengnomesale.com/Gnome_Pranks, accessed March 2019.
Graham Seal, *Great Australian Urban Myths*, pp. 142–3.

HER MAJESTY RESPONDS
A version in Fred Daly, *The Politician Who Laughed*, Melbourne, Hutchinson, 1982, p. 77.

TIGGA'S TRAVELS

www.awwnews.com/aww/tigger-australian-cat-00112.html, accessed
    March 2019.

RUNNING NAKED WITH THE BULLS

The Mansfield Courier online, 26 January 2002.
Susan Kurosawa, 'Horse by northwest', *The Weekend Australian
    Magazine*, 5–6 October 2002, p. 33.
Sophia Constantine, 'Pilbara Spirit at Cup', *The West Australian,*
    7 July 1917, www.thewest.com.au/news/north-west-telegraph/
    pilbara-spirit-at-cup-ng-b88519003z, accessed March 2019.
Australian Associated Press report in *The West Australian*, 14
    December 2002, p. 55.

YOU NEED MINTIES

'Modern Catch Words', *Morning Bulletin* (Rockhampton), 19 July
    1927, p. 8.
'Moments Like These You Need Minties!', *The Labor Daily*, 7
    February 1930, p. 5.
'An announcement concerning supplies of "Sweetacres"', *The Mercury*
    (Hobart), 10 November 1943, p. 6.
See also Vane Lindesay, *It's Moments Like These: Cartoons Behind
    a Nation's Catchcry*, Melbourne, Sun Books, 1979.

PHOTO CREDITS

are Mary Regan, Flo Colls, Kath Regan and Gin Regan.'
Photographer unknown. Courtesy the State Library of
NSW.

Page [200] 'Two swaggies strike a pose! Local graziers, Jabez
Nicholls and Sam Nicholls, dressed as swaggies in front of
Ryans Boots and Shoes, Gundagai, NSW, late nineteenth
century.' Photograph by Charles Louis Gabriel. Courtesy
the National Library of Australia.

Page [242] 'Mr V.J. White, Assistant Chief Protector of
Aborigines in the Northern Territory, with "Paddy" the
camel, near Ayers Rock (Uluru), 1935.' Photograph by
Charles Mountford. Courtesy the State Library of South
Australia [PRG 1218/34/71].

Page [280] 'A cart of memories: young lads gallivanting
for the day, South Australia, circa 1909.' Photographer
unknown. Courtesy the State Library of South Australia
[PRG 1364/1/36].